Library Services
to the Incarcerated

Library Services
to the Incarcerated

Applying the Public Library Model
in Correctional Facility Libraries

Sheila Clark and Erica MacCreaigh

LIBRARIES
UNLIMITED
A Member of the Greenwood Publishing Group
Westport, Connecticut • London

Library of Congress Cataloging-in-Publication Data

Clark, Sheila, 1956–
    Library services to the incarcerated: applying the public library model in
correctional facility libraries / by Sheila Clark and Erica MacCreaigh.
        p. cm.
    Includes bibliographical references and index.
    ISBN 1-59158-290-3 (pbk.: alk. paper)
    1. Prison libraries—United States.   2. Libraries and prisons—United
    States.   I. MacCreaigh, Erica.   II. Title.
Z675.P8C55 2006
027.6'65—dc22   2006017621

British Library Cataloguing in Publication Data is available.

Library of Congress Catalog Card Number: 2006017621
ISBN: 1-59158-290-3

First published in 2006

Libraries Unlimited, 88 Post Road West, Westport, CT 06881
A Member of the Greenwood Publishing Group, Inc.
www.lu.com

Printed in the United States of America

The paper used in this book complies with the
Permanent Paper Standard issued by the National
Information Standards Organization (Z39.48–1984).

10 9 8 7 6 5 4 3 2 1

To the inmates and staff who walk the difficult paths in jail and prison and who humble and humor us every day. They show us what we need to share and teach us how to teach others. (S. C.)

To Kathy Krape for training me how to write "for reals," and to Marcie Rahn for more than twenty years of "cheerleading." Not one word would have been possible without you. (E. M.)

Contents

Acknowledgments

This is the first book either of us has written, and although it's certainly no *War and Peace* (although that would have made an interesting subtitle), the undertaking was monumental for both of us. Seventy thousand words doesn't sound like that much, either to an aspiring novelist who has been writing all her life or to a born storyteller with an awe-inspiring gift of gab. Now we know better!

We also now recognize our outrageous naiveté in thinking we could write this book all by ourselves. Many people have generously given of their time to share their experiences "inside" with us, and to them we are most grateful.

For their stories and input about Arapahoe County Jail, we want to thank Candice Brown, Brenda Carns, Cindy Chadwick, Susan Oakes, Bobbie Patrick, Gwen Proctor, and Bob Tenny. For their daily shouldering of many trials and triumphs with us, we thank our amazing colleagues, Tania Beck-Loftis, Ginger Bilthuis, Robin Broome, Sue Buck, Sarah Danielson, Lynn Dyba, Angie Greer, Christine Kreger, Monica Owens, and Phil Rahn. For the same kind of input about the Colorado state prison libraries, many thanks to Nina Aldrich, Holly Jo Butt, Darlene Cole, Ladell Marta, Vicki Osborn, and Teresa Silveria.

With respect and a great deal of professional pride, we want to thank the many contributors to the Association of Bookmobiles and Outreach Services' listserv for their sage advice over the years. Although our jail-related questions have been slightly off-topic, this extraordinary group has never failed to give us the answers we needed; in particular, we are indebted to Helen Bolton, Jeannie Dilgier-Hill, Melanie Johnson, Libby Moore, and Lou Spicer. We have benefited, as have our patrons, from the tireless advocacy of Satia Orange and Glennor Shirley; our conversations with you have been few, but always productive. Finally, special thanks to Diane Walden for the whirlwind tour of southern Colorado's finer correctional library establishments—what a ride!

Thanks to our editor, Barbara Ittner, who walked two greenhorns through the book-authoring process for over eighteen months. Much gratitude to the officers of the Arapahoe County Sheriff's Office, particularly Lieutenant Joe Ferro, Lieutenant Chris Manos, Captain Jeffrey Spoon, Captain Frank Henn, and Captain Tom Bay for their vision and support of our library. The same thanks go to Chris Brogan, Donna Walker, Reed Osborne, Marlu Burkamp, and Eloise May of Arapahoe Library District for upholding librarianship's highest ideals by supporting equitable access for our most chronically underserved patrons.

We know we have many more people to thank. If we have inadvertently omitted anyone here, we assure you it is only due to inevitable limitations of time, space, and memory; be assured that we do gratefully recollect your contributions in quieter hours.

At last, special thanks to Carl and Carolan, and Carol, Earl, and Curt for their patience, support, and encouragement on the home front. We couldn't have done any of this without you.

Introduction

Jails and prisons are microcosms of a world many of us will never see on the outside. It is a tough world, a street-smart world. It is an ethnically, culturally, and religiously diverse world. It is a world of high school dropouts and college graduates. It is a world of men, women, and, in some cases, children. It is a world of many languages and many homelands. It is the barrio, the ghetto, the suburbs, and the country club, thrown together in a strangely coherent culture of rules, order, and schedules. It is a world of despair and a world of possibility.

It is a world librarians can serve with the skills, principles, and ethics practiced in public libraries.

The construction of correctional facilities of all kinds is increasing at an unprecedented pace. In the last twenty-five years, the number of state facilities has increased by 70 percent. Of the top ten states in terms of prison expansion, Texas saw a 706 percent increase between 1979 and 2000, and Florida saw a 115 percent increase; the average increase of all top ten states was 210 percent (Lawrence and Travis 2004). One in thirty-seven Americans is or has been incarcerated at some point in his or her life (Chaddock 2003). The Federal Bureau of Prisons updates prison population statistics every week: as of December 1, 2005, more than 188,000 persons were incarcerated in federal or private facilities (Bureau of Prisons 2005). Federal and state prisons together, at the end of 2003, held 1,387,848 inmates; local jails held 691,301 (Bureau of Justice 2004). However, because jails "take and release" inmates, compared to prisons, which "take and hold," the admission rate in jails is between ten and thirteen times that of prisons. In other words, America's prison population turns over once about every two years, whereas the jail population turns over up to twenty-five times annually (Schlanger 2003). The relative stability of the prison population as opposed to the extremely high turnover in jails has considerable implications for the types of services librarians can provide. But regardless of facility type, the numbers point to an enormous population of people in critical need of access to legal information and recreational library materials.

Most incarcerated people will ultimately be released. Short-term offenders usually find themselves back in exactly the same environment in which they were arrested. Long-term prisoners increasingly find themselves

1

confronted by a world of technology—ATMs, Internet, cell phones, iPods—that most of us take for granted, but with which they have had little or no experience. Reemployment is always a concern, as is reconnection with family and friends on the outside.

Public libraries, as agents of social change and as institutions of learning, can help inmates and prisoners adjust to the realities of their lives within a correctional institution. We can also help prepare inmates and prisoners for their eventual release by supporting their personal goals. Everything the public library can provide (with a few obvious subject matter exceptions, like lock-picking) can be provided in correctional facilities. This includes:

- Recreational reading, viewing, and listening materials
- Life-enrichment materials and classes on everything from parenting to interpersonal communication to learning foreign languages
- Literacy and ESL materials, classes, and support
- Legal information about criminal law, civil rights, lawsuits, and family law
- Resources for job seekers
- Intellectual stimulation
- A place to feel safe and to free the mind

Finally, corrections librarians are ambassadors for the public library. We know the value of public library resources for people in need; but because public libraries are governmental institutions, many marginalized people in our society approach the library with extreme suspicion, if they approach it at all. Good corrections librarians build bridges that connect facility libraries to the public library world.

Why Correctional Libraries?

The first question we must ask ourselves, not only as librarians but also as taxpayers and members of a public who will probably not experience incarceration, is this: Why is correctional library service important? We think the reasons libraries in prisons and jails are important are the same reasons that educational, spiritual, and life-enriching programs in prisons and jails are important. A philosophy professor who teaches classes to inmates in Texas states, "It is impossible to exaggerate the power of ideas and concepts—for example, justice, truth, goodness, virtue, beauty—to grab a human mind and redirect a person's life" (Jablecki 2000). A librarian and criminal justice professor states, "They [the books] do more than keep prisoners out of trouble. They accomplish mental therapy; they relieve tension; they carry the prisoner outside the confines of his own thought; they keep him from turning his mind in on itself. They give indirect education to men who could never be lured into a classroom" (Sullivan 2000). We can think of a lot of other reasons, and will discuss many of them in detail when we look more closely at applying the public library model outside the public library. But first, let's take a quick look at the history of correctional libraries in the English-speaking world.

History of Correctional Libraries

Writing in 1995, *Down for the Count* author Brenda Vogel stated that while the purpose and mission of public libraries is not in question, there is ongoing philosophical debate about the role of libraries in prisons. Ten years later, we propose that the role of public libraries actually is up for reanalysis. As public libraries evolve, so too may their counterparts on the inside. But while public libraries seek to redefine their place in their communities in response to social and technological changes at the societal level, the overriding influence defining prison library services is the prevailing stance of the penal administration community about what a correctional facility is intended to accomplish.

Indeed, for the last 100 years in this country, we have seen the pendulum swing forward from a predominantly punitive penal philosophy to a more rehabilitative position, and back again. The question at the center of this ever-evolving concept concerns how many and exactly which rights prisoners should retain upon incarceration. Scarcely more than a century ago, the answer was zero. Imprisonment was viewed as a means for moral and spiritual reflection and atonement. Indeed, confined as they were to solitary cells under abysmal conditions, prisoners were still allowed access to reading material . . . as long as it was religious in nature and written with the intent of leading the reader back to the straight and narrow. Fast forward a few decades and we see a shift away from physical punishment and spiritual reclamation to emotional and psychological rehabilitation and behavioral reeducation. Prison and jail programs in general moved away from religious influences and adopted a position more in line with the psychology field. Prison and jail libraries opened up in a similar vein, from carrying strictly "redemptive" materials to more general interest and recreational reading collections. Early in the twentieth century, the American Library Association (ALA) joined forces with the

American Correctional Association to create a recommended reading list for prisoners.

Inmate and prisoner access to the justice system and to legal research materials is another evolving concept. In 1969, a federal district court ruled in *Johnson v. Avery* that the state of Tennessee's policy on not allowing prisoners to help other prisoners with legal research was unconstitutional, because it effectively barred illiterate prisoners from accessing federal habeas corpus. The verdict was appealed, reversed, and then landed in the United States Supreme Court, where the decision of the federal district court was upheld. However, due to the reluctance of prison administrators to allow extensive contact between prisoners (citing security reasons), the actual application of the provision of *Johnson v. Avery* was extremely limited.

In 1974, two Massachusetts cases, *Wolf v. McDonnell* and *Stone v. Boone,* mandated that prisons provide on-site law libraries. These rulings paved the way for *Bounds v. Smith* in 1977, in which the Supreme Court ruled that correctional facilities were obligated to provide prisoners with adequately stocked on-site law libraries. An alternative was also provided by the ruling, which stated that individuals experienced in legal research and writing procedures could assist indigent and illiterate prisoners in drafting legal proceedings (Wilhelmus 1999).

Everything changed in 1996 with legislation that, at first glance, seems to guarantee the provisions of *Bounds v. Smith*. In *Casey v. Lewis,* the Supreme Court responded to accusations against the Arizona Department of Corrections that prisoners were experiencing a system-wide dearth of access to adequate legal reference materials. The Supreme Court upheld prisoners' right to said resources; however, it also ruled that for offenders to claim a rights violation under the provisions of *Bounds v. Smith*, they must be able to prove that they experienced "actual harm" due to inadequate prison law libraries or legal assistance. Inmate and prisoner recourse to sue a facility for violating *Bounds v. Smith* was essentially hamstrung by *Casey v. Lewis.*

Today, we see many jail and prison library programs reverting to the American penal system's philosophical infancy and a nationwide trend toward tougher sentencing and tougher time served. However, in spite of this bad news, there are many rays of hope. The state of Maryland's motto regarding prison programs is "The Heart of the Maryland Prison System is the Library." Several family literacy programs are thriving all over the country, including Hennepin County Library's *Read-To-Me* program and Arapahoe Library District's *Begin With Books in Jail.* Arapahoe Library District also created the acclaimed *Choose Freedom—READ!* program, in which public librarians present book talks to county jail inmates several times per year (Clark and Patrick 1999). Nationwide, public library outreach staff regularly visit their county jails with rotating collections of donated books; other public libraries, like Arapahoe Library District and Monroe County Public Library, operate on-site contractual libraries with their own budgets for purchasing materials (de la Peña McCook 2004). Clearly, there are cracks in the walls through which public libraries can reach the underserved incarcerated.

To reduce confusion, we need to briefly mention the organizational and functional differences between jails and prisons because those differences dramatically impact the kinds of library services that can be offered to inmate patrons. Common parlance allows interchangeability of the terms "jail" and "prison." However, dramatic differences include the way the two types of entities are funded, who governs them, and the term of stay for their residents. Jails are funded at the county and municipal levels, as are most public libraries. Their organizational hierarchy very well might include an elected official—usually the sheriff—at the top with sworn law enforcement comprising much of the staffing. Jails detain people awaiting trial, convicted prisoners awaiting transfer to state prison, and inmates serving short sentences, usually less than a year.

Prisons are usually state or federally funded, although private prisons are becoming much more common. State departments of corrections govern state prisons; a state prison warden is usually not an elected official, and state prison officers are not necessarily law enforcement officers with authority outside the prison system itself. Federal prisons are governed by the Bureau of Prisons, an agency of the U.S. Justice Department; as in state-run facilities, the directors tend to be appointed and the guards are not necessarily law enforcement. Convicted persons facing longer sentences, usually over a year, typically go to prison.

We will talk in greater detail about the differences between jail and prison in Chapter 4.

The Importance of Correctional Libraries

Now let's revisit the question about why correctional libraries are important in this day and age. A colleague of ours, Lynn Dyba, retired librarian and cocreator of the *Choose Freedom—READ!* project, often said, "Reading is a civilized act we do for ourselves." Libraries lend a measure of *civilized normalcy and familiarity* to an otherwise regimented and often frightening environment that by design segregates its inhabitants from the rest of the world. Librarians can work wonders by treating their prisoner patrons with the simple civility taken for granted by library patrons on the outside.

One of the principle roles of public libraries in the U.S. is as a "university of the common man." In jail and prison, with a lot of hard time on their hands, many inmates rediscover an *opportunity for learning* they either never had, or never fully embraced in school. "The people in here are starving for information," one inmate told us.

As we've already mentioned, most jail and prison libraries are required by law to provide inmates some level of access to legal research materials. But wading through statutes and case law written in elaborate legalese is a daunting proposition. Librarians inside can provide the kind of bibliographic instruction inmates need to exercise their constitutional right to judiciary access.

Over the years, we've heard many of our colleagues, friends, and family members express doubt about whether library service is necessary, or just an expensive "perk" for the incarcerated. In response, allow us to paraphrase the sentiments of Erica's father: "You can't read and riot at the same time." The obvious implication is that library service inside a correctional institution might have demonstrable *security* benefits. Though we know of no systematic studies comparing the rate of violent incidents between correctional facilities with good libraries and those without (and this is a research question we'd very much like to see pursued), we can say that library services tend to be better funded, better staffed, and more comprehensive in facilities governed by innovative and compassionate wardens and captains. Thus, good library service can be an integral part of progressive correctional operations as a whole, which makes library service a benefit to facilities looking to improve their accreditation scores, if nothing else. Further, offering library services to correctional facility staff, as well as to inmates, creates opportunities for fostering the requisite goodwill for connecting inmates to library resources.

Library outreach programs in general provide a *model of service* when considering the mission and the future of public libraries. Public libraries are facing radical changes, largely because of the cultural impact of technology. In a depressed economy, they also face staffing shortages and severe financial constraints. In the midst of transition and uncertainty, public libraries must reevaluate their roles and how they do business. Some libraries are responding by shifting their outreach endeavors into high gear. Reaching out to the disenfranchised—such as non-English speakers, immigrants, lower-income families, at-risk children, and prisoners—embraces a fresh public service ethic while preserving the library's mission of equal access for all.

Why This Book?

An obvious publishing gap on the subject of correctional libraries, particularly those in jail, revealed a need for this kind of book. The *ALA Policy Manual* (n.d.) specifically identifies services to jails and other detention facilities as the responsibility of public libraries in the same taxing districts. But the financial and personnel resources to meet this end are limited, as are professional guides and advisory materials. The scant number of out-of-print and out-of-date publications represent almost everything currently available, and everything currently available focuses all but exclusively on prison, not jail, librarianship. ALA and the Association of Specialized and Cooperative Library Agencies (ASCLA) have a handful of printed standards for correctional institutions, but they are out of print and outdated.

There are two excellent how-to books on correctional libraries, *Libraries Inside: A Practical Guide for Prison Librarians* by Rhea Joyce Rubin and Daniel Suvak, and *Down for the Count* by Brenda Vogel. Both, however, are out of print, somewhat out of date, and focus on prison libraries to the exclusion of jail, juvenile, and community corrections services. The dearth of support material published by professional library associations is probably one reason that less than 20 percent of American jails have library services provided by the local public library.

Changing trends in incarceration patterns, especially the inverse correlation between reduced rates of crime and increased rates of incarceration, call for current perspectives on library service in and to incarcerated populations. While all jail and prison librarians deal with their share of difficult inmates, and while many prison librarians provide service to the worst imaginable offenders, policies such as mandatory sentencing and the war on drugs have resulted in state prisons virtually overflowing with nonviolent offenders, 95 percent of whom will ultimately be released (Gainsborough and Mauer 2000; Bureau of Justice 2003). With the public library profession emphasizing greater outreach, the time is ripe for a fresh look at this oft overlooked—but expanding—opportunity for library service.

This book differs from other works on correctional library service in a couple of important respects. First, we hope it reflects our passion for jail librarianship. As librarians, we have found this unique niche of public library outreach to be the most exciting, enriching, and edifying experience of our professional careers. The challenges we face every day on the inside take on a strangely epic scope when considered in relation to the daily civ-ilized realities of the public library world. The work satisfies soft corners of our hearts—those corners housing our internal social workers, teachers, and ministers—while strengthening our characters, our principles, and our resolve.

"Why do you do this job?"

As we wrote this book, our evangelical glee intensifying with every page, we paused to wonder, "Are we the only people who feel this great about working in a place like jail?" So we hit the streets to find out. Here are some of the things people working inside are saying. Names have been changed, here and throughout the book, to protect the innocent—and the not-so-innocent!

Terry (youth offender prison librarian): "I do this job because people care that I'm here. There aren't a lot of people who want to do this job, and it has to be done."

Barb (former county jail librarian, now in an urban public library): "I did the job because it meant serving an underserved population without judgment, in a kind and dependable manner. It also entailed inventiveness in providing the best possible resources and programs within limited confines, as dictated by budget, staffing constraints, and facility use."

Valeri (women's prison librarian): "I do this job because it gives me the chance to do absolutely everything in a library. And unlike adult services in a public library, inmates have the enthusi-asm usually only seen in children's services. We are celebrities, heroes, because we give them what they want and what they need."

Sabrina (county jail librarian): "I do this job because I get to see changes in people. I actually see the light bulb going off in people's heads. I love intense one-on-one discussions on finding the answer, either to a reference or question or the harder question of how to become a real person worthy of respect."

Donna (prison librarian): "I do this job because prisoners are the most wonderful, grateful audience I've ever served. No day is ever the same, and you can never expect to get through your list of things to do today because thirty other things always come up."

Emily (former county jail librarian, now in public library outreach): "I do this job because I get to interact with people who would probably never make use of my skills as a librarian in the course of their daily lives. Our library provides opportunities for expanding people's understanding of the world."

Linda (maximum security prison librarian): "I do this job because when my patrons come to me, they've been in solitary for a long time. They have a deer-in-the-headlights look and are completely unsocialized. After a couple of weeks, I explain what they can get from the library and they relax a little."

Bill (former county jail librarian, now in a suburban public library): "I did the job because it meant helping the down and out and feeling good about it."

Second, we wanted to write a book that could capture some of the fun of being a librarian in a correctional facility. That's right. Fun! Many of the vignettes and anecdotes we'll share with you are poignant; many more are humorous. We include these personal glimpses for two reasons. First, we want to emphasize the humanity of jail and prison, the correctional culture, its residents, and its staff. It is far too easy to overlook that part. Second, we include these stories as a mild acid test for our readers who may be considering a job in a correctional library. The environment rewards a certain sense of humor; if you come away from reading our stories feeling more shocked than amused, we strongly encourage you to spend some time observing a correctional library's daily operations firsthand before committing yourself to working there. Our stories are not intended to be sensationalistic; we employ them to add depth to our message that even though jail can be frightening, exasperating, challenging, and infuriating, it can also be hugely enjoyable.

Organization

Library Services to the Incarcerated shows you how to provide exemplary library services to inmates by applying the public library model. The book addresses four kinds of correctional library services: prison, jail, juvenile, and community corrections. However, we readily admit that our personal expertise is jail libraries. We will discuss all aspects of library service, since a disproportionate number of correctional libraries are one-person operations requiring a broad range of skills. Thus, we will try to cover everything from user needs studies, purchasing, cataloging, and weeding to hiring, budgeting, program planning, and advocacy.

The book consists of two parts. Part One spotlights the human side of jail librarianship—of the librarians, the prisoners, and the staff. We will expand upon our concept of the public library model and what we believe its application means for those working inside correctional libraries. Then we look at personal qualities and professional skills that characterize good jail librarians, explore helpful resources, describe the rewards of jail librarianship, and discuss common challenges. We expose some of the myths and stereotypes surrounding inmates and examine their demographics, diversity, and information needs. Here we offer advice on establishing fair practices, identifying and avoiding inmate games, and building appropriate personal boundaries. Finally, we describe how to function within the correctional facility culture, including comparing how different kinds of facilities operate, what regulations and standards can guide you, ethical considerations, and some good ways of working with law enforcement and nonlibrary civilian staff.

Part Two explores the logistical side of jail libraries, including facilities, equipment, and technology; collection development; services and programming; managing human resources, including volunteers and inmate workers; budgeting and funding; and advocacy within the facility and in the community.

A Word of Caution

It's a mistake to walk into a correctional facility with the idea that you, the librarian, are there to redeem anyone. If there is redemption inside such a place, it resides in the hearts of its occupants, not in the content of its library or the good intentions of its staff. The reality of jail and prison librarianship is that we make small but meaningful differences in many lives every day, differences that may not be long remembered, but that are immediate and are immediately recognized. Inmate patrons are quite probably the most overtly appreciative patrons a librarian could ever work with, and the rewards of serving them are the closest thing to instant gratification any job on this earth can offer.

Scope and Audience

Correctional libraries are not everyone's cup of tea. That said, we consider our primary audience to be you hardy souls who have already discovered that correctional libraries are, in fact, your cup of tea or who are interested in exploring the possibilities. You may be a practicing librarian; or you may be a dedicated paraprofessional doing everything a librarian is trained and expected to do, learning it by doing it on the job, and doing it for peanuts. You may have no public library experience, but want to do more for your patrons and don't know where to begin. To this end, we extend our insights and advice, as well as a conceptual framework with which to start considering new modes and methods of service. Public librarians and correctional facility administrators wanting to initiate or enhance library services to inmates and prisoners are another audience for this guide. We hope this book will help you think outside the very large boxes that are jails and prisons.

Whoever you are and whatever your motive, if you have an interest in library outreach and services to nontraditional patrons, we invite you to read this book. We invite you to consider whether your passion for learning, coaching, and teaching, your ability to envision greater possibilities beyond present circumstances, and your desire to serve the most chronically underserved library patrons in this country mark you as one of those amazing souls who, to put it quite frankly, belongs behind bars.

References

American Library Association. N.d. Services and responsibilities of libraries: Services to detention facilities and jails. In *ALA policy manual* (sec. 52.1). Retrieved January 30, 2005 from http://www.ala.org/ala/ourassociation/governingdocs/policymanual/services.htm.

Association of Specialized and Cooperative Library Agencies. 1980. *Survey of library services to local correctional facilities.* Chicago: American Library Association.

Bureau of Justice. 2003. *Reentry trends in the United States* (August 20). Retrieved August 31, 2005 from http://www.ojp.usdoj.gov/bjs/reentry/reentry.htm.

Bureau of Justice 2004. *U.S. prison population approaches 1.5 million* (November 7). Retrieved January 30, 2005 from http://www.ojp.usdoj.gov/bjs/pub/press/p03pr.htm.

Chaddock, G. R. 2003. U.S. notches world's highest incarceration rate. *Christian Science Monitor* (August 18). Retrieved January 30, 2005 from http://www.csmonitor.com/2003/0818/p02s01-usju.html.

Clark, S., and B. Patrick. 1999. Choose Freedom Read: Book talks behind bars. *American Libraries, 30*(7), 63–64. Retrieved December 3, 2005 from InfoTrac Web: General Reference Center Gold database.

de la Peña McCook, K. 2004. Public libraries and people in jail. *Reference and User Services Quarterly, 44*(1), 26–30.

Federal Bureau of Prisons. 2005. *Weekly population report* (December 1). Retrieved December 3, 2005 from http://bop.gov/news/weekly_report.jsp.

Gainsborough, J. and M. Mauer. 2000. Diminishing returns: Crime and incarceration in the 1990s. *The Sentencing Project* (Fall). Retrieved April 20, 2005 from http://www.sentencingproject.org/pdfs/9039.pdf.

Jablecki, L. T. 2000. Prison inmates meet Socrates. *Humanist, 60*(3). Retrieved May 9, 2005 from http://www.findarticles.com/p/articles/mi_m1374/is_3_60/ai_62111876#continue.

Lawrence, S. and J. Travis. 2004. *The new landscape of imprisonment: Mapping America's prison expansion* (April). Washington, D.C.: Urban Institute Justice Policy Center. Retrieved May 8, 2005 from http://www.urbaninstitute.org/UploadedPDF/410994_mapping_prisons.pdf.

Schlanger, M. 2003. *Differences between jails and prisons.* Paper presented at Prisons Seminar, Harvard Law School.

Sullivan, L. 2000. The least of our brethren: Library service to prisoners. *American Libraries, 31*(5). Retrieved January 3, 2005 from InfoTrac Web: General Reference Center Gold database.

Vogel, B. 1995. *Down for the count.* Lanham, MD: Scarecrow Press, Inc.

Wilhelmus, D. W. 1999. Where have all the law libraries gone? *Corrections Today, 61.* Retrieved January 3, 2005 from InfoTrac Web: General Reference Center Gold database.

The Public Library Model

Before getting into how the public library model has been applied at the Arapahoe County Detention Facility (ACDF) library and how it can be applied elsewhere, let's elaborate on what we mean by "the public library model." ALA has identified eleven core values of modern librarianship; we believe three of these are particularly pertinent when applying the public library model in prisons and jails: access and intellectual freedom, privacy and confidentiality, and social responsibility (in which customer service can be defined as a commitment to equitable treatment of all library users). Throughout this book, you'll see how these values often conflict with values generally governing correctional facilities, namely restriction, surveillance, and punishment. In an *American Libraries* article about building a juvenile detention facility library from scratch, Veronica A. Davis (2000) notes:

 Libraries are portals to new worlds. They serve up possibility, learning, and, in a word, freedom. In this sense libraries run counter to the spirit and intent of the average prison, where jailers scrutinize every portal, every possibility, and every freedom, including the figurative ones offered in the quiet refuge of the library.

Probably the most critical element in applying ALA values to a correctional library setting is your own willingness to do so. If your own core values do not mirror those of the library profession at large, everything we are about to tell you is meaningless. Brenda Vogel (1995) states:

 Differences between library service in prison and in the outside community are created both by a suspension in the belief

13

of the value of library service in a democracy when applied to a prison situation, and by librarians choosing not to apply consensual theory and practice to an institutional environment.

The prison librarian is not there to add to anyone's punishment. (Leffers 1990)

If you really are committed to bringing the public library model into prison or jail, your belief in equal access and equal treatment of all library patrons, regardless of where they live or of the circumstances of their lives, must be unwavering. As a correctional librarian, you will be called upon at some point, and probably more than once, to defend these values.

Access and Intellectual Freedom

The whole point of incarceration is to cut offenders off from the rest of the world, to punish them for their crimes, and, in some cases, to protect the general public from any future criminal actions through the imposition of life—or death—sentences. In jails, deputies scrupulously monitor inmates' movements; except for a few trusties (inmates who work in the facility), no one walks outside the cell blocks unaccompanied. Inmates are discouraged from speaking to other inmates outside their own dayrooms. While inmates can close the doors to their cells, they cannot open locked cell doors; only the deputies can do that.

Prisons are long-term facilities that usually house more homogeneous populations in terms of security level than jails. (In jail, inmates charged with capital crimes may be housed right next to inmates in for misdemeanors.) Consequently, prisons sometimes permit prisoners more freedom of movement than is allowable in jail. But regardless of the level of unaccompanied movement these people enjoy on the inside, every prison and jail has a wall around it. Telephone access is restricted, as are outside visitors. The types of mail inmates can receive are strictly regulated, even down to certain newspapers over others. While some inmates have televisions in their cells, a common television room for all is more likely, so no one person can watch precisely what he wants exactly when he wants to.

Public libraries, "the people's university," are all about unfettered access, not only to the world of information, but to information specialists. Extended hours are not enough; now we have online 24-hour access to catalogs and reference librarians all over the country. Some public libraries have initiated 24-hour hold pickup boxes and paperback and DVD vending machines. Inside a correctional facility, access takes a backseat to the daily imperative of keeping track of who is where, and when. Yes, the facility runs 24/7, but that does not mean it is adequately staffed to provide an officer for every prisoner who wants to look up case law in the library. Nor is there always sufficient staffing to ensure adequate protection for civilian staff, including the librarians, entering prisoner living units. Other priorities compete for officers' time and attention as well, like medical, educational, and pastoral services. There are never enough officers to go around.

In public libraries, the Internet has revolutionized how we provide reference services. But most inmates and prisoners do not have access to even offline computer resources, let alone the Internet. And while access to both public defenders and the courts is a guaranteed right, access to legal information resources is not uniformly provided because there are few guidelines to help determine what kind of access is adequate. In some jurisdictions, giving inmates just one hour a week to use dated print materials fulfills the legal requirement. And today, all over the country, correctional facility law libraries are closing, the justification being that since inmates have legal representation, the provisions of *Bounds v. Smith* are satisfied without law libraries.

In terms of information access, the ALA's Freedom to Read statement affirms access to a limitless diversity of views and expressions, subject matter, and authors and publishers, with or without controversial personal lives or political affiliations. It affirms the responsibility of librarians to challenge any encroachment on the freedom to read by individuals, groups, or government entities, and the responsibility of librarians to provide books that encourage diversity of thought and expression. At the same time, the Freedom to Read statement rejects using personal moral, political, or aesthetic preferences as a standard for what should be published or circulated, coercing the reading tastes of adults, and labeling any expression or author as subversive or dangerous (ALA 1994). But in an environment that denies inmates even the most basic of democratic prerogatives—the right to vote—the Freedom to Read statement rings a little hollow. How do you get to "yes" in a culture built on "no"?

Correctional libraries are not independent agencies, nor are their patrons free human beings bearing all democratic rights thereto. Correctional libraries, be they a department run by the facility or a contract operation from the outside, fall under the absolute authority of a nonlibrary agency. The art of bringing the public library model into this environment consists of honoring the spirit of ALA's highest ideals while following the correctional facility's rules. It is an interesting and daily challenge that demands common sense, diplomacy, patience, and not a little give-and-take.

Unlikely Allies

Several years ago, one of our detention facility's chief purchasing agents demanded—through his assistant—that we remove several titles from our recreational reading collection. He objected to titles that included the words "death," "kill," or "die." So much for *To Kill A Mockingbird, Death of a Salesman,* and *Never Die Alone*!

So I employed a tried and true diversionary tactic: I stalled.

"Please ask him to visit us the next time he's in the building so he can see what we do," I told his assistant. As soon as I hung up the phone, I began cataloging newly arrived titles like a maniac, hoping to get them into patrons' hands and out of our office before they were taken away.

The purchasing agent did come over. And he was duly amazed at the depth and breadth of our collection. And he still walked away with about half a dozen books he found offensive and unceremoniously pitched them in the dumpster behind the facility.

Fortunately, his assistant's cubicle just happened to overlook the aforementioned dumpster. After her boss left for the day, she went outside and retrieved all of our books. Shortly thereafter, the purchasing agent was fired and our "incendiary" items were placed back on the shelf.

Privacy and Confidentiality

ALA's Core Values Task Force project lists confidentiality and privacy second only to access as central professional values, stating, "Protecting user privacy and confidentiality is necessary for intellectual freedom and fundamental to the ethics and practice of librarianship" (ALA Council 2004). In ALA's statement, "Libraries: An American Value," the preservation of privacy and confidentiality is characterized as a part of a "contract" with library patrons (ALA 1999). The ALA Freedom to View statement, as well as the ALA Code of Ethics, also cites privacy as a fundamental professional value (ALA 1990, 1995).

But inside a correctional facility, privacy and confidentiality take a backseat to surveillance and scrutiny. Incoming mail may be carefully examined to prevent conspiracy with outsiders to traffic contraband or arrange an escape, and to prevent harassment of people on the outside. Telephone calls may also be monitored for content. Jail and prison buildings are surrounded by and are full of cameras; barely an inch or corner cannot be observed through lenses transmitting images to screens in central control rooms.

Aside from security concerns, privacy is easily compromised by the inmates themselves. Apart from administrative segregation and administrative lockdown, few inmates have a cell to themselves. Confined to small rooms equipped with bunk beds and floor mats, inmates literally live on top of each other. During routine lockdowns, the only personal space an inmate may have in a room with two or more people is his or her bed. Personal effects may be stored on shelves, or in cabinets or trunks, but not locked up. Inmates' reading choices are therefore open for all to see.

Sometimes, the physical size and layout of the library or the expediencies of bookcart service preclude complete confidentiality. The ACDF law library has never had more than a few dozen square feet of floor space for its legal reference local area network (LAN). Essentially, no matter how quietly inmates and staff speak, pretty well everyone in the room is privy to the conversation. Our bookcart service in the dayrooms is usually so rushed that inmates must browse the carts shoulder to shoulder, and there is no way to hide titles during checkout when the work space consists of the cluttered top shelf of a typical book truck.

But that's not all. Privacy and confidentiality must sometimes be breached by library staff as well. In order to establish a reasonable limit to the volume of patron requests for photocopying services, the ACDF library only photocopies documents going to the courts. This requires at least a cursory glance at a patron's originals to prevent abuses of this policy and to preserve equity of service. If inmates have access to word processing software in a facility with policies governing the content of inmate-created documents, staff needs to monitor what inmates are typing. In those very rare facilities that allow prisoners to access the Internet, monitoring what's happening on the screen becomes especially critical.

All of these compromises to privacy and confidentiality demonstrate daily the following basic corrections principle: security comes first. One aspect of successful jail librarianship comes from knowing how to tailor public library values in order to fit within the institutional environment. Some challenges to privacy, such as a deputy's demand for access to law library attendance records or to a list of a particular inmate's checked-out items, can be handled in much the same way they would be in the public library. Court orders work the same way inside, but because of the intricacies of building relationships with other facility staff, it's imperative to try to talk the requestor out of such a request before falling back on due process. Some challenges, especially those created by living and working in close quarters, must simply be tolerated until environmental or procedural changes accommodate improvements. The bottom line is to try to preserve as much privacy and confidentiality as possible, with the understanding that the degree to which this is possible in public libraries is not a realistic expectation inside.

Social Responsibility

The ALA Policy Manual (1986) states:

> The broad social responsibilities of the American Library Association are defined in terms of *the contribution that librarianship can make in ameliorating or solving the critical problems of society*; support for efforts to help *inform and educate the people of the United States on these problems* and to encourage them to examine the many views on and the facts regarding each problem; and *the willingness of ALA to take a position on current critical issues with the relationship to libraries and library service* set forth in the position statement. (Emphasis ours.)

In our introduction, we cautioned librarians against undertaking the role of redeemer. But corrections librarians everywhere can ameliorate problems every day in many different ways. Claudine O'Leary states: "Having a library in jail means there are community members in a place where they largely don't like to have civilians. There are many times when we'll hear officers say horrible things or threaten to beat someone up and they turn around and see us and they have to quickly change what they're saying. They don't want it to get out. Just our presence there made a difference" (Mantilla 2001).

Simply making books available gives inmates a lifeline. "What is seen as a sedentary leisure activity that wouldn't constitute a normal part of an inmate's life 'on the out,'" says prison writer-in-residence Martyn Waites (2004), "becomes inside a vital tool for survival, escape and enrichment." Waites goes on to say, "Prison is a seedbed for growing future readers. It may be the only time some prisoners have ever come into contact with a book." In our high-tech era, this is an extraordinary opportunity for public librarians to advocate the value of the printed word!

Good solid customer service offers you an opportunity to rehumanize a chronically inhumane environment in which inmates and most facility staff interrelate according to a tension-generating paradigm of "us versus them." Good customer service in jail depends upon two things: civility and fairness. A disproportionate number of inmates come from impoverished backgrounds; many do not speak English. In these cultures, the public library doesn't always have much impact. Part of this may be due to the impression residents of poorer communities have of the library as government institution. Certainly behind bars, if you're not in prisoner garb, the inmates automatically lump you in with the security staff. It takes time to build trust as you walk the delicate line between advocating for inmate patrons and honoring the facility's rules. Friendly, competent professionalism is a hallmark of public library customer service; traditional library patrons expect it. For prisoners, many of whom may never have set foot in a public library, this kind of customer service is alien. And it will be treated with skepticism at first. That's where fairness comes in. In this environment, as in the public library, it pays to have well-considered policies governing materials selection, conduct in the library, means of accessing library services, and the extent to which services will be provided. These policies protect you by establishing boundaries and guiding your actions, but also by ensuring that everyone plays by the same rules. When inmates see that everybody will be treated in the same way, they will begin to trust your good intentions. If they come to accept your kindness and professionalism, you will have broken through a barrier of suspicion and misunderstanding that many of these people have harbored their entire lives. And maybe, when they get out, they won't be afraid to utilize the resources of their local public libraries.

While we reiterate that librarians are not avatars of social redemption, you cannot ignore your role in improving the status quo within the correctional facility community itself. If that means nothing more than providing a bright moment in an otherwise bleak day, you've positively impacted the status quo. If you can support the inmate who is learning to read or is attempting to get her GED, you've positively impacted the status quo. If you help someone research his case in the absence of a private attorney and that person can prove his innocence as a consequence, you have positively impacted the status quo. If you diffuse potentially dangerous situations by providing prisoners with diversionary reading, you have positively impacted the status quo.

Models of Service

In-House Service

The Heart of the Maryland Prison System is the Library (from the state of Maryland's Correctional Education Libraries Web site).

The wide range of possibilities for providing service in jails and prisons largely depends upon two factors. Facility administration determines *quantity* of service, specifically what level of service will be staffed and funded, and by whom. The presence or absence of a civilian librarian and that person's opinion of and approach to library service to inmates strongly influences *quality* of service.

Most correctional facilities provide some kind of on-site library service that can range from the provision of battered donated paperbacks on a couple of dingy shelves in each living unit to spacious, full-service libraries replete with recreational, reference, and legal collections, several civilian and inmate staff, computers, listening (and viewing) stations, and year-round programs. In between is a public library outreach services model, where inmates do not actually visit the library, but book trucks restocked regularly from the library's collection are taken into the living units for patrons to browse.

Library as Destination

The library is the one place where young inmates should not be reminded of their confinement. After all, the library is the heart of any academic environment; and isn't home where the heart is? (Davis 2000)

The service model for most prison libraries—and a few jail libraries—is that of library as destination. It is a place for prisoners to go. All of the challenges, trivial and large, that face public librarians in their library buildings are present here. ADA compliance, lighting, plumbing, furnishings, and anything having to do with physical space happens here.

But *space* doesn't create the concept of *place*, although it certainly influences it. A sense of place is generated by people's feelings about a space. This is what we mean when we talk about library-as-destination. In an environment as sterile and industrial as most prison and jail complexes, the library is often the one place where inmates can go to forget about being behind bars.

Librarian as "Information Concierge"

This concept of "concierge marketing" states that in the presently evolving business economy, more and more customers will turn to "concierges," essentially to outsource basic functions of life such as food shopping, arranging travel, and managing utilities for homeowners too busy to negotiate their own long-distance calling plans, wait around for cable TV repair technicians, or change service providers when necessary (Ettenberg 2002). In a prison or jail environment, residents have nothing but time on their hands, but they also do not have control over most of the conditions of their lives. In that sense, everyone working in a correctional environment provides a concierge service of some sort. Contracts for food services, cleaning services, maintenance, and, yes, even library services, are negotiated for inmates on their behalf. We are deliberately stretching the concierge metaphor here, just to give you an idea of what it means.

In the library world, the concept of "information concierge" is especially relevant when considering any kind of library outreach. If a patron walks into your library, he or she has already done half the work. But the nature of outreach assumes that you go to your patrons. And obviously, you can't carry an entire library with you when you go, no matter how big your bookmobile is!

So building relationships with off-site patrons is important. They must be able to trust you to understand their needs and your responsiveness to them. This is particularly true when your patrons absolutely can't visit the library. It's true of homebound public library patrons, of many rural and urban poor bookmobile patrons, and of inmate patrons who do not have a destination library they can visit. These patrons could comprise an entire facility, as ours does, since we don't have that kind of library. Or these could be patrons temporarily in "the hole" for facility rules infractions or those serving long periods of time in lockdown as part of their sentences.

The concierge model also works to serve inmates—and this is most of them—who do not have access to the online databases or specialized print resources that most public library patrons can access conveniently. If you serve a population who, for whatever reason, cannot do for themselves, you must adopt a concierge-style role. You go forth on their behalf and find them the information they need. They need, therefore, to be able to trust your judgment and responsiveness to their needs. To be truly terrific at this kind of service, you learn to read the real needs behind the expressed needs. That is the heart of exceptional reference service and readers advisory.

Librarian as Educator

Curriculum support is the main function of the juvenile facility library. And just as in schools, the better the librarian is as a school media specialist, the better the library will support the educational goals of the school system. Juvenile facilities are required to follow the curricula of the public school systems in which they are located, so their libraries ideally reflect their counterparts on the outside.

But juvenile facility libraries are not the only places librarians play an educational role. Many adult facilities run their libraries out of the education programs department. Libraries tend to reflect the passions and priorities of the people running them, so the collections of libraries governed by educators may contain more strictly educational and vocational support materials than libraries run by public librarians who try to cater to patron preferences for popular materials. These libraries may also be less likely to stock media.

Many adult facility libraries, regardless of which department they belong to, offer their own educational programs, adjunct to the GED and vocational programs nearly always offered by the programs department. These classes can be almost anything you'd see in a free university catalog, anything of interest to adult learners. These include but are certainly not limited to classes on basic computer skills like Windows, Word, and keyboard typing, conducting legal research, filing briefs, and writing business correspondence, using the library, parenting children from a distance, and subject-specific book talks. Libraries interested in adult education also offer classes to help prisoners learn job and interpersonal skills to prepare them for reentry into the community.

Outreach—On the Inside

Library as Community Outreach

Legions of municipal, county, and even state correctional facilities maintain cooperative relationships with local public libraries to provide some level of service to inmates and prisoners. This kind of outreach supports the emphasis public libraries place on equitable access for all. A librarian committed to that ethic is a value-added component to any correctional facility library service, because he or she knows what to advocate for on behalf of inmate patrons. Public library outreach to jails and prisons also streamlines the facility's operations by positioning professionals who know how to "do libraries good" in roles for which they are properly trained, including the stewardship of budgetary funds for collections and programs.

This kind of partnership takes many forms. Sometimes, correctional libraries are run entirely by inmates. Professional librarians are brought in to train them and troubleshoot the circulation/cataloging software. Some county libraries provide weekly or biweekly bookcart service; some provide deposit collections which they periodically refresh. Some park their bookmobiles, usually at minimum security and juvenile supervision facilities, where the inmates are allowed to come aboard. And some, like ours, are contractual arrangements in which librarians employed by a public library work as contract staff in full-service on-site correctional libraries.

Some correctional libraries are built on donations and discards from the local public library. A librarian at the helm can make reasonably good selections from these sources if they're plentiful enough, and patrons who have access to selected-for materials are always better served than those who make do with a random mishmash of others' castoffs. Some correctional libraries draw entirely from the public library's cataloged collection; inmate patrons in these facilities, consequently, have as much access to public library materials as any patron walking free. The only disadvantage to this model is that all of the materials must be hauled between locations, but essentially, that is no different from any bookmobile or deposit collection service.

Still other correctional libraries have their own budget line items for their own materials. We believe their patrons are especially well served. On-site collections improve patron access. And collections selected with specific communities in mind become more relevant to members of that community. Even the best public libraries don't always carry the materials most in demand by prisoners, especially when you consider how far removed most prisons are from prisoners' communities of origin.

Library as Window to the World

As public libraries place more emphasis on marketing themselves as community focal points, as gathering places, and as forums for programs, correctional librarians need to pursue the same, if for different reasons. Public libraries are reinventing themselves to respond to the needs of a fast-paced culture that becomes more alienated every year, and to emerging generations that are more print-averse than their predecessors.

Even though jails, and especially prisons, are self-contained communities, their residents are not self-selected. In a volatile, security-conscious environment, they do not make connections with each other easily. The library, as neutral ground, can help build bridges between people by offering interactive programs, such as checkers tournaments and spelling bees. The library can also keep inmates somewhat plugged in to the outside world by bringing outside presenters in. Our patrons often express how touched they are by people's willingness to donate their time and expertise to alleviate the tedium of incarceration.

Conclusion

Good correctional libraries built on solid principles of public library ethics and service can't help but be a boon to incarcerated communities. As prison superintendent Walter A. McFarlane states, "Better libraries mean better inmates. We hope that education opportunities will improve the average inmate and help him turn from crime. This change has benefits that reach far beyond the prison walls and ultimately has a payoff for any would-be crime victim" (Davis 2000).

Perhaps Kathleen de la Peña McCook (2004) puts it best in her recent article on public library presence in jails: "While we may not be able to change the prison-industrial complex that has grown so much over the last decades we can, as working librarians, take first steps. We can seek to ensure that people held in local jails have library service. There are some public libraries and projects that provide guidance in this path. If we help even one person, we help all."

References

American Library Association. 1986. Mission, priority areas, goals: Introduction. In *ALA policy manual* (sec. 1.1). Retrieved May 9, 2005 from http://www.ala.org/ala/ourassociation/governingdocs/policymanual/mission.htm.

———. 1990. *Freedom to view statement.* Retrieved May 9, 2005 from http://www.ala.org/ala/oif/statementspols/ftvstatement/freedomview-statement.htm.

———. 1994. *Freedom to read statement.* Retrieved December 15, 2004 from http://www.ala.org/ala/oif/statementspols/ftrstatement/freedomreadstatement.htm.

———. 1995. *Code of ethics of the American Library Association.* Retrieved December 15, 2005 from http://www.ala.org/ala/oif/statementspols/codeofethics/codeethics.htm.

———. 1999. *Libraries: An American value.* Retrieved February 7, 2005 from http://www.ala.org/ala/oif/statementspols/americanvalue/librariesamerican.htm.

American Library Association Council. 2004. *Core values task force II report.* Retrieved December 15, 2004 from http://www.ala.org/ala/oif/statementspols/corevaluesstatement/corevalues.htm.

Davis, V. A. 2000. Breaking out of the box: Reinventing a juvenile-center library. *American Libraries* 31(10). Retrieved January 3, 2005 from InfoTrac Web: General Reference Center Gold database.

de la Pena McCook, K. (2004, Fall). Public libraries and people in jail. *Reference and User Services Quarterly, 44*(1), 26–30.

Ettenberg, E. 2002. *The next economy.* New York: McGraw-Hill.

Leffers, M. J. 1990. Prison library—one day. *Special libraries* 81(3), 242–246.

Mantilla, K. 2001. Windows to freedom: Radical feminism at a jail library. *off our backs, 31*(2). Retrieved January 3, 2005 from InfoTrac Web: General Reference Center Gold database.

Vogel, B. 1995. *Down for the count.* Lanham, MD: Scarecrow Press, Inc.

Waites, M. 2004. Readers behind bars: Books can make a huge and positive difference to men and women in prison, as writer-in-residence [Editorial]. *The bookseller.* Retrieved January 3, 2005 from InfoTrac Web: General Reference Center Gold database.

2

Understanding Yourself

A correctional facility is an intense environment with a perhaps unnaturally heterogeneous mélange of social classes, educational attainments, economic backgrounds, ages, nationalities, and creeds. At the absolute nadir of human experience, at the bleakest point in the lives of many of the people who pass through, there are extraordinary opportunities for librarians to serve. The opportunities all begin with relationships.

Obviously, the qualities that make for a good corrections librarian are not identical to those that make a good corrections nurse, a good corrections guard, or a good corrections therapist. For one thing, of all the civilians who work directly with inmates, librarians are perhaps the only ones without any power whatsoever. (This is called "the bottom of the totem pole.") The upside of ranking so low is that we have very little authority over inmate patrons—just like our dealings with patrons on the outside. The playing field is more level, and that helps us to establish trust right out of the chute.

Trust is a rare commodity behind bars. Before anything else can happen, you must gain the trust of the facility's administrators. Then there is the process of gaining the trust of the deputies or officers you'll see every working day. Finally, winning and maintaining the trust of the inmates is a delicate dance between hard-line rules, friendly accessibility, and over-familiar compromise. Without trust and trustworthiness, the best collection in the world won't make it into inmate patrons' hands. So, to boil it down to the least common denominator, everything that can make you a successful corrections library is based on healthy professional relationships.

In this chapter, you'll learn about the qualities that great corrections librarians bring to the job. Naturally, no one is going to possess all of these qualities, but effective corrections libraries, like public libraries, are run by people well suited to the communities they serve. The more of the following attributes you already have, or are relatively sure you can learn, the better suited you'll be for an institutional working environment.

Five Types of Corrections Librarians

As we stated in the previous chapter, librarians' attitudes toward inmates' freedom of access to library materials makes or breaks the application of the public library model. Indeed, some of these attitudes preclude applying such a model at all. Mongelli (1994) identifies three types of corrections librarians, upon which we base the first three types below, and the kind of service inmates can hope to receive from each. We will add two additional types for your consideration.

The Terminator

The terminator believes that all liberties should be suspended the minute a person is incarcerated. Forget innocent until proven guilty in jail, forget basic civil liberties in prison; this librarian admits distaste for inmates in general and sees no logical need for inmate access to the courts or expensive law library collections. There is an obvious resentment of inmates who file suit against the facility and for jailhouse lawyers. This librarian may also believe he or she is there to uphold the punitive tradition of incarceration to the exclusion of purely recreational pursuits; thus, a pleasure reading collection under this librarian's care will usually be skeletal, often consisting of unselected donations. (Although many correctional facility libraries' recreational reading collections are built on donations, certainly not all of these are subpar.) If the collection is selected instead of donated, this kind of librarian will select "redemptive" literature of the religious, self-help nonfiction, and squeaky-clean-type fiction. Nothing incendiary, controversial, or violent on this worthy librarian's shelves! Nothing much of interest, either.

The Church Lady

The church lady librarian may not despise inmates, but does distrust them profoundly, seeing any inmate hard at work in the law library as a lawsuit crazed problem child whose possible eventual release due to a loophole betrays the need for a law library in the first place. This librarian knows that inmates retain some rights upon incarceration. The problem is, she can't imagine why. This librarian might approach collection development in much the same way the terminator does, approaching it from a position of moral superiority, assuming that good wholesome reading is only appropriate, considering the environment.

The Realist

The realist is a librarian who recognizes both the need to provide inmates with the legal resources to which they are entitled and the fallibility of the criminal justice system. While this librarian may dislike certain types of inmate patrons (described in greater detail in the next chapter), he or she will accept them as a fact of life. Fairness and equity of access rule the realist's thinking. This librarian will be more likely than the other two types to build a varied recreational reading collection based on inmates' actual reading interests. The realist knows that a collection full of nothing but what the librarian believes is worthy reading material is not likely to see a lot of use. This phenomenon would probably not faze the first two types of librarians, but the realist wants inmates to enjoy the civilized act of reading. To ensure this, the realist stocks the shelves with relevant subject matter and popular authors and genres.

The People Pleaser

The people pleaser poses a very real security risk because his or her boundaries are too porous and are highly susceptible to manipulation, not only by the inmates, but by other nonlibrary staff. These librarians will bend themselves into the professional equivalent of outrageous yoga postures to accommodate absolutely every request that comes their way. Of course, since the inmates and officers want precisely antithetical things, this sets the stage for conflict that the people pleaser simply cannot tolerate. The people-pleaser librarian is in jail to be everybody's friend. But making nice is a one-way ticket to disaster in a correctional environment. The people-pleasing librarian will bend (or break) any rule, resulting in serious compromise of professionalism and trustworthiness and very likely putting himself in danger of losing his job, or worse.

The Crusader

This is the type whose passion for correcting the many injustices in the world can be harnessed and focused to great effect. But unharnessed and unfocused, the crusader, surrounded by the bleak daily reality of jail or prison, will come to one of two ends. On one hand, a crusader will disregard the hierarchy of authority and publicly challenge the line staff. This librarian will not accept his or her place in the organizational culture and will spend a lot of time going over deputies' and officers' heads in order to get the administration to support his or her reformative goals. The result is decimation to the working relationship between librarians and officers that is so critical to the library's success. On the other hand, a crusader will be like a meteor, descending upon the facility as though on fire with transformative intent, and then quickly burning up and withering in the face of the tough realities of life and work on the inside. In any kind of library outreach, there is an element of social work, but the crusader is more social worker than librarian. This person cannot focus on the work of the library, cannot achieve the requisite emotional distance from the problems of incarceration, and probably won't last long behind bars.

Do You Belong Behind Bars?

What kind of person can and will work successfully with inmate patrons? As our discussion has already shown, it takes a certain type of person to create and maintain, in a correctional setting, "a mirror of free and honest society as it exists in library service throughout the United States" (Vogel 1995). We've always said that a good jail librarian needs the mind of an educator, the heart of a social worker, the spine of a Navy SEAL, and the stomach and sense of humor of an eighth grader. The following personal and professional qualities and an understanding of the environment can be effectively combined to make for a great corrections librarian.

Personal Qualities

Determination
If at first you don't succeed . . . that doesn't mean you won't tomorrow! Applying the public library model in a correctional facility is all about "getting to yes" in an environment built on "no." No second phone call, no visitors this week, no choice about what to watch on TV tonight, no more dinner, no more meds, no more commissary today. Since public libraries are all about access, you, as a correctional librarian, can bridge the cognitive and logistical chasm between "yes" and "no."

Getting the information you need to succeed in this task takes perseverance and adaptability. The key is figuring out the facility's routines. We'll explore that further in Chapter 4.

Know Your Limits
Jail is weird, prisons are weird, and if you're working in these weird worlds, things will get to you from time to time. Within the limits of

generally consistent behavior, give yourself permission to not be 100 percent all of the time. The ten-hour, four-day work week is a brilliant way to ensure you have enough time to reenergize, because the intensity of the corrections environment can wear you down. (This is precisely the reason many law enforcement professionals work four-day schedules.) If you're completely wiped out and you have no one to hand tasks off to, your patrons will probably be better off if you go home than if you stagger around at half-wattage.

> *It's Time to Go Home When . . .*
>
> It's time to go home when your mild-mannered library volunteer says to you, "Whoa, look who got hit with the ugly stick this morning!"
>
> It's time to go home when the crankiest sergeant in the entire jail says to you, "You know, you are being very negative. Perhaps we should work on a little reframing."
>
> It's time to go home when the nicest sergeant in the entire jail says to you, "How about a little cheese with that whine?"
>
> It's time to go home when thrice-convicted axe murderers hold up their hands when they see you and say, "I swear I didn't touch the pencil sharpener—please don't look at me like that!"
>
> It's time to go home when your inmate clerk says, "You're beginning to make me feel like that librarian in *Ghostbusters* after she saw the apparition."
>
> It's time to go home when the chaplain says to you, "Talking to you just makes me want to put myself in lockdown."

Some days, even if you stick around, it's going to be obvious to everyone that you're not going to get anything accomplished with a certain situation, inmate, or guard. If you're lucky enough not to be a one-person operation, that's when you get to play a little game we call "Tag, You're It." The object of the game is simple: Find ways to provide reliable, professional service to people (or in spite of people) who are making you nuts.

The rules are as follows. When you've hit the limit of your sense of humor, coping ability, or skills, you let a coworker (Contestant #2) know that 1) the situation is simply more than you can professionally deal with today, and 2) you're either going to avoid the situation entirely (by rescheduling or canceling the services) or pass it off to your coworker. He or she then has the choice of passing or playing. If your coworker decides to play, he's it!

For "Tag, You're It" to be successful, you need sufficient clarity and self-awareness to recognize when you've hit your limit. It's not necessary to heap judgment on yourself; we just call it "having a fragile day." You also need a team in which any member is competent to pick up wherever another leaves off. This requires an investment in cross-training.

Tag, You're It!

There was one particular inmate patron, a highly distractible 19-year-old in for a laundry list of offenses, who drove me to apoplexy. Every interaction between us degenerated into testing behaviors and unsuccessful attempts to establish proper boundaries or, at best, pointless exchanges of time-consuming banalities having little or nothing to do with the task at hand. It got to the point where the dislike we had for each other began to crack my professionalism. I invariably got so worked up after each encounter with this guy that my emotional upset began to deenergize the rest of the staff. In other words, I became a royal pain in the neck. At that point, Sheila and the other team members stepped in and essentially tagged themselves, if for no other reason than self-preservation! For some reason, and it doesn't really matter what that reason was, the patron's annoying habits were easier for other staff to just blow off.

Sheila had a similar experience with a deputy who stonewalled us for awhile. He had been blocking our access to inmates for bookcart and routinely refused to let them attend law library. After a particularly ugly exchange between him and another librarian, Sheila decided to intervene. The conversation between her and the deputy was even less productive than the first had been. At that point, another staff member offered to take over, since she had developed a friendly professional relationship with the deputy. Soft-peddling and strategic kowtowing often go a long way, and it was easier for the other staffer to handle the situation since she had not been directly involved when the situation degenerated. After a few weeks, things were back to normal.

Know Thyself

Based on an inordinate interest in pop psychology, we introduce the ever-popular "family of origin" concept to effective jail librarianship. The reason we bring it up is that in situations of stress, human beings tend to fall back on whatever imperfect behaviors helped us survive as children within our imperfect families. Problems arise when we apply those same behavioral responses to adult situations. Most situations we find ourselves in as adults are not replicas of the familial crucible in which our personalities were formed. But stress triggers adaptive behaviors that are probably not the most appropriate responses to the present situation. And stress and lack of control are a daily reality in jail.

Family Ties

We knew a very talented jail librarian with otherwise excellent personal boundaries who began showing a marked preference for an inmate in the Behavioral Control Unit. Fortunately, because we have a tight and highly observant team, we noticed this and asked about her interest in this inmate. She hadn't realized she was getting drawn into the inmate's experience. Upon reflection, she confessed that she liked him in spite of herself and perhaps because of his laundry list of personal problems because "He reminds me of my dad."

Another colleague of ours was startled one day to discover that her own father, from whom she'd been long estranged, was incarcerated in our facility. Both of these women experienced a great deal of ambivalence in these situations because of the intensely personal issues they entailed. But both were also professional—and wise—enough to know they had to distance themselves from these inmates in order to maintain their own emotional balance and continue to do their jobs effectively.

There's not a whole heck of a lot of literature devoted to understanding one's emotional developmental underpinnings as applied in a jail or prison setting. Despite this publishing gap, we have recommended several mainstream titles to each other and our colleagues over the years, which are listed in Suggested Readings at the end of this book.

Patience

Simply barreling through social, cultural, and logistical barriers to your provision of library services isn't the best strategy in jail. Jail is a complicated system, with a lot of internal interest groups often working at cross-purposes, and safety is always an overriding concern. Sometimes it's best just to wait things out. Anything that isn't an immediate security concern can probably wait. Some problems, especially with particular inmates if you're in a jail setting, will disappear when those inmates move on. Some problems, though, are relative constants, like technical difficulties with your computers, high staff turnaround, and tight budgets. They are part of the job, and if you can come to peace with them in jail, you will have learned an important lesson about life in general.

> Confucius say: Wise the librarian who does not anger deputy with library door keys.

The Weakest Link

I was working one Saturday by myself, making the rounds to the cellblocks to renew library books before beginning the day's law library sessions. Time was of the essence, but the deputy in central control decided to have a little fun. Every time I came to a cellblock door, he would drone over the intercom, "You . . . are . . . the . . . weakest . . . link." (Apparently, he thought I looked like the host of the show with the same name.) As the morning wore on, law library loomed and the renewals still weren't done. I came to another locked door and again, the deputy's disembodied voice intoned, "You . . . are . . . the . . . weakest . . . link." I finally lost my patience and despite warnings never to do so unless I was literally on fire, I pressed the intercom button.

"YOU are the MISSING link!" I retorted. The deputy laughed and laughed, and once he collected himself (finally), he let me through. Game over. (Erica)

> One of our deputy colleagues warned us not to get hooked on the idea that all of our problems will be solved when challenging patrons or coworkers leave the facility. "Sooner or later, someone just like him will come in here to take his place!"

Healthy Lack of Perfectionism

You're probably looking at this prodigious list of personal qualities and thinking, "I can't possibly be all those things!" Of course you can't, so get over it. Jail and prison either cure perfectionists or devour them. And really, what is perfectionism anyway? It's the irrational belief that everything is, in fact, under our control. Ha! Jail and prison are all about control. And, earnest civilian employee, unless you are a nurse, you don't have any of it. So give it up. If you can't, fake it till you make it. Striving for excellence, while not getting too hung up on your weaknesses, will preserve your sanity and keep you from alienating everyone you work with. As we like to say, "We don't gotta be perfect, we just gotta be good!"

> Sometimes your arrow hits the target. Sometimes, it hits the nearby sheep.

Good Boundaries

Let's elaborate. By "good," we don't really mean good. We're talking iron-clad, rock-solid, impervious. The line is drawn as soon as you walk in the door, and it's drawn somewhere about three feet around your person. You also have to draw some lines around your heart and brain. This is where the social worker aspect of the jail librarian personality can get seriously burned. You'll need to leave some of your more tender aspects in the parking lot.

Names

The language you use is an essential tool in establishing your boundaries. This begins with considering how the inmates will address you and how you will address them. We have always operated as follows, and we'll explain why. Call the inmates by their last names and use proper titles, such as "Mr." and "Ms." At the same time, encourage them to call you by your first name, unless facility policy prohibits this. There are both practical and philosophical reasons for doing this.

Encouraging inmates to use your first name may, at least in theory, help you keep your surname from becoming public knowledge. This is not a bad idea, since most of these folks will be getting out someday. Also, since librarians on the inside as well as the outside tend more often to be female, and since women's names frequently change, having the inmates use your first name preserves some of your privacy. It's really nobody's business if you've just gotten married—or divorced—and the less inmates know about your personal life, the better able you'll be to maintain your professional detachment.

This philosophy is not universal by any means, and it's important to clearly understand your facility's policy about names. For example, the

Colorado Departments of Corrections (DOC) insists that inmates and staff address each other by their *last* names.

Using inmates' last names draws a psychological boundary of formality. It's simply less likely that you'll be tempted to get chummy with "Mr. Perkins" than you will with "Tommy." Also, the other facility staff refer to the inmates by last name. It's less confusing for everyone to use the same language, since you need to stay up to speed about what's going on in the facility.

From a philosophical point of view, using inmates' last names adds a measure of professionalism to your interactions; they are your patrons and there is absolutely no reason you should not treat them with the dignity and respect you would afford regular public library visitors. Our biggest hope is that our interactions with our patrons will be so positive, they won't want to wait to get to the public library for more of the same once they are released. When they get there, they will know to expect the kind of service they received from us behind bars.

> *The Way I Want It*
>
> You can maintain good boundaries and still be respectful of the inmates. It helps to show your sense of humor. One day an inmate patron said to Sheila, "You call us by our last names, but we call you by your first names. Why don't you call us by our first names?"
>
> Sheila replied, "We want you to know that we respect you and we want to treat you all fairly and as equals. By using your last name respectfully, we hope we convey to you that we are here in a service capacity in order to help you."
>
> "Well, then," the patron asked, "why don't we call you by your last name?"
>
> This is a situation in which it would be all too easy to retort, "Because you are a con and I am a law-abiding citizen and the more formal our interactions the less likely our relationship will degenerate into something that could get me sacked or killed." But you don't have to go there. Without missing a beat, Sheila cheerfully and simply replied, "Hmm, I guess it's because that's the way I want it."

Touching

Physical touch is one of the most precious and controversial commodities behind bars, and it certainly raises a worthy host of concerns for officers. For the most part, we strongly discourage touching of any kind, since even something as seemingly innocuous as a bump to the shoulder can be a way for an inmate to test your boundaries. We do think shaking hands is okay, but be warned: it definitely pushes the line and may invite strong censure from other staff. It may also defy strict policy.

You are responsible for understanding exactly what your facility's policies state about touching inmates (or even other staff). By and large, we have found that such policies don't appear in state departments of corrections' administrative rules and regulations for entire penal systems, but do appear in employee and inmate conduct manuals at the facility level. For example, Arapahoe County Detention Facility's inmate handbook ranks "intentionally touching a staff member" right up there with gambling, refusing to obey direct orders by officers, theft, and indecent exposure. The penalties for an inmate who intentionally touches a staff person include loss of visitation time, loss of facility "good time" (days deducted from an inmate's sentence), extra work details, the filing of criminal charges, and even time spent in lockdown. The penalties for a staff member range from disciplinary action to termination to endangerment.

If your facility doesn't have an expressly stated policy about physical contact, your own boundaries are strong, and you have earned the trust of your supervisors, we think hand-shaking can be very beneficial. For one thing, shaking hands brings a bit of normalcy from the outside, and applying the public library model is about bringing as much normalcy into jail as is safely possible. For another thing, you don't have to get really close to shake hands. Conceivably, you can comfortably shake hands with a good five feet of space between you! Our rule of thumb: touch nothing but hands, and don't be the one to initiate the contact. If an inmate patron offers you his or her hand, you may respond in kind or not as the situation warrants. Ultimately, the purpose of shaking hands is this: It is a relatively safe and appropriate way of bridging a gap (and these gaps are legion behind bars) that denies our shared humanity. And remember, if all else fails, nothing beats a smile.

> *Doing the Wave*
>
> If you want to keep your patrons coming back, you must assiduously preserve their dignity and humanity. There's nothing quite as insulting and demoralizing as offering to shake someone's hand and having that person rebuff you. By the same token, as a corrections employee, you need to maintain the boundaries that will keep you safe. So if you're not comfortable or are forbidden to touch the inmates in any way, what can you do? We find that the following line works absolute magic when an inmate wants to shake hands:
>
> "Mr. So-and-So, I can't shake your hand, but I can wave very enthusiastically!" An exaggerated wave with a sincere smile on

your face conveys your respect for the other person, inserts a little comic relief into the situation, and preserves appropriate physical detachment.

Flexibility and Adaptability

Things change all the time in a correctional facility. As the lowest-ranking civilian employees, librarians usually don't have a lot of people soliciting them for input. For example, we recently lost over half of our library space when the court services department needed more room. Over one-third of our circulating collection of recreational reading materials had to be weeded in under a year, and our eight-station intranet containing the bulk of our legal reference resources had to be dismantled. We made a lot of hard choices about what we would have to sacrifice for the good of the order. A lot of old, neglected titles went out the door, but so did a sizeable chunk of our popular science fiction collection. Hardback books, representing a considerable financial investment, were also sacrificed since they take up more room than paperbacks. The upside of the situation was a rare opportunity to wheel and deal for a little consolation prize. That prize was the fulfillment of a reference concept that Sheila had long been jockeying for. Now, we have a sixteen-station wireless mobile reference unit that can be rolled into the inmates' living areas, allowing us to serve three times the number of patrons, even though our print collection was slashed and inmates can no longer leave their living units to visit (what is left of) the original library.

Even under the worst possible contingencies, flexibility and adaptability—which entail not a little patience and creative thinking—can deliver enormous returns. You have to be willing to go with the flow and think outside the box, even on very short notice.

High Tolerance for Ambiguity

To continue the woeful tale of our lost floor space, the court services department had foreseen taking over our space for years. Every now and then, a deputy would come into the library with a tape measure and dire predictions that the wrecking ball was on its way. When the final decision finally came down, the library staff quickly adjusted. But it took *sixteen months* from the laying down of the edict to the actual erection of the new wall splitting the library in half. And when the wall did finally go up, library staff received about forty-eight hours of advance warning. The warning was a surprise; the fact that it preceded action by such a short span of time was not. Going with the flow, come heck or high water, is definitely your best survival mechanism. It also goes a long way in establishing your cooperativeness and *esprit de corps*, even in extreme situations that look like the end of you.

Agoraphobics, Please Apply!

The inmates aren't the only ones confined in small places. Often as not, jail and prison librarians are squashed into whatever neglected broom closet happens to be available. The chances of having an office window are about as good as the chances we will be invited to star on the next "Celebrity Survivor" show opposite George Clooney. (But hope springs eternal.) For you seasonal affective types, this means you'll have to go outside to get your recommended dose of sunlight. Another sometimes challenging part of working on the inside is that there are doors, often important doors—like the ones that get you in and out of the facility—that you will not be able to open and close. Someone at a video screen, possibly in a remote part of the building, gets to decide when those doors open and close for you. If you have even a mild case of claustrophobia that requires nothing more complicated than ready escape routes, a corrections environment will have you climbing the walls. You must be able to tolerate not only the confinement, but the discretion of others regarding when you can leave.

Sense of Humor

A deputy once told us, "Stay here only as long as you can laugh." Jail can be a miasma of human misery, and there are a lot more people who don't want to be there than there are those who do. With its locked doors, artificial light, and lack of windows, it can be physically oppressive even to those of us who get to leave at the end of the day. And the potential for physical danger is always present.

Without a sense of humor, the environment can eat you alive. Being able to find the humor in just about any situation, no matter how grim, is not generally something you can be taught. An appreciation for sarcasm, absurdity, surrealism, and irony definitely makes it easier to relate to the collective comic consciousness behind bars. Those who are easily offended won't last long here.

If you do not have a sense of humor, you will not make it. (Librarian at maximum security state penitentiary.)

Humor in all human groups is a shared cultural concept. Humor behind bars, regardless of how earthy, adolescent, or grim, helps keep the organization running smoothly by alleviating tension. Humor allows people to decompress and let off steam, it delays or even prevents severe delayed emotional fallout, and it gives people a way of connecting with each other and showing care for one another. Believe it or not, when you've just about hit the wall and are ready to dissolve into a blubbering mass, a well-timed one-liner can be all it takes to get you back on your feet and your sense of perspective back in place.

Debbie Does Dewey?

I had only been supervising the jail library for a couple of months when one of our staff resigned and we began searching for a replacement. Thinking myself terribly insightful, I insisted that all applicants visit the facility prior to their interviews, just to see how the walls felt.

The afternoon two of them were scheduled to visit, there was an emergency drill in the inmate workers' pod, resulting in the transfer of all our inmate workers to another facility for the day. That left us desperately short-staffed for bookcart. I struck on the bright idea to have the two hopefuls work bookcart.

I was so focused on solving the problem of staffing bookcart, I failed to take a good look at the applicants. After they'd been in the cellblocks for several minutes, I noticed that the patrons were paying a lot of attention to the younger of the two. Since inmates tend to scrutinize new staff (we consider it a hazing ritual), I didn't think much of it, until the other librarian in the pod hollered, "Hey! We're not staring at you guys, so stop staring at us!" That's when I finally clued into what the buzz was all about.

The younger applicant was wearing a tight, low-cut wrap-around blouse in flimsy fabric that more than accentuated her natural endowments. Every man in the pod was foaming at the mouth, and I went home that day convinced that I would get fired, the library would be shut down, and the sky would fall from the heavens. But Sheila was the Voice of Reason that day and she convinced me that often, things like this become the big deal we make of them, and to just wait for it to blow over.

The next day several deputies asked me if I was hiring the barely dressed candidate. When I said no, a few of them said, "Can I at least have her phone number?" The punch line was when my coworker sent a one-line e-mail reporting the previous day's fallout: "We broke a circ record in Pod 3. Seventy-six percent of the inmates checked books out!" (Erica)

Professional Qualities

Trustworthiness

As a general rule, suspicion is a great quality to exercise behind bars. As a staff member, you want to be very cautious about whom you allow yourself to trust. The inmates aren't the only ones to be wary of! Other civilian staff and even officers are capable of sexual harassment and stonewalling, and they may have ulterior motives for helping you. But to be effective as a librarian to the inmates and as a coworker to the officers and other civilian staff, your own trustworthiness must be impeccable. You must behave with consistency, fairness, and impermeable personal boundaries to build that rarest of commodities: credibility.

Don't say anything you don't mean. It's perfectly all right to admit to not knowing something, rather than scrambling to make something up.

Don't make promises you can't keep. There's nothing wrong with not promising anything at all, except that you will do your best.

Do your best not to play favorites. Let's face it, there will always be some patrons you really enjoy and some you just can't stand. (This is no different than working in a public library!) Just take care in making sure your preferences for some do not impact the quality of service you provide for all.

Strong Customer Service Ethic and Skills

Correctional facilities are not generally known for the superlative, outstanding, and personalized service they provide their residents. If you're serious about applying the public library model, you'll need a solid customer service background, because you're sure as shooting not going to get customer service training in jail.

Good customer service in jail answers the perennial question: "How do we get to yes in an environment built on no?" Even on the public library side, there are times when you have to say no. No, that book is not available right now; no, you may not check out any more items until you pay your fines; no, you can't make copies because the copy machine is broken; no, you can't attend the origami program because we have the maximum number of participants already. Honoring the patron's frustration and disappointment is where you begin. People want to know you empathize, even if you're the reason they're upset in the first place! Explain why their request can't be accommodated; this establishes credibility and fair practices. Finally, think of alternatives that might reasonably make up for whatever the patron can't have. Yes, I can put you on the waiting list for that book; yes, I can hold your items for you for a few days until you get your check; yes, I can call you when the copier is fixed; yes, we have videos on origami and several good books that you can check out.

Ability to Cope with Criticism, Confrontation, and Conflict

Tensions run high on the inside, and you will find yourself dealing with many staff—civilian and officer alike—who have strong philosophical aversions to libraries inside correctional facilities. Even staff who support the library's mission will from time to time question certain choices you make. Challenges are a good thing. They show you that people care. They help you understand another's point of view, which works toward relationship building. Challenges also give you opportunities to review what your library is doing and how you might do things differently.

You also must be able to work well with people you really dislike. Most public libraries are warm, welcoming, touchy-feely places, governed by a feminine culture of mutual care and concern. Correctional facilities, with their masculine paramilitarism, are as far away from that world as you can get. People will make you angry, and you'll certainly make them angry. You may even exchange verbal blows. When this happens, you have to be able to get over it and get back to business.

> *"Nobody ever fell on rice."*
>
> I rolled into one of the pods one morning to get ready for law library. Rice was scattered all over the multipurpose room (MPR) floor, so I asked Deputy N to assign an inmate worker to clean it up before the program. Deputy N refused. So I asked for a broom. Another refusal.
>
> Not to be deterred, I started scrounging around the sally port for a broom. At that point, the deputy bellowed, "What is the big deal? I've never known anyone to fall on rice!" He tromped into the MPR and proceeded to kick the rice off to the side with his big black combat boots.
>
> At that point, one of the nurses arrived to distribute meds and ran into Deputy N's bad mood herself. I hollered, exasperated, "I thought he was just being crabby with me!"

> The very next day, Deputy N was working overtime and I had a special event to prepare for in his pod. There was no way to move the inmates into the MPR without his help. So, I figured, "Yesterday he was unpleasant and I let him know. Today, I suck it up." I made nice, ruffled feathers were smoothed over, and Deputy N made sure the room was packed for my program. (Sheila)

Good Boundaries

We already mentioned this under personal qualities, but we cannot emphasize it enough. Inmates, and sometimes other staff, will do their best to cajole, compel, and convince you to bend or break the rules. Some will try to intimidate you. Some will try to charm you. This is why you must have clear vision about why the rules are in place, so you can stick to your guns in an intelligent way. You don't necessarily need written policies—but it doesn't hurt to have something in print to hand someone, either. Just be sure that if you do decide to be formal and write down the library's policies and rules, you get the administration's stamp of approval.

> *Thor's Hammer as Behavioral Control*
>
> I received a written complaint one day from a patron who had been dismissed from law library by one of my newer staff for some form of misbehavior or other. In his complaint, he wrote, "I was stricken from the library by the new librarian!"
>
> This was an accusation to be taken seriously. I went to our new librarian and gravely asked, "Did you have a problem with Mr. I yesterday?"
>
> She answered in the affirmative and I asked quietly, "Am I to understand then that his allegation that he was 'stricken from the library' is true?"
>
> At this point the veteran staff started rolling their eyes.
>
> "Listen," I said, "I don't ever want to hear that you've *struck* a patron from law library." She gulped. I continued, "If someone's getting kicked out, I want to hear that you SMOTE him. THAT'S the way to exceed expectations around here!" (Erica)

Boundaries are not just about preserving your safety; they're about preserving your ability to relate to the inmates as library patrons, no more, no less. You will have myriad opportunities to delve into the grisly particulars of your patrons' charges. You may have some access to the facility's computer records, you will certainly find yourself in a position to overhear other staff discussing inmates, and you may even be offered juicy gossip or lurid details during your own conversations with people. Remember, your ability to give inmates good library service will not improve with your knowledge of their criminal histories.

Our public library HR director once said to Sheila, "I think I understand how you can work in that place. You pretend that it's normal." Bingo! We rely on our ability to create daily interactions that are normal and routine in a decidedly contrived environment. In essence, we "pretend" the place is normal. We think of the inmates in terms of our professional relationship to them: they are our patrons. Relative ignorance of their personal lives is something public library patrons take for granted; we couldn't look up those details if we wanted to. In jail we can, but we usually don't.

Stem your curiosity. Keep it on the level and keep it professional.

"They're Crooks"

Shortly after I started working in jail, I was shooting the breeze with one of the deputies in the library. After several minutes, I asked him if he was planning to go down to the pods and bring some patrons back for law library. He didn't exactly answer the question. Instead, he retorted, "They're not patrons, Erica. They're crooks." I responded, "I can't do my job if I think of them that way. It's a mental game I play so I can do a good job as a librarian."

The deputy said, "Don't play a mental game that will lead you to believe you can turn your back on these guys." It was a good reminder, but not one that ever led me to stop thinking of our library users as patrons first. (Erica)

Diplomacy, Tact, and Salesmanship

If we were writing a job description, this quality might also be described as "an ability to develop and maintain cooperative relationships with nonlibrary agencies." In jail vernacular, that means "ability to let criticism, insult, and sometimes inscrutable control issues roll off your back like rain off a duck." As a librarian in a correctional facility, you are working in an environment unlike public libraries, in that at any time, for any reason (or no reason), your operation can be shut down by an outside agency, for an hour, a week, or entirely. Justification for the library's existence and operations will be questioned, challenged, and sometimes stonewalled; and over-worked civilian staff and officers will confront you, sometimes out of the blue. You need to be able to distinguish between someone having a bad day and someone who is legitimately threatening what you're trying to do. Overreaction can be as detrimental to your credibility and trustworthiness as underreaction.

As in all public libraries, diplomacy is especially crucial in any situation involving a complaint about library materials. We will discuss this later in the section on how the system works.

> *I don't think they learned that in here."*
>
> I once received a challenge from a lieutenant about a Spider-Man comic book. Apparently, an aspiring inmate artist had taken it upon himself to elaborate upon the illustrations of Spidey's anatomy. What troubled us was not the challenge, but the manner of it. The lieutenant handed his complaint to me in writing . . . on a sticky note. And he fully expected us to pull the book off the shelf.
>
> "Sticky notes do not make policy," I said to the library staff. What I said to the lieutenant was, "Will you meet with me to discuss this?" At the outset of our meeting, I asked the million-dollar question: "Has this harmed anyone?" The answer was no. "Does this constitute a security threat?" Again, the answer was no.
>
> "But they're drawing things where only tights should be!" the lieutenant insisted.
>
> "Yes, sir," I said, "but I don't think they learned how to draw that in here."
>
> The lieutenant took the point, which was that the books we owned were not in fact inspiring inmates to err. The issue then simmered down to what it really was—one defaced book. We removed the book from our collection and replaced it a few weeks later without further ado. (Sheila)

Stamina: Or, the Ability to Work Alone for Long Periods of Time

A disproportionate number of special libraries of all kinds are solo libraries, that is, they operate with only one staff member. That stalwart soul could be in charge of collection development, providing reference assistance, shelving, acting as liaison with facility staff and administrators, managing the budget, ordering supplies, repairing damaged materials, and any other of myriad more basic library functions that are often shared in the public library world.

There's more to working alone in a correctional library than just working alone, however. Correctional facilities are strangely cliquey places; every day we observe Enhanced Disturbance Control Unit (EDCU) deputies sitting with other EDCU deputies and avoiding the court services deputies who crowd around a single table; the nurses sit apart from the administrative assistants, the teachers sit apart from the maintenance crews. While our experiences with most of the people belonging to all of these groups tend to be perfectly friendly, for some reason, lunchtime is the time to congregate with one's own tribe. It may have something to do with uniforms attracting like uniforms, but that doesn't explain the nonuniformed civilians' inclination to eat with their own. Even if you work in a library with other librarians, there will be days you'll find yourself working—and, consequently, eating—alone. It can be psychologically and emotionally unsettling. We advise you not to take the cliques personally. It's just the way of things in jail.

As a corrections librarian, you are often physically and philosophically isolated from the library community at large. You may often be marginalized and even stigmatized by other library professionals. If others see your patrons as undeserving, they may consider your work a waste of time and money. Furthermore, the corrections library cohort is scattered throughout the country, working underground, behind walls, below the radar. Since many are paraprofessionals, they often do not plug in to the meager online and association resources available to them. Those who do find relatively few peers and resources readily available to help them. One look at ALA's and most state library associations' conference itineraries tells you that outreach is still a feebly acknowledged function of libraries. In Chapter 11, you'll find a list of resources that will help you tap in to a community of peers. We also hope you'll become a beacon yourself, to find and draw local, state, and regional corrections library staff together. In Colorado, we've been trying for some years to form a jail/prison subcommittee of our state library association. One of these days, it will happen!

Ability to Reinterpret Library Bill of Rights and Freedom to Read Statement for a Correctional Environment

If you're a librarian by education or trade already, you may be surprised at how often you'll be asked to leave your profession's ethics at the door. Sometimes, this is completely appropriate. Sometimes, it is not. You have to know when to fight for inmates' rights to information and when to back off for the good of the order. Books about martial arts and locksmithing are universally banned in jail and prison; getting yourself worked up about this kind of censorship is an open invitation to losing your input in materials selection for your library.

By the same token, as the Spider-Man anecdote shows, there are times when you have to stand up for yourself, your patrons, and your materials. There's really no need for a civilian librarian to roll over and comply with every challenge he gets from other staff. The assumption we'd like to make is that you are in charge, not one of the line staff, because of your library expertise. The officers, deputies, and facility administrators don't have that expertise, and though they may have reason to challenge you, you have your own profession's ethics and methods to support what you're doing.

Defend your patrons and your library with common sense and you'll build bridges, not walls.

Broad Knowledge of Library Functions

In a jail or prison library, chances are good that you will work either alone or incredibly understaffed. You'll have to be able to assess your users' information and recreational needs, purchase materials for them, classify and process those materials, get the materials to the shelf, answer readers advisory and reference questions, check materials out and in, track down missing items, repair damaged items, weed your collection, and discard your weeds. In the meantime, you'll prepare and monitor your budget, supervise civilian and inmate staff, arrange special programs for inmates, troubleshoot recalcitrant computer and office equipment, build good working relationships with uniformed staff and facility administration, and hopefully keep abreast of developments in correctional facility administration and in public library trends. You not only need this range of skills and a breadth of understanding of how libraries function from top to bottom, but you'll need to be able to prioritize functions according to daily, weekly, and annual calendars. The ability to devise a three- to five-year plan won't hurt, either, and understanding trends influencing both libraries and corrections will help you do that. Be advised that patience is a virtue; when drawing up a plan, take into account how slowly things seem to change inside correctional institutions. But also remember that correctional facilities often see a lot of conspicuous change when a new sheriff is elected or a new warden steps in. You'll want to be prepared to step up the pace if that happens.

Rewards of Service to Inmate Patrons

Instant Gratification

A colleague of ours, a public librarian who has presented several book talks in our jail, put it best: "Working with those guys (the inmates) gives you the closest thing to instant gratification you can get in this business."

What she's talking about is the inmates' obvious and overt gratitude for services that in a normal public library would be taken for granted, but which in a correctional facility are altogether too rare: services like photocopying, providing the latest paperback bestsellers, notary services, and answering reference questions. But there's something even more fundamental to public library service that works absolute magic in jail. It's a good, solid customer service ethic. Respectfulness, consideration, and responsiveness are not hallmarks of the correctional culture. Simple courtesy brings a much-needed measure of dignity to the librarian/inmate interaction. And dignity is in very short supply on the inside.

Some patrons have such low self-esteem that if you say hello, it makes their week. It's such a simple way of acknowledging your patrons' humanity in a very dehumanizing situation. Another great public librarian skill, which is relatively easy to practice in smaller facilities, is remembering particular types of books that particular patrons like. It's the library equivalent of a great business tactic: meeting the customer's need before he knows he needs something. Other customer service skills, such as making eye contact and reading body language, can also help you determine which of your patrons might be struggling with their legal research but are too embarrassed to ask for help. Just like patrons in the public library, "May I help you?" will be met with relief and gratitude from someone who needs assistance.

A corollary to instant gratification is immediate feedback. In jail, you know at once if you got it right (whatever "it" is) or if you blew it. Of course, it's great getting that positive feedback right away! As for the negative feedback, at least you get the opportunity to correct the problem quickly.

"Yes, Mr. V, There is a Santa Claus"

Awareness of which patrons like what, responsiveness to their suggestions for purchase, and making sure we expeditiously get the right materials into the right patrons' hands are basic public librarian functions. Since correctional facilities are closed communities and you're just about guaranteed to see your patrons on a regular basis, you get to see a lot of transactions through to the end. And believe us, it's a big deal for an inmate to be the first person to get his hands on a new book that doesn't smell like toothpaste!

One day, one of my staff approached me and said, "Sheila, it's time we ordered those Madeline Baker books. It looks like Mr. V is going to be here for awhile and he's been requesting them for months." I told her to talk to Mr. V and have him choose ten different titles, which we'd promise to get for the library when we placed our next order. A couple of weeks later, she presented Mr. V with the much-anticipated titles. "Did you see his face?" she asked me later. "It face lit up like a kid's at Christmas!" (Sheila)

Service to the Traditionally Underserved

Public library outreach is all about reaching those people who either would not or cannot otherwise make full use of library services. Bookmobiles rolling into remote farm communities or sprawling urban projects, library volunteers delivering books to the doors of the homebound, and children's librarians conducting literacy-based story times for low-income families are among the more "traditional" public library outreach services. Jail and prison libraries as a rule have not followed public library models of outreach, but the inmate population definitely fits the description of a traditionally underserved community. And just like outreach on the outside, outreach on the inside presupposes a collaborative, mutually beneficial relationship between the library and the hosting non-library agency. There are gatekeepers in jail, just as there are gatekeepers in non-English-speaking neighborhoods, senior assisted living facilities, and Head Start daycares. The ability to reach members of those communities is largely based on the librarian's ability to sell the service to the people in charge—activities directors, daycare administrators, property managers, wardens, and lieutenants—and work within the scheduling and staffing parameters of the hosting facility.

Opportunities to Develop Cooperative Relationships with Nonlibrary Agencies

In these days of shrinking budgets and a diminishing general impression of libraries as a natural public good, libraries are banding together to provide materials and services to their patrons. The consortia library model, with different library systems sharing a common database and the cost of a common courier, is probably the best known of these cooperative arrangements. But we should not limit ourselves to collaborating with our own. Public library outreach services of all kinds—bookmobiles, homebound delivery, deposit collections, and ESL and childhood literacy classes—demonstrate the power of shared responsibility.

Inside a correctional facility, the first relationship must be with the facility itself. If you are an employee of that facility, this relationship is pretty straightforward. But if you are a public librarian working on contract, as we are, there are some hurdles to jump even if the correctional facility administration and staff are thrilled to have you there. The biggest hurdle is learning to be a contributing member of an alien culture, so different from the culture of education and access that is the hallmark of public libraries. Learning the routines, rules, and rituals, and building constructive alliances along the chain of command, lay the foundation for a collaborative endeavor based on trust and mutual respect.

When the going gets tough, we like to remind ourselves that even though a relationship between different agencies is complex and requires a commitment to maintain, two agencies working toward a common goal will naturally blend their best resources and provide much more together than either could have provided on its own.

Something New Every Day

One of the most cited reasons library staff give for loving their jobs is variety. It's always a new patron with a new question, new technologies, new resources. But it's also true that libraries in general are not traditionally known for their nimble, immediate responses to changing environments. (How long did it take for most of us to abandon card catalogs? How many of us still have them???) Fortunately, in the public library sector at least, that's changing. And in correctional libraries with their relatively finite populations (as dictated by the size of the facility) and captive (no pun intended) audiences, it's actually okay to try new things toward which the public libraries may not have yet ventured. For example, the ACDF library was the first Arapahoe Library District library to be open on Sundays. We were also one of the first, when our staffing and finances fell on thin times, to mindfully focus our talents and resources toward a very specific operational mission: to provide legal reference resources and recreational reading materials at least once a week. Period.

Understanding Your Role

Let's not beat around the bush. Special libraries, be they corporate or hospital research centers, church reading rooms, or correctional libraries, are always the last line item and the last priority. We take pride, therefore, in being in good company!

As correctional librarians, our most important role is **gatekeeper to information** in an information-hostile environment. We spoke earlier about getting to "yes" in a culture built on "no." Part of being able to do this is understanding different levels of information access. There are three kinds of information on the inside:

- Information to which inmates are legally entitled—law resources such as state statutes and case law

- Information to which inmates are not legally entitled, but that does not pose demonstrable security risks—general reference resources such as world atlases, encyclopedias, and dictionaries; most nonfiction subject matter; most fiction

- Information to which inmates would definitely be entitled in a public library setting but that often pose demonstrable security risks inside a jail or prison—nonfiction titles on martial arts, locksmithing; directory assistance; interlibrary loan materials; Internet access

In Chapter 6 you'll find more about writing a collection development policy in cooperation with the facility's administrators that will permit inmates the greatest degree of information access while preserving the greatest degree of personal safety.

Another role of the correctional librarian is that of *facilitator*. As in the public library world, the librarian is the bridge between patrons and information. Here is where the public library model is most easily expressed: in the reference or readers advisory interviews. Inside, as in the real world, patrons don't have good research skills, which can be seen in the way they frame their questions. The infamous phrase "I read this book once and I don't remember the title or the author or what it's about, but I really liked it and it had a blue cover" is as prevalent in jail as it is in the public library. Helping patrons to think about their information needs and to frame their requests in ways that allow us to find what they need is all in a day's work, inside as it is outside.

We call our third role *"the face of the library."* In jail, it's not just about the information; it's about the library as well. As a correctional librarian, you can be an emissary for librarians everywhere! Uphold the value of education by providing access to literacy materials, study guides, and information on community resources. You are a promoter, marketing the value of libraries as lifelines to opportunity and enrichment. You are also an advocate, especially when you consider yourself in terms of library outreach programs.

Personal Challenges and How to Surmount Them

Fear

If you are flat-out afraid of being inside a jail or prison or working around criminals, this is NOT the job for you! Fear in certain situations is appropriate. As the saying goes, caution is not cowardly and carelessness is not courage. But there is a critical distinction: While caution will see you through to safety and success in a correctional environment and imprudence will probably compromise your safety (unless you're very, very lucky) flat-out fear will hobble you and make it far too easy to compromise your principles AND your safety. Frightened people are easily manipulated and, as we've said many times, boundaries are paramount in jail.

Conjuring the Monster

In a correctional facility, emotions often precipitate the very things we want to avoid. We knew a corrections librarian who became so rattled by a particularly unpleasant patron, she began to perceive him as a threat. What actually might have been no more than the patron's own bad attitude and disagreeable personality was understood by the librarian as dangerous. Ugly altercations between the two ensued to the point at which our colleague became too afraid to return to work. Things like that can happen. And while you can train people to deal with difficult customer service encounters in ways that are jail-appropriate, you can't train people to not be afraid.

So what is frightening on the inside? Nine times out of ten, we are afraid of things that never happen. Kathryn S. Thompson (as quoted by Vogel) has observed in prison, as we have in jail, that the culture of violence that so pervades a correctional facility's atmosphere is by and large left behind at the library door. If one of the services provided by the facility library is indeed a measure of noninstitutional normalcy, that may explain why inmates avoid disrupting it. We have noticed when providing bookcart services in the dayrooms that inmates known for volatility and physical altercations with each other can stand elbow to elbow in front of the fiction cart and choose their books in relative peace.

Uniforms can be intimidating. Officers and deputies wear a lot of equipment. Some of this you can identify (flashlights, radios), some you'd rather not identify (handcuffs, pepper spray), and some you couldn't identify if they were served to you with breakfast (tasers). In our jail, inmates wear uniforms that to a certain extent classify them by the severity of their charges; for example, inmates in orange are facing felony charges, inmates in blue are misdemeanor offenders. Inmates in red are "security risks," which could mean anything from an escape risk to an assault risk. Parts of some inmates' uniforms, outside their cells, are foot shackles. Seeing armed officers and shackled prisoners can be as scary as it is psychologically distressing. But both speak to safety and security concerns. If the right people are armed and the right people are restrained, chances are you're in pretty safe company. This is very different from the public library, where everybody looks the same walking through the front door.

The energy inside a correctional facility can also be frightening. There's something about a six-foot, six-inch, 300-pound man in a red uniform and shackles excitedly approaching you that can be a little unsettling. What the heck does HE want? If he's in the library, chances are good he wants some information or the latest John Grisham novel. There are a lot of extroverted prisoners out there; extroverted people coming to you *en masse* in a very confined space gives anybody pause! But you don't necessarily need to be afraid, just aware. The flip side of that extroverted energy is the intense, oppressive energy of many people who have hit emotional rock bottom and begun to dig. Severe depression, occasionally combined with other mental disorders, is not at all uncommon in an environment like jail. These deeply troubled, obviously suffering people can really hit an emotional nerve for compassionate library staff. Their grim intensity can seem threatening. But they will be very unlikely to do anything to compromise their access to the library, which may very well be the one ray of promise and joy in their lives.

Media images of jails and prisons are sensationalistic and definitely frightening. When we first set foot in the Arapahoe County Detention Facility, we were amazed that there were actual doors on the inmates' cells and not black iron bars. The facility was well lit, the white linoleum floors gleamed, the walls had fresh cream-colored paint. None of the deputies were walking around with Uzis, and there weren't vicious Dobermans leaping at fences. Rather, the deputies were very friendly and the most dangerous animal in the facility was a good-natured, drug-sniffing German shepherd named Denny. Frankly, the only really scary thing about jail that the media actually gets right most of the time is the mealtime mystery meat!

Since a correctional facility is a self-contained world, unpleasant people are harder to avoid. And incarceration does not exactly bring out the universal best in people! The fact is, in jail or prison, as in the world at large, there are some not-so-nice people. Some will be your patrons, some will be your coworkers. This is no different from public library work. It just seems different because of the intensity and the fact that you're working in an enclosed space with these people. Just as you try not to take someone else's bad attitude personally on the outside, you should try for the same inside. And like folks on the outside, few people in jail are genuinely bad tempered. They just have a lot of bad days.

Let's face it, it's not just the inmates who threaten us. We get a little nervous when we introduce a new author or new line of titles we think the deputies might take exception to. Triple Crown publications, classics on the art of warfare, and books on how to draw exaggerated comic book characters—especially women—can be high on challenge hit lists. But usually, aside from a little grousing, intelligently selected library materials are tolerated by the line staff. And basic tolerance is all we need in order to give our patrons books that will delight them!

Intimidation

Correctional facilities are all about one overarching theme—control. The officers maintain control over inmate interactions and movements in order to protect everyone inside. The inmates jockey for control over contraband supply lines, access to services, each other, and the staff. Civilian staff fight to control their schedules and budgets.

In a correctional facility, there is a formal hierarchy of authority. But there is an equally powerful informal hierarchy of influence. Without genuine respect, authority will have little influence and, therefore, control. Inmates respect other inmates who buck the system, successfully sue the facility, and carry out threats of physical force. On the flip side, inmates tend to respect staff who refuse to play rule-bending inmate games. If you earn the respect of your patrons by exercising consistency and fairness, it's unlikely they will try to intimidate you into doing anything. Subtle attempts at manipulation will always happen, but manipulation is usually more annoying than physically threatening, *if* you know it's going on.

> *"I'm not just any inmate!"*
> I had been working at ACDF for all of a week when I made the acquaintance of the facility's most notorious inmate, Mr. S. Well over six feet tall, well over 300 pounds, scarcely a week went by when an emergency call wasn't issued because Mr. S was threatening some violent mayhem or other. When Mr. S was brought into law library the morning I met him, shackled and wearing a high-security red uniform, he made a beeline for the front desk with a thick pile of papers in his hands.

"I need all of these copied in duplicate, immediately," he said, without preamble.

I eyed the one-inch-tall stack of documents, fully aware of the library's policy to only copy twenty pages at a time. I also knew that Mr. S was fully aware of the policy and, not incidentally, fully aware that I was the new kid on the block.

"Sir, I'm sorry, but if you want that many documents copied, you'll have to leave them here and I'll bring them to you later."

Mr. S gave me a look not unlike those I've received from sales clerks at high-end cosmetics counters after I've sampled every shade of eyeshadow and every perfume tester with the obvious intent of not actually buying anything.

"Miss," he said, voice dripping with pained condescension, "I understand that you're new. My name is Mr. S."

"Yes, sir," I said, shaking his hand. "Your reputation precedes you."

"Then you'll understand that I have a court date coming up."

"Yes, sir. A lot of other people here do, too."

Mr. S looked positively affronted.

"Miss MacCreaigh, I don't think you have a clear grasp of the situation. I am not just any inmate. I am Mr. S, I am here on a double-homicide charge, and I need these copies now!"

With what I hoped was my sincerest "Your wish is my command" smile (perfected during years as a public library circulation clerk), I relieved him of his prodigious stack of papers, and repeated, unequivocally, "Mr. S, I believe you know our policy about copies. I'll be happy to get these back to you later today." After a few more moments of indignant squawking, Mr. S sat down to do his research and I delivered his copies to his cell, per policy, later that day. (Erica)

Sexual Harassment

Most librarians are women. Most residents and employees of correctional facilities are men. And many of those men have been locked up for a long time or work shift hours that preclude a normal social life. Any questions?

True premeditated sexual harassment can be a little difficult to pin down in a correctional facility. The prevailing sense of humor tends to be pretty earthy to begin with. But basic common sense applies. If you would not tolerate certain comments or types of speech outside, you have to draw the same line inside. This may be easier to do with inmates than it is with other staff, because the balance of power is in your favor in your relationship to the inmates. If something is spoken amiss, your job requires you to nip the behavior in the bud and report it if necessary. There's very little room for analysis or interpretation. An offhand innuendo is as likely to be a form of testing as it is an off-the-cuff comment. Do NOT tolerate it.

With staff, however, it can be tricky to identify where the line is crossed between the facility's culturally acceptable casual conversation and outright harassment. Either way, you should not have to listen to talk that offends you. If certain kinds of comments offend you on the outside or if your internal radar suddenly starts going off, you must respond at once. If you tell someone that you'd rather not hear a certain kind of talk and that person persists, report that person's behavior to your supervising officer. Don't go straight to the offending staff person's supervisor; let yours talk to his or hers. If it's your supervisor who is harassing you and you've already tried working it out with your supervisor, figure out the facility's grievance process and begin following it immediately.

The point we're trying to make is that sexual harassment is whatever the victim feels it is. What is casual or harmless flirtatious banter for one might be all-out attack for another. Things can get out of hand very quickly inside. Take whatever action you must to protect yourself and your professionalism.

> *The Early Jailbird Gets the Worm*
> My experience with overt sexual harassment was limited to an incident with an inmate who informed me that he'd be taking dreams of me back to his cell that night. A prompt report to the deputies resulted in the inmate being written up and locked down. Other than the exchange of a few scowly looks, that inmate and I had no further problems. However, subtler forms of sexual harassment are common, such as the time I gave a book about songwriting to one inmate in 23-hour lockdown who informed me, "You know, there's just not a lot of inspiration inside these cold walls . . . and then you walk in . . . with your books." (Hint, hint, nudge, nudge.)
>
> One day, Mr. D came into law library with obvious mischief on his mind. After fooling around for close to forty minutes at the computers, he came up to the desk and asked me if I was married.

"Mr. D, I'm just about books. Nothing but books. You wanna talk about books?"

He gave me what I'm sure was intended to be an irresistible come-on look.

"Nothing but books? That sounds sad to me. But okay, tell me what you like to read."

Not to be baited, I said, "Mr. D, why don't YOU tell ME what you like to read?"

Mr. D grinned wolfishly.

"I read loooooove poetry."

Drat! Outfoxed! Maintaining my cool, I said, "Right. Well, I'll be sure to bring you some books about that when bookcart comes to your pod."

"Actually," he said, leaning in closer for emphasis, "I'd really like to read some of my loooooove poetry to you."

Aargh! Outmaneuvered at every step! The lesson I learned from this exchange was this: If a patron (and this applies to those oppressively flirtatious types in the public libraries as well) starts a conversation with a personal comment, you will not deflect his/her interest by being charming and amusing! At the outset, after the marriage query, I should have said simply, "My personal life is none of your business." Draw the line, and stick to it! (Erica)

Physical/Romantic Attraction

Since jail and prison deputies and officers are, by and large, men and civilian staff inside correctional facilities are often women, a certain measure of office romance is to be expected. Work relationships usually begin in small ways and proceed cautiously. In an environment as charged with tension, adrenaline, and sexual frustration as correctional facilities are, many people, both single and married, find the temptation extremely compelling. To a certain degree, correctional facilities are self-contained worlds; what happens here, stays here. But here is the caveat.

Your first priority must be the library. An indiscreet (or inappropriate) work relationship has the potential of undermining your professionalism, which in turn undermines your credibility and trustworthiness. Be advised that everything you do inside is observed by someone and that the correctional facility environment is exceptionally gossipy. As a jail librarian, you will spend much of your time in jail justifying your right to be there in the first place. If you do begin a relationship with another staff person, save it for after hours. Anything that becomes grist for the gossip mill distracts people from your real mission of running the library.

And now a word about relationships with inmates. Many inmates are good looking, intelligent, articulate, and very charming. Librarianship of any ilk is a humanistic endeavor, and the human experience is magnified behind bars. In this scenario, that doesn't matter one whit. Do NOT get involved with an inmate. This includes close platonic friendship as well as physical and romantic attraction. You get involved at the risk of your job, the risk of your credibility, the risk of the library service, and the risk of your safety. You will get fired. The library service itself could be abridged or terminated completely. Most importantly, you could get injured or worse. Do not do it.

> Even the most innocuous acts can be misconstrued as inappropriate behavior in jail. A jail librarian we knew used to close the library door when she was working alone. Alone without other paid staff, that is. She also closed the door if she was alone with inmate workers. She was stunned when the rumor mill got back to her that she was fooling around with the trusties in the library!

Conclusion

In Appendices B and C, you'll find the job descriptions and interview questions good for hiring salaried staff and inmate workers. These documents succinctly illustrate what we've described in the last several pages: Applying the public library model inside a correctional facility demands a rare combination of personal and professional traits and attainments. But overriding all of these is one key element we have not mentioned. You must want to be there. That is not something anybody can advise or teach you about. It is also something that you might not even know about yourself yet, especially if you have never worked inside a correctional facility.

Therefore, we encourage you to get in contact with one or two jail or prison librarians near you (your state library might be able to direct you if you get stuck) and see if they'll let you shadow them for a day. You'll want to make sure you're there on a day with lots of patron interaction; we generally figure the busier the better. If you're considering applying for a correctional library job, we definitely urge you to spend at least a few hours in the environment, just to see how it feels to be surrounded by all the demands of public library patrons in a confined windowless space behind locked doors. It's not for everyone. But those of us who know we belong in here think it's the best place in the world to work.

References

Mongelli, W. D. 1994. De-mystifying legal research for prisoners. *Law library journal* 86(259), 277–298.

Vogel, B. 1995. *Down for the count*. Lanham, MD: Scarecrow Press, Inc.

3

Understanding the Patrons

Over the years, people have often asked us, "What kinds of people are in jail?" The glib answer is a resounding "Everyone. Because everyone is welcome!" The follow-up refrain goes something like this: People in jail represent every color and nationality, every religion and creed, a multitude of languages, both sexes and every sexual preference, ages ranging from early teens to old age, and academic achievement ranging from illiteracy to Ph.D.s. They represent the world in small. So why are they on the inside? Are they any different from people on the outside?

Inmate Demographics in the United States

The most reliable common denominator for all prisoners is a history of poverty (Sullivan 2000). Other distinguishing features of prison populations include a predominant number of people who grew up in single-parent households, people of nonwhite ethnicity, and a disproportionate number of people with learning disabilities and reading difficulties.

According to the Bureau of Justice, there are over two million prisoners in jails and prisons across the country. Two-thirds of these are housed in state and federal prisons; the rest are held in local (county or municipal) facilities (Bureau of Justice 2005). A staggering 6.9 million people were either on probation or parole or in jail or prison in 2004 (*Facts about Prisons* 2005). That number represents one out of every thirty-two American adults. If recent incarceration rates remain stable, approximately one out of every fifteen people in the United States will serve time in state or federal prison at some point in their lifetime (Bureau of Justice 2004, December). This statistic does not include the millions of people who will avoid prison, but will serve time in jail, community corrections, or on probation.

61

Here are some other quick facts about the American inmate population.

- In 2003, of those inmates sentenced to serve more than one year, 44 percent were black, 35 percent were white, and 19 percent were Hispanic (Bureau of Justice 2004)
- Between 1995 and 2003, inmates between the ages of forty and fifty-four accounted for over 46 percent of the growth of the entire U.S. prison population (Bureau of Justice 2004)
- At the end of 2003, two-thirds of all prisoners were younger than forty (Bureau of Justice 2004)
- More than half of all prison inmates have obtained a high school diploma or GED (National Institute for Literacy n.d.)
- Over 50 percent of convicted inmates state they were under the influence of drugs or alcohol at the time of their offense, and 83 percent of convicted state prisoners admit drug use at some point in their lives (Cooke 2002)
- Sixteen percent of the entire corrections population is female; of these, nearly half report being physically or sexually abused (Greenfield and Snell 1999; Snell 1994)
- More than half of state and federal prisoners have minor children; of those children, over half are ten years old or younger (Mumola 2000; National Institute for Literacy n.d.)

"I'm not really a bad guy."

The stereotypical inmate is male, nonwhite, young, chemically dependent, uneducated, and unemployed; the Bureau of Justice statistics certainly seem to bear that out. But describing an inmate is not that easy. The statistics do not even begin to tell the stories about "being a bad guy."

In jail or prison, the first things you see are the uniforms that distinguish law enforcement staff from civilian staff and so-called good guys from so-called bad guys. But give it a week and you realize that you're surrounded by people just like yourself. During the 2000 presidential election, inmates on all political sides followed the recount with the fervor of any free citizen. On 9/11, inmates wept alongside civilian and uniformed staff. When Jessica Lynch was rescued, inmates cheered; when Martha Stewart was indicted, they jeered. Just like the rest of us.

One inmate told us, "I'm not really a bad guy. My life just spiraled out." His story is a common one, both inside and outside jail: laid off, bitter divorce, drinking problem. It's a story of feeling alone and up against a wall with few human or economic resources to call upon. It's a story that doesn't belong to prisoners alone.

What differentiates their version of the story from ours is how they dealt with the challenges of life. The life of the future inmate is rarely marked by evil, malice, or even mental illness. It is, however, almost universally marked by chronically bad decision-making.

Perhaps a more pertinent question is how the prison population—legions of potential library patrons—compares demographically to librarians. The library profession, unlike the graying prison population, is already gray, with 75 percent more librarians over the age of forty-five than comparable professions (Wilder 1996). Librarians tend to be white, well-educated even without the MLS, and overwhelmingly middle-class. And women still dominate the profession. Contrast this with the relatively youthful, disproportionately ethnic, less-educated, economically disadvantaged men who comprise the majority of correctional facility populations, and the stage is set for some interesting interpersonal relating.

When we walk the halls of jail, we see the toll taken by poverty, drug and alcohol abuse, and lack of medical attention. We see a defeatist attitude thinly veiled with homeboy bravado. Many inmates walk very slowly, "treading air." On the other hand, there are those inmates who spend time in jail like some people spend time at camp. Jail is a place where they live clean (physically and behaviorally), where their time is constructively structured, and where they meet new friends. All inmates are eager to see a friendly face, which is why basic civility counts for more in jail than anywhere else.

We agree with Vogel (1995) in thinking that the ultimate, defining difference between inmates and the rest of us is this: Inmates are confined in a formidable place. And that, too, makes a corrections librarian's job very interesting. Where do the hallowed credos of the American librarian feature in a world where the civil right to information challenges the human right to safety?

Female Inmates and Prisoners

Women represent a fraction of the number of imprisoned persons in this country, yet they are among the fastest growing segment of the arrested and incarcerated (Snell 1994). Eighty-five percent of women under the supervision of correctional agencies are on probation or parole. The overwhelming majority of women are arrested for drug-related offenses.

Incarcerated women are somewhat less likely than men to have a history of prior convictions and are half as likely as men to have been juvenile offenders (Greenfield and Snell 1999). Women and men are almost equally likely to have high school diplomas or the equivalent, but women are more likely than men to have some college education (Snell 1994).

Incarcerated women are less likely than their male counterparts to have been employed at the time of their arrest; and well over one-third of women (compared to less than a third of men) had incomes of less than $600 per month at the time of their arrest. While about 8 percent of men were receiving welfare assistance before their arrest, 30 percent of arrested women were on welfare (Greenfield and Snell 1999).

Almost half of women under correctional authority reported being victims of physical or sexual assault, with nearly 70 percent of those women reporting that the assault occurred prior to age eighteen. Nearly half of the women in state and local custody have never married, a substantially higher percentage of never-marrieds than in the general population. Approximately seventy percent of women either in jail or on probation, 65 percent of women in state prison, and 59 percent of women in federal prison have children under the age of eighteen (Greenfield and Snell 1999).

A librarian's professional relationships to women in jail vary greatly from those with the male inmates. In general, women are less likely to come to law library to seriously research their own cases. Instead, they overwhelmingly express the need for information about marital law and child custody and support. Women also seem to be less likely to sue our facility over library access. We suspect it's because fewer women are doing legal research in the hopes of getting long sentences reduced, perhaps because their sentences tend to be shorter and less severe than men's (Greenfield and Snell 1999).

> *Mars and Venus Behind Bars*
>
> Unquestionably, gender issues are alive and well between inmates and corrections librarians. One librarian at a medium security state prison described her experiences with male and female inmate workers this way:
>
> "When I worked at the men's prison, the men rarely argued when I gave them instructions. There was some chivalry there. If I was walking out of the library with my arms full, they would offer to help carry things. Unless they are openly gay, they keep their relationships quiet. They have to keep up a 'macho' image, which actually isolates them more. Racial divisions are also more pronounced among men.
>
> "Women are different. They will argue with you. The gender sameness means if my arms are full, their attitude is 'carry your

own stuff.' They are needier, more emotional, more talkative, and more likely to bring their personal problems to work. But women aren't isolated like men are because they don't have the macho thing going on.

"When women come to prison, they don't come with the external support system that men do. Guys have moms, wives, girlfriends, and sisters who visit them—and take care of their kids. Many incarcerated women are abandoned by the people they knew on the outside and their kids are often sucked into 'the system.' To compensate, female prisoners create 'family groups' that cross racial barriers, groups of 'aunties' and 'sisters'. Some women are even considered 'brothers.' "

Because family law is much more complex than criminal law, and because women in general are more inclined to share intimate details of their lives with others, we hear more about women's life stories than we do men's. Bookcart and law sessions with women are far more social than men's; it's more difficult to keep women's conversations on the subject of books and legal research because women's communication and interrelational styles are more sociable than men's, whose communication styles tend to center around information exchange and task orientation.

But because women behind bars have usually experienced a disproportionate degree of trauma in their lives, their high energy socializing combined with the tragic content of their communication can be very draining. We have been fortunate to always have at least one person on our staff take ownership of the library needs of the 140 or so women in our facility. Those librarians illustrate how well challenging populations can be served by people who really want to give them the best library services and materials possible.

One of our colleagues is a library school student whose interest in children's librarianship carries over into her working relationship with female inmates. By helping incarcerated moms, she feels like she's helping kids. Another coworker was a criminal justice major from a law enforcement family who was able to provide consistently good customer service without getting emotionally involved. Yet another was a social worker in a former life who used to remove abused children from their homes; working with female inmates was easy compared to her previous job. What all of these librarians have in common is the ability to feel and express empathy without feeling sorry for the inmates and without getting sucked in. In certain measure, this quality is necessary for anyone working with any incarcerated population, regardless of age or gender. But we find it's particularly useful for those working with imprisoned women.

Juvenile Offenders

Juveniles can be found in all kinds of correctional facilities and programs, although according to a 1997 study by the Bureau of Justice (Strom 2000), over 85 percent of them are in juvenile-specific facilities. Kids sentenced to adult prisons generally have three correctional housing options according to legislation in each state: solely adult incarceration, graduated incarceration, and segregated incarceration. Most states allow incarcerated minors in adult correctional facilities to live fully integrated with the adult community, although a few states prohibit shared housing assignments for adults and juveniles and stipulate that inmates under the age of eighteen must be housed in separate units. Even fewer states mandate that no prisoner under age sixteen can be housed in an adult prison, regardless of the nature of his or her offense. Several states employ graduated incarceration, which basically means that youthful offenders begin serving their sentences in juvenile facilities until they reach a certain age, usually eighteen, at which point they can be transferred to an adult facility. Some states apply segregated incarceration with particular underage offenders, assigning juvenile offenders to specific facilities or programs based on their ages and need for substance abuse treatment and life skills training (Strom 2000).

Juvenile facilities can resemble anything from boot-camp military-style programs to public high schools. Local public school systems often administer the education programs inside juvenile facilities so they are in step with the kids in the community. However, not all teens in juvenile facilities are in school; some have already graduated or achieved their GEDs.

Incarcerated kids share some common characteristics. They tend to exhibit lower-than-average intelligence scores. Verbal performance and reading ability tend to be lower than those of the general public. Academic achievement consistently rates at least one year and often several years below grade-level; and incarcerated youth have high rates of grade retention (Foley 2001).

All of these factors make juvenile offenders the least likely of all inmates and prisoners to make voluntary use of a correctional library's resources. The challenge for you as a librarian, then, is to figure out how to "turn them on" to the printed word. This challenge is no different from the challenges teens pose in the public libraries, although the source of the challenge is different. Teens in the public libraries, with their myriad entertainment choices and high-tech preferences, are a tough audience for libraries to reach, although any teen services specialist will tell you it's worth the effort. We think so, too, and will share some ideas for reaching incarcerated teens in the section on library programming.

Pass the Patterson, hold the Koontz

Sheila staged a customer service coup with one of our juveniles that began rather dubiously. One day at bookcart, as Sheila was recommending books she thought any teen boy would like to read, Mr. H exclaimed indignantly, "I hate Koontz! I don't want to read anything by a white guy!"

Sheila, characteristically unruffled by the outburst, said calmly, "Well, what DO you want to read?" And in an equally characteristic display of frustration witnessed by many public library readers advisors, Mr. H threw up his hands in disgust and said, "I just don't know!"

So Sheila decided this was a good opportunity to build some trust. "Mr. H., let me try a few things out on you," she said, handing him a few titles (none of which were by Dean Koontz.) "You have to tell me if these books are good or bad. If you like the book, then it's good."

Several weeks and several favorably received titles later, Sheila offered Mr. H. *Along Came a Spider* by James Patterson. "Just to warn you," she said solemnly, "the author is a white guy. But the main character is a black guy, so I hope you'll give it a try."

It was a bit of a gamble that Sheila blithely played, having won Mr. H.'s trust by suggesting several books he'd enjoyed. A couple of weeks later, she received a kite from Mr. H., thanking her "for that good book."

Girls detained in adult facilities are in perhaps the worst position of any class of prisoner in the country. For their protection, they cannot be housed with juvenile males, nor can they be housed with adult females. There usually aren't enough girls, especially at the county level, to warrant their own cellblocks. Consequently, girls do their time in adult facilities in solitary confinement (Chesney-Lind and Sheldon 1998). Since nearly two-thirds of girls in correctional settings have experienced physical abuse and over half have experienced sexual abuse, they are far more vulnerable to depression and self-destructive behavior. This is exacerbated by their isolation in adult facilities. Girls in adult facilities can be the most emotionally exhausting patrons for a librarian to deal with, assuming the librarian gets to see them at all.

Here is a special note about minors in an adult detention facility. If a minor winds up in one, a line has been crossed. In prison and jail, you don't usually see minor-league minors, even if they have been arrested more than once. The kids detained in adult facilities generally aren't in for burglary, vandalism, or even drugs. They are in for rape, murder, robbery, and assault. Juveniles who have been sentenced to adult facilities are almost half again as likely as adult prisoners to be serving time for a violent offense (Strom 2000).

Just as it takes a special kind of person to work with adult inmates and prisoners, it takes a special kind of person to work with juveniles accused of the worst possible crimes. Teresa, a librarian at a state-level juvenile detention facility, says that teen boys in prison are challenging to work with because they don't talk and they try very hard to be tough. They require a firm touch, and you must be unwaveringly professional in your dealings with them. "These kids are slower to trust and have trouble making connections with people," she says. "It's harder to get a sense of progress or professional gratification when working with them." Patience with their guardedness, their subpar social skills, and their learning disabilities must be paired with a real liking of kids and, perhaps most importantly, an educator's heart.

"I'm essentially working in a school media center," Teresa states. Her library looks like any public high school's; the day we toured seven Colorado prisons, the only bank of computers we saw was in her library. (Other libraries had only one or two computer catalogs for patron access.) As with any school media specialist, a juvenile center librarian must be part librarian, part teacher. In prison, he or she must also be part corrections officer.

Love 'em or leave 'em

We recently heard a story from a prison librarian about a teen inmate. He was slated for release, anticipating a job interview, and asked Teresa if she would write him a reference.

"I'm only asking because you are a very reputable person," he said, mistakenly placing emphasis on the second syllable of "reputable."

His comment speaks to the respect a librarian must command when working with teens of any ilk, but particularly incarcerated teens, who at a young age have already expressed profound contempt of authority. To earn their respect, you must be consistent, fair, and respectful toward them. In that sense, good customer service to teens is no different from serving adults! So what is the key to working well with incarcerated teens? We think it's probably the same quality that makes for great teen librarians in public libraries. You have to like teenagers!

Profiles of Inmate Behavior

Many factors contribute to the internal culture of a jail or prison. These factors include but are not limited to how the facility is administered, the size of the facility, the quality of life inside the facility, and the facility's budget. Donald Clemmer (Rubin and Suvak 1940/1995) pioneered the idea of a "prisoner culture" based on prisoners' feelings of being rejected by society. According to Sykes and Messenger (Rubin and Suvak, 1960/1995), the prisoner culture exists at a subsistence level that actually reinforces prisoners' experience of alienation and low status. All of these authors describe the "inmate code" of behavior, designed primarily to challenge the authority of the facility or system administrators and officers.

The problem with the idea of an "inmate code" and "prisoner culture" is that they only apply to some of the people who are incarcerated. Clemmer himself admitted that even though prisoners are aware of the general tenets of the inmate code, some prisoners choose to participate in certain aspects of the culture, while others elect not to become part of the prisoner culture at all. In 1977, Gordon Hawkins hammered the final nail in the concept of "prisonization," citing behavioral studies that clearly showed how every prisoner's personal social history directly influences his or her behavior behind bars (Rubin and Suvak 1995). In other words, every prisoner is a full-fledged individual with his or her own motivations. As librarians on the inside, you need to remember that, because in environments like prisons, which emphasize conformity, it's easy to forget. Rubin and Suvak (1995) state: "Just seeing inmates as people with a wide range of human characteristics and qualities can make a prison librarian's job more joyful and hopeful. The lesson is: Know the inmate code, but do not make it dogma."

Something else to bear in mind in the midst of our humanistic rendering of the correctional library experience is that we are in fact talking about working with criminals. Inmates and prisoners who say, like Morgan Freeman in *The Shawshank Redemption*, "Everyone's innocent in here!" (King 1982) are truly a dime a dozen behind bars. And, shortcomings of our legal system aside, most inmates aren't. The Bureau of Justice states that over half of jail inmates were on probation, parole, or pretrial release at the time of their arrest; 40 percent had served or were serving at least one sentence for a violent offense, and nearly that many had served at least three prior sentences prior to their most recent incarceration (2004).

In their now-classic book *Games Criminals Play* (1981), Bud Allen and Diana Bosta, a corrections lieutenant and an educator, respectively, studied cases in which an inmate set up and used a correctional facility staff person for further criminal gain. The authors found nothing to indicate that certain personality features, ethnicity, gender, or job assignment predispose an employee to being successfully set up. But length of service in corrections was an indicator of susceptibility. Fully 63 percent of the victims of inmate setups had been in the corrections business for less than eleven months. Another 21 percent had been corrections employees for less than three years. Allen and Bosta (1981) speculate:

 Perhaps this occurs because of the transition lag from free society values and expectations to the confined society values and expectations. Inmates try to coerce new employees before staff-encouraged professionalism is established or before the procedures, rules, and convicts communication code are known by the staff member.

If you truly want to apply the public library model behind bars, it is absolutely critical that you reconcile constant mindfulness of criminal intent with a commitment to provide equitable—and excellent—library service to criminally minded people. *Games Criminals Play* contains a must-read chapter on how four types of prisoner—the observer, the contact, the runner, and the turner—team up to sting staff. In addition to those types, William D. Mongelli (1994) has identified five other types that are specific to correctional library patrons—narcissists, loopholers, hustlers, writ writers, and lost souls. In a virtually one-of-a-kind article in *Corrections Today,* prison librarian Stephen Mallinger (1991) identifies seven more. We strongly advise that you read all of the above as soon as you can, especially if you're brand-new to the environment or returning after a lengthy hiatus.

We've encountered a few characters of our own. As you consider them, bear in mind the one overarching commonality they all share: They want to control the librarian and/or the library. Whatever their angle or their motive, the ultimate goal is about taking control away from you. Let's take a brief look at some of these types and how your behavior, as outlined in the previous chapter, can either derail nefarious intentions or so fully compromise your position that your job and your safety will be at risk.

The Bully

This is a person who, exactly like schoolyard bullies, spends an inordinate amount of time picking fights with and lording over those he or she perceives as weaker. Bullies on the inside are absolutely no different from bullies on the outside and were probably themselves victims of bullying at one time or another. Their defining feature is fear; they bluster about in an effort to make themselves seem ferocious because they are secretly terrified of the other inmates, of the outcome of their upcoming trial, and of the staff.

Bullies will manipulate, coerce, verbally abuse with insults and sexual harassment, and threaten to sue you if you don't bend the rules for them. The difference between the bully and the narcissist is that bullies find it very difficult to stand up to stronger people. You can demonstrate your own strength in a number of ways. Refuse to get rattled when they start making demands. Stick by your guns; keep the rules consistent for everyone and offer the bully the same kind of respect you insist up receiving from him or her. If the inmate is physically intimidating, insisting upon physical distance ("That's close enough, Mr. So-and-So") can ameliorate the feeling of being at a physical disadvantage. Intimidation simply does not work if you refuse to be intimidated.

But as with so many things in prison and in life, things are not always that simple. If a bully intimidates you, get help from an officer! Also consider the benefits of learning some personal safety tactics. Prisons conduct extensive personal safety training, including self-defense courses, in their new staff orientation programs. If you are in a facility that does not offer such training, or if you are a contract employee as we are, you might have to pursue such training on your own. It's probably worth the energy and money if you find yourself intimidated inside. Anything that increases your self-confidence will enhance the way you carry and express yourself. Many bullies can recognize a self-confident bearing as something they don't want to challenge.

Who's Afraid of the Big Bad Wolf?

In Chapter 2, we told the story of Mr. S, the physically intimidating inmate patron with a penchant for manipulation and intimidation. He also had a legendary and violent temper. Scarcely a week went by during his incarceration at our facility when deputies weren't rushing *en masse* to Mr. S's pod to defuse some volatile situation he'd cooked up.

One day, some nurses and I were having lunch when the deputies' radios blared out the emergency signal and all the uniformed staff leapt up from their tables and bolted out the door to, you guessed it, Mr. S's pod. I made some offhand remark about murderers who just couldn't behave themselves. The nurses looked at me like I was nuts.

"Who told you he was a murderer?" one of them asked.

"He did," I replied. "In law library the other day when he was trying to get me to make a bunch of copies for him."

Both nurses rolled their eyes.

"Don't believe everything these guys tell you," they advised. "Mr. S never killed anybody. He's a sex offender and he's scared to death in here. He probably told you that he was a murderer so all the other inmates in the library could hear. He's hoping they'll be scared of him now!" (Erica)

The Narcissist

Mongelli (1994) uses this term to describe an almost pathologically self-centered inmate who harbors a vendetta against the correctional facility or a department therein. States Mongelli: "Often considered model inmates in terms of submission to law library rules of behavior, they smile warmly and tell a topical joke while handing the librarian a photocopy request describing a complaint naming the librarian as a defendant."

The defining feature of narcissists is exaggerated egotism that probably covers up dangerously low self-esteem. Anything that frustrates them is grounds for a lawsuit. Because their ego is a blinder, they often don't know as much about the law as they think they do, and they often have a difficult time prioritizing their needs since they run on a relentless imperative of immediate gratification. Of all the many different types of people you'll meet in jail, narcissists are the only ones who will make you feel like the paid help. They are also the only ones who are absolutely impossible to satisfy.

You could spend fifteen hours working on a narcissist's seventy-two different requests, hand-deliver the fruits of your arduous labors to his cell, and then lay down and set yourself on fire while singing "The Star-Spangled Banner," and the narcissist would threaten to sue you because the pages you photocopied came out too dark (which will adversely affect the outcome of his trial) and you're singing off-key (an obvious human rights violation).

Two tricks can help you deal with the narcissist. First, you will have to remind the narcissist practically every time you see him or her that the library's rules and policies apply to everybody. The narcissist will want to have the same argument with you over and over about this; don't get sucked in. ("We are not discussing this again. Period. If you want to discuss it further, take it up with the sergeant.") Second, document absolutely everything you provide to the narcissist. Because when you do get called into court to face the narcissist's accusations that he or she suffered demonstrable harm because you weren't responsive enough, you will be able to present the judge with documented evidence of everything you have provided.

The Narcissist in Action

We had an inmate patron whose incessant demands for extravagant law library access and reference assistance (especially printing and photocopying) resulted in our having to inform him that his "unreasonable requests" fell outside the scope of our service. Not to be deterred, Mr. F sicced his attorney on us; before we knew it, we had become Mr. F's own personal legal reference gophers.

Then, he fired his attorney and went *pro se,* at which time we were able to go back to treating him like all of our other patrons—fairly! His requests continued to be demanding, excessive, and unmanageable. When we returned some of his written requests unanswered, he began waving the lawsuit flag.

About this time, he clocked a deputy and went into lockdown. Library staff agreed that he was too unpredictable to allow into the law library. About the same time, the lieutenants drew up a new policy stating that inmates in administrative or disciplinary segregation would not be able to attend law library, but would have their reference requests answered via kite.

The library staff discussed the implications of this. We knew we needed to do everything in our power to provide library service to these inmates as equitably as possible. This would be no mean feat, since they had no way of doing their own legal research and our ability to conduct reference interviews was virtually nonexistent. Nonetheless, we agreed to expedite any kite request from an ad-seg inmate within three days, which was more than twice as fast as we could promise answering any request from inmates in the general population. We felt this was only fair. Since these patrons could not do for themselves, we would meet them 95 percent of the way.

In spite of our efforts, Mr. F blew a gasket when he found out that he would not have direct access to the law library. A few days later, he convinced a judge that his federal rights as provisioned for in *Bounds v. Smith* were being violated. Not surprisingly, he didn't say anything about the jail's new administrative policy! The judge issued a court order specifying Mr. F's right to access law library resources in person.

Our lieutenant intervened and explained the new facility policy, which the judge upheld, and for a few days Mr. F was silent. Then suddenly kite requests began pouring in, as many as twenty kites a day with multiple requests written on each. Fearing he would follow through on his threat to sue, and contrary to our better judgment, we prioritized his requests, sometimes printing more than five hundred pages of material for him each week.

Fortunately, I had been doing a little record keeping on the side. Months earlier, when Mr. F had established a pattern for wasting time in law library on non-research-related activities, had been caught stealing library supplies, and had abused the kite-request process by submitting multiple kite requests a day for random information not remotely connected to his case, I began documenting his behavior. This turned out to be positively providential, because eventually Mr. F found a judge who would entertain his complaint about "completely inadequate library service." The judge asked us if we had documentation to support our claim that we had gone far above and beyond what was reasonable to provide. And we did.

As luck would have it, our winning argument came from Mr. F himself. When asked what exactly he expected of us, he replied, "The librarians have provided me with a four-and-a-half-foot stack of printed material. But I need more." The judge decided he didn't need more and dismissed the complaint.

The Charmer (aka "Romeo")

This inmate is truly God's gift to the opposite sex, although we've heard about gay charmers sidling up to same-sex staff with similar techniques. Charmers overuse one weapon in their social arsenal, hence their nickname. They are often physically attractive and are usually intelligent. Less refined charmers usually come across as flattering and self-impressed; it's easy to detect and deflect their manipulative intentions. But really good charmers, the ones who are patient, the ones who pretend to be cooperative, reasonable, and modest, and who pretend to actually have a sincere interest in who you are, probably cause more staff to get fired than any other type.

Charmers will keep their eyes and ears open for any details about your life that they can use to draw you in. If they learn you have a dog, they will do their best to draw you into a conversation about your pet. If they learn you have a child, they will share their own parenting experiences in a spirit of camaraderie. If they learn you have an interest in poetry or religion or hockey or cooking, they will try to connect with you by reciting e. e. cummings or discussing the finer points of the Book of Hezekiah or analyzing the stats for your favorite team (which will always be their favorite team, too!) or engaging you in reminiscences of your grandmothers' exceptional Sunday afternoon dinners. They are masters at making you feel special. And in an environment as alienating as jail and prison, that can be extremely seductive.

"Oh, Lord, it's hard to be humble . . . "

During bookcart one afternoon, Mr. G, who clearly considered himself a heaven-sent gift to women, asked me if he could check out "just one extra book."

"Mr. G, you know the limit's three."

"I know," he said, leaning against my cart in what I'm sure he thought was a classic *GQ* pose. "But I thought a beautiful woman like yourself . . . "

"What, Mr. G? Can't count? You've got three books. You're done!"

With a veritable twinkle in his eye, he thrust his arms dramatically out to his sides and went down on one knee.

"What if I were to kneel here before you and beg, Miss MacCreaigh?"

In a rare moment of perfect clarity and timing that Sheila would have been proud of, I said blandly, "Mr. G, if you had any idea how many times a week I see men on their knees begging, you'd know that it happens too often to impress me anymore!" (Erica)

Not all charmers are entirely insincere, but that doesn't matter. They are in the game for personal gain. The more closely involved you become with the charmer, the more power he or she gets and the more compromised you become. The rule here is to avoid becoming to attached to inmates. Our motto is "Be friendly, but not familiar."

The Suck-Up (also known as The Brown-Noser)

Fawning. Smarmy. Obsequious. All of these are accurate terms for the suck-up, one of the most easy to spot of all the types. For some reason, a disproportionate number of sex offenders fall into this category, so dealing with their treacly sweetness can be just this side of nauseating.

The suck-up positively effervesces with gratitude for everything you do for the "residents of this facility." In the beginning, he or she will practically kowtow to you, lavishly (and loudly) extolling the myriad virtues of the library to any nonlibrary staff person within earshot and writing letters of commendation to the warden. Their testing of the rules will begin in small ways, an extra sheet of blank paper here, an extra bookmark there. If you say no, the suck-up will apologize profusely. Then the next day, she will ask you again.

The thing about suck-ups that will get under your skin the most is their tendency to consider themselves better than other inmates and of the same mind frame as the staff person to whom they're ingratiating themselves. If you allow yourself to be sucked in by the suck-up's flattery and professed desire to please and accommodate you, his or her self-perception will eventually evolve from sycophantic serf to lord of the manor. Suck-ups, given enough rein, begin to identify themselves as your equals. Their demands will become more obvious, more imperative. They themselves will become plaintive, cross, exasperated. They will appeal to what they think is your shared intellect and sympathy. Beware. If frustrated at this stage of the game, suck-ups can get very nasty, throwing tantrums in the library and threatening to sue.

As with all the types, be fair, consistent, and professional and you'll be fine. With suck-ups particularly, though, you also want to nip the game-playing in the bud. Because suck-ups are more annoying than threatening, it's easy to overlook the way they push the envelope. Don't let them waste their time or yours with their excessive praise or false obligingness.

> *Just Between You and Me*
>
> Mr. M had been playing the library staff off each other for a few weeks, assuring staff that so-and-so had given him special dispensation to print personal letters on the law library computers, because "we came to an agreement about the importance of this task." He'd then give staff a knowing wink. You and me, kid, he was obviously thinking. We're in this together.
>
> When one of our coworkers put the kibosh on his game, he wrote a two-page letter of complaint to the library supervisor. In it, he carefully explained why he was entitled to special privileges not accorded to other inmates. After generously praising the many virtues of the library service and other library staff, he instructed us to "please inform our new librarian of this arrangement so I may pursue my legal obligations unfettered."
>
> What made us mad was his use of the word "our." Our? His choice of words reflected the classic suck-up tendency to identify with staff, especially those with authority.

The next day, uncharacteristically dressed as if I was going to a board meeting, I called Mr. M out of his cell. I carefully explained library policies and informed him that I had cleared up any misunderstanding among the staff about what the rules were, and told him there would be no further confusion because all staff would be enforcing the same policies. I also clarified who was in charge.

"Mr. M, I was especially disturbed by your use of the phrase 'our new librarian,'" I began.

Mr. M interrupted, saying most contritely, "Oh, ma'am, I thought about that after I sent you that kite. I sincerely apologize. I obviously made an incorrect assumption. Is she, in fact, a volunteer?"

Seeing as how he missed the point entirely, I wearily informed him that the new librarian was *my* employee, not *his* employee, and I expected him to afford the same level of respect to all the staff that he'd shown to me that morning. (Erica)

The Jailhouse Lawyer

No stereotypes here; this guy really exists. This patron devours all the legal material he can get his hands on and, as he digests it, will begin honing an understanding of the legal (typically criminal justice) system to rival that of any paralegal or law school student.

The jailhouse lawyer takes his or her access to law library very seriously. This person will often step in to help you if another patron's reference question has you stymied and will often coach other inmates on which of your titles or databases can best help them. Some jailhouse lawyers actually have lively little cottage industries in the legal brief-writing biz, exchanging their expertise for goods and favors from other inmates.

Jailhouse lawyers tend to present themselves as slightly more intellectual than other inmate library patrons, and they tend to make use of law library resources for the sole purpose of winning their own criminal cases, unlike the narcissist, who just wants to sue somebody. They command a certain level of respect from other inmates and may even elicit a certain amount of respect from you. But beware; jailhouse lawyers, just like many inmates, are intent on personal gain and will try to manipulate you. They are among the most likely of all inmate patrons to try to form a bond with you based on common interest (researching the law) and compatible intellect. Ultimately, every jailhouse lawyer asks to be "worked in" for extra or longer law sessions, or to be allowed to check out more than the maximum number of books. Remember that anything you do for one must be allowed for all. Remain consistent and fair in your dealings with the jail-house lawyer; he or she will test you but probably won't challenge you. They don't want to risk losing access to a service they very much value.

> *Is There a Lawyer in the House?*
>
> I had been employed at our jail library for a whopping five days when suddenly every veteran jail library staffer and all of our public library counterparts skipped town. Sheila and one of her former jail employees, now a public librarian, were attending a conference. The part-time jail library assistant and Bob, the former jail librarian whom I'd been hired to replace, had gone on vacation. I faced three full days with no backup and no one to help me navigate the myriad reference questions I would receive.
>
> Well, almost no one. By the third day, my reputation for clue-lessness had become the stuff of legend. One patron, Mr. W, had visited the library a couple of times in the preceding days and, upon asking me for yet more research assistance that I could not provide, asked gently, "Are Sheila or Angie anywhere in the building?" When I said no, he asked hesitantly, "What about Bob? Is Bob ever coming back?"
>
> To this I replied wearily, "No, Mr. W. Bob's not coming back. I'm all you've got now."
>
> Mr. W. visibly wilted. Dolefully staring at what seemed (to both of us) an incomprehensible bottomless pit of case law books, he said, "I miss Bob."
>
> "So do I, Mr. W!" I cried, at which point the rest of the inmates in the room burst out laughing. At that point, our resident jailhouse lawyers, who had stood silent witnesses of my pitiful efforts over the last few days, took over. I was so relieved, I decided to ignore the final word of the conversation, when another patron glibly quipped, "Hey, at least she's better lookin' than Bob!" (Erica)

The Pod Father (or Mother)

We have deliberately not referred to media portrayals of inmates because they tend to be one-dimensional and sensationalized. But we will make an exception in this case because the Pod Father (or Mother) is a rather exceptional inmate. The character of Red in Stephen King's *Rita Hayworth and the Shawshank Redemption* is a Pod Father. He's a man "who knows how to get things," how to bribe officers, how to "grease the wheels." He's been in the system for forty years. He's a go-to guy, and the people who enlist his services include the staff.

Of all the aforementioned types, the Pod Father (or Pod Mother) is the most polished, the most intelligent, the most reliable. Pod Fathers are like chieftains of the dayroom and often have influence over entire cellblocks, units, and wings of facilities. They know every name and have multiple informants bringing them the skinny about other inmates, the staff, and the facility. The amount of semiclassified information about staff and facilities that Pod Fathers know speaks volumes to the almost telepathic way information travels behind bars. And if there's a Pod Father in the building, much of the information will travel in his direction.

We're not really sure how Pod Fathers establish their influence. We know it's not through physical intimidation or obvious threats of violence. Often, they are an intellectual notch or more above most other inmates (and some staff), with the social graces and people skills to get things done. Sometimes, they have been in a facility long enough to have achieved a position of trust with the staff and of respect with other inmates. They know how to advise other inmates about facility-sanctioned educational and recreational programs and services. They also know how to advise others on how to get around the system.

The Pod Father (or Mother) does make use of library services, but his usage is carefully calculated. He only checks out the most intellectually stimulating reading material—classics, histories, business, and finance books—and he uses the law library in a careful, systematic way. But his primary motivator is not self-edification or even, we suspect, winning his case. The Pod Father's primary motivator is personal reputation. He wants his intelligence to be recognized, to be seen as someone who can make things happen and someone who can advise. And in most cases, he can.

Where the relationship with the Pod Father becomes sticky is when you rely on him—and you can—to help you with things like getting the word out about a library program or finding long lost books. Pod Fathers will always graciously acquiesce to any reasonable request, and the degree to which they can effectively help you with whatever you're asking for is downright spooky.

As with any of the other types, you have to be consistent, professional, and fair when dealing with the Pod Father. Although he is an inmate who can help you and whose influence other facility staff probably rely upon, too, you still don't want to get chummy or make any promises. Offer him sincere appreciation when he helps you. Because he is reputation-driven, you can repay him by referring other inmates to him for help and counsel.

Staying Safe

Creating Your Safety Net

So how does a new corrections librarian stay out of the red zone when it comes to manipulative inmate behavior, especially when said behavior is often incredibly subtle? Ideally, you will step into a position where you have someone working beside you to coach you while you learn the ropes. Unfortunately, more often, new library staff are on their own.

Professional connections inside are paramount because you need people who will watch your back. You need to get to know the officers. The first step is to introduce yourself and learn the officers' names. Dale Carnegie (1990) said that "a person's name is to that person the sweetest and most important sound in any language." Knowing names is a deceptively simple yet profoundly powerful tool of influence that works especially well in the dehumanizing environments of prison and jail. Once you know their names, keep the officers informed about what's going on in the library, emphasizing every positive outcome you can.

Building social ties outside of work is another rehumanizing activity that can deliver big dividends at work. Most prisons and many jails have staff picnics and parties; attend as many of them as you can, if for no other reason than to learn more names! As with any social activities outside the workplace, remember that on Monday, you still want your coworkers to see you as a professional. No table dances with a lampshade on your head, please. Your mission is to be friendly and to be seen. Consider it an ambassadorship. You are there to be yourself, but also to represent the library and build some loyalties. Staff parties are a great opportunity to ask for other people's stories and advice, too.

It's okay to have friends in the facility to talk to. If you're part of a prison system, there are likely other librarians doing the same job as you but in different facilities. Consult the system's administrators to figure out who those folks are, and solicit their support and advice. Also, get to know civilian staff in other departments, like the nurses, counselors, chaplain, and teachers. Inmates try to set them up, too, and veteran corrections employees will be able to advise you on what to watch for. If your paths cross with any regularity, you might also ask them to watch you as you interact with the inmates and request that they immediately point out any of your behaviors that may compromise you later.

The prison library listserv can be an excellent support resource. Check with your state library association to see if they have an outreach services subchapter; they may be able to connect you with others in your state who are doing the same job. ALA's Office of Literacy and Outreach Services may be able to refer you to people and organizations out of state, too. The Association of Bookmobiles and Outreach Services listserv members sometimes bring up service to prisoners; its members are among the most passionately committed library professionals in the country. Members of your tribe are out there. Finding them will make your professional life much easier and more enjoyable.

Fan Clubs and Fan Mail

Anyone who has worked in a small public library will tell you that patrons always have their "favorite" librarian. We know a very gifted readers advisor whose patrons are so fond of her, they simply stop reading when she's on vacation and not around to recommend books!

Corrections libraries have in common with small public libraries the fact that we really can get to know our patrons pretty well. And they get to know and like us a lot. It's okay for patrons to rely on some staff more than others; often this is an accident of scheduling when certain staff are simply more available when certain patrons are around. Sometimes it's due to consistently productive librarian/patron exchanges, often based on a good match between a particular librarian's areas of interest and expertise and the patron's information needs. And some librarians are simply people with pleasing personalities; everybody, even the incarcerated, likes to work with them.

But sometimes, it's more than that. Inmate crushes on corrections staff are common, particularly on civilian staff who provide a humanistic service. The most obvious and common red flag is surreptitious communication, and the easiest manner of it is note passing and letter writing. We've intercepted the most earnest of correspondences, which usually contain admissions like "I know I'm not supposed to be writing to you" and "I know you probably aren't allowed to write to me." These statements are invariably followed with "but . . . " But, I hope you'll write to me anyway. I hope you won't report me. I hope we can at least be friends.

Sheesh. The best approach is to immediately report the behavior and surrender the note or letter to the deputy or officer on duty in the inmate's living unit. If a letter arrives from an inmate in another facility, let your commanding officer know at once. And under no circumstances should you lead any admirer to believe that their expressions of affection are acceptable or welcome. We don't advocate you become suspicious or start reading double meanings into every interaction with inmates who are friendly and seem to seek you out. Suspiciousness contains too much preemptive defensiveness that can interfere with good customer service. As we mentioned before, often inmates prefer working with you simply because you've proven your competency at helping them. Rather, the mindset we advocate is skepticism. You can distrust the purity of your patrons' motives without anticipating problems by maintaining healthy skepticism. Skepticism supports vigilance without tipping over into the fear that can actually precipitate what it means to avoid.

User Needs

Now that we have shed some light on whom and what to pay attention to, we turn our focus back to the public library model. The key to providing good library service to inmates lies in our willingness to think in terms of public libraries. For example, we have always referred to our inmate clientele as "patrons." It is a word that clearly establishes our relationship to inmates, our professional purpose, and our role in the facility. Another strategy is to think about how inmate patrons and library patrons on the outside are the same. These are people with information needs, simple as that. Inmates, like most library patrons, are inexperienced information users. Their position to you, the librarian, is an unequal one. They usually don't formulate adequate research strategies, they are bewildered by information technologies and resources, and half the time their stated questions have little to do with their actual information needs. And believe us, the very last inmate you see as you're trying to close up shop for the day will be the one who isn't a registered patron yet.

So what are their information needs? Without jumping the gun too much, since we will discuss this in detail in Part Two, inmates' information needs are as varied as those of public library patrons. But since inmates represent a closed society whose members have a single overriding point in common—they've all been arrested for something—you will definitely field a preponderance of legal queries. In an informal user needs survey conducted in 2002, we found that out of the forty-six inmates studied, fourteen wanted answers to legal questions and fourteen wanted directory assistance, usually for courtrooms, attorneys, or other correctional facilities. Inmate-specific queries regarding prison facilities and correctional facility administrative charts, along with business, medical, career/job, and Social Security queries made up most of the remaining questions. Other questions ranging from religion and art history to author biographies and tax information have also crossed our desks.

As for recreational reading needs, there's a standing joke among jail and prison librarians that you could stock your leisure reading collection with nothing but Stephen King and satisfy most of your patrons. It's certainly true that Stephen King enjoys enormous popularity in jail, but if the New York Times Bestseller List is any indicator, the same can be said on the outside. The fact is that inmates read everything, just like public library patrons—everything from Eric Jerome Dickey to Charles Dickens, from Carlos Castenada to Carl Sagan, from Danielle Steel to Daniel Defoe. Inmates read at all levels, just like folks on the outside, so R. L. Stine has a place right next to John Steinbeck, and Laura Ingalls Wilder next to Oscar Wilde.

The important things to remember when applying the public library model to your patrons' recreational reading needs are as follows.

Designated Budget

Many jail and prison libraries are built on donations. We believe there is a proper place for donations: as filler for your otherwise specifically selected collection. You simply cannot provide patrons with timely, relevant materials if you don't have the money to respond to their specific needs.

> Bookcart can look like naptime if the collection is bad. Ours looks like feeding time.

Library materials budgets can be publicly tax-supported, but are more often provided via inmate commissary funds, which are monies generated through the regular sale of personal items and snack foods, usually by a private company under contract, to the inmates. In this sense, the inmates are your taxpayers and you have a duty to provide them with a collection that meets their needs. Actually, we take it as our duty regardless of where the money comes from. If you have no budget for books and the facility's administration doesn't look to fork over any time soon, start writing grant requests.

Patron Input

Inmate patrons should be encouraged to suggest titles, authors, and subjects for the collection, just as public library patrons on the outside do. Avoid the temptation to build your collection with the intent of "redeeming" your users. This strategy doesn't fly in public libraries, because it precludes the development of a balanced collection representing many points of view. It's also likely that those materials considered "worthy" by middle-class, middle-aged women with master's degrees won't reflect the tastes of the public at large. This disparity is magnified tenfold behind bars.

Many, many inmates say, "I haven't read a book since high school!" They rediscover reading behind bars. A fair number discover a love of books for the very first time when they're incarcerated. All of these folks, as well as avid veteran readers, love the chance to discuss the books they've read. This is an opportunity—take it! Dialogue with your patrons, as you would with public library users. What did they like about the book they just read? What didn't they like? If you're getting requests from all over the building for Triple Crown publications, you need to invest in multiple copies. But also be receptive to the patron who tells you that the fiction collection is starting to look a little one-dimensional with all those Triple Crowns in there! Your patrons can tell you if you're missing the third book in a four-book series, they can tell you about authors you never see on suburban or rural public library shelves (and often not even in urban libraries), and they can tell you if they're seeing the same old tired titles week after week. The beauty of working in a closed environment is that everyone is forced to look at the same things. Perceptions vary, however, and the more feedback you get from your users, the stronger your collection will be.

The Reformer

One afternoon after our inmate workers had gone back to their cells for the daily head count, one of our coworkers decided to take a quick glance at the book trucks to make sure the guys had selected good titles for bookcart later that afternoon. A couple of minutes later, she came into the office chuckling.

"You need to see what Mr. K did to the nonfiction cart."

Always ready for show-and-tell, we followed her to the cart in question. Nearly every book on all three shelves dealt with Christian subject matter. Since Mr. K had made a name for himself with his inimitable way of encouraging other inmates to use the library, namely by greeting every patron who approached his cart with a booming "Welcome to the finest library establishment in all of Hotel Arapahoe!" we knew his intentions were honorable. Still, his selections hardly did justice to our well-rounded, balanced nonfiction collection.

So, later that day, when the inmate workers came back, we gave them a brief tutorial on librarianship's nobler tenets, namely the representation of many points of view and a responsiveness to expressed user needs. However, Mr. K obviously thought we were out of our minds.

"You ladies don't understand how much reformation is needed around here!" he said. We assured him that we could appreciate the sentiment, but still had to be librarians about it, not social workers. He shook his head at our misguided liberalism and thereafter stocked the shelves according to our specifications.

But somehow, those books he believed most worthy of jail's many fallen souls always wound up on the top shelf.

Response Time

Several factors influence the speed at which we respond to inmate patrons' requests for purchase. The big factor that distinguishes jail from prison is the length of time inmates stay there. Sometimes in jail, a one-week turnaround isn't fast enough, whereas in prison, you might have twenty-five years to respond to an inmate's request! Again, it all goes back to applying customer service principles just as other public libraries do.

In our public library district, we have a general rule about how quickly we will fill a patron request for purchase. The turnaround time for an in-print item is usually less than a week. While we would dearly love to be able to respond to inmate requests in kind, the reality of a small library environment precludes that. Because we are a self-contained unit with only five people to perform all library functions from selection to weeding, we simply don't have the manpower to respond to every individual request immediately. But we think we do the next best thing. We collect requests in writing and place about six book orders a year, largely composed of specifically requested titles. While our patrons are waiting, we try to keep them apprised of where we are in the selection and acquisition process. There is nothing more fun than telling an inmate patron, "We got the latest John Grisham in the mail today and I'll have one for you next week!" except, of course, for actually delivering the book. If we cannot get a requested title, we check back in with the patron who asked for it, with apologies.

Ask your patrons how long they're in for (if they're in prison) or how long until they're released or taken to prison (if they're in jail.) We never assume that our patrons will have access to what they've requested after they leave our facility, whether they're headed for prison or set to be released. If the patron is a short-timer, we expedite. If we don't get them what they want to read, it's a lost opportunity for them and for us.

Some books are requested over and over (e.g., *The Claiming of Sleeping Beauty* and *Gettin' Buck Wild: Sex Chronicles II*), and for security reasons have been banned from the facility. In rare cases like that, we are upfront with the inmates and let them know that we simply don't have permission to purchase some titles. This is where your readers advisory skills come in handy; there is almost always something you can suggest as a reasonable substitute.

New Books that Don't Smell Like Toothpaste

The toothpaste reference is a standing joke because, not infrequently, inmates try to repair books by "gluing" them back together with toothpaste. Needless to say, it doesn't work very well. And the last thing someone wants is a book that smells like someone else's minty-fresh dentifrice.

The point is to maintain your collection, which correlates to the materials selection process. You never know quite when the money for materials will run out, so it's worth investing in whatever supplies you need to keep the books in reasonably good shape. Demco is our favorite source, but Office Depot will suffice for tape and glue, which is what 95 percent of your repair efforts will require. At the same time, try not to hang on to books that have obviously outlived their time. As in the public libraries, a well-weeded collection will be better utilized than one that's been allowed to go to seed. Patrons will judge books by their covers—or lack of them. If the book is in such disgusting shape that you wouldn't choose it if it was the last book on earth, your inmate patrons shouldn't have to settle for that either.

Conclusion

Jails and prisons are weird places. They force together people who would likely never meet each other on the outside and who certainly wouldn't be friends. But behind the locked doors and within view of the cameras, you find that even though the environment is weird, the people in it are pretty much like folks on the outside. This is especially true when you start looking at inmates as library patrons.

Much of your success as a corrections librarian rests in your mindset. It is very easy to walk into a correctional setting with a clear mindset about who prisoners are or what they are like. That mindset, if you've never worked inside a jail or prison, is probably wrong. For you and your library to succeed, you've got to be willing to change your mind about prisoners.

Recently, a highly experienced public librarian expressed disapproval at the level of programming we were offering our patrons. We were thunderstruck by her criticism since we see inmates as library patrons first, inmates second, and assumed other librarians would, too. This illustrates how easy it is to assume that others, even other experienced public librarians, will automatically accept that point of view. When confronted by that kind of philosophical resistance to seeing inmates as deserving human beings, we are reminded of why we as librarians are in jail in the first place. We are there to uphold inmates' right to comprehensive and equitable library access, as passionately and legitimately as we would any underserved patron group in the county. And as Satia Orange, director of the Office of Literacy and Outreach Services, is wont to say, empowering the underserved is what library outreach is all about.

References

Allen, B. and D. Bosta. 1981. *Games criminals play.* Sacramento: Rae John Publishers.

Bureau of Justice. 2004. *U.S. prison population approaches 1.5 million* (November 7). Retrieved January 3, 2005 from http://www.ojp.usdoj .gov/bjs/pub/press/p03pr.htm.

———. 2004. Lifetime likelihood of going to State or Federal prison. In *Criminal offender statistics* (December 28). Retrieved May 21, 2005 from http://www.ojp.usdoj.gov/bjs/crimoff.htm#inmates.

———. 2005. *Corrections statistics* (November 13). Retrieved December 3, 2005 from http://www.ojp.usdoj.gov/bjs/correct.htm.

Carnegie, D. 1990. *How to win friends and influence people.* New York: Pocket Books.

Chesney-Lind, M. and R. G. Sheldon. 1998. *Girls, delinquency, and juvenile justice.* Belmont, CA: Wadsworth Publishing Company.

Cooke, C. L. 2002. Understanding incarcerated populations. *AORN Journal* (March). Retrieved May 14, 2004 from http://www.findarticles.com.

Facts about prisons and prisoners. 2005. Retrieved December 3, 2005 from http://www.sentencingproject.org/pdfs/ 1035.pdf.

Foley, R. M. 2001. *Academic characteristics of incarcerated youth and correctional educational programs: A literature review* (Winter). Retrieved May 14, 2004 from http://www.findarticles.com.

Greenfield, L. A. and T. L. Snell. 1999. *Woman offenders.* Retrieved May 21, 2005 from http://www.ojp.usdoj.gov/bjs/pub/pdf/wo.pdf.

King, S. 1982. Rita Hayworth and the Shawshank redemption. In *Different seasons* (15–106). New York: Penguin Books.

Mallinger, S. 1991. Games inmates play. *Corrections today* 53(7), 188–192.

Mongelli, W. D. 1994. De-mystifying legal research for prisoners. *Law library journal* 86(259), 277–298.

Mumola, C. J. 2000. Incarcerated parents and their children. Bureau of Justice (August). Retrieved November 2, 2005 from http://www.ojp .usdoj.gov/bjs/pub/pdf/iptc.pdf.

National Institute for Literacy. N.d. *Correctional education facts.* Retrieved November 2, 2005 from http://www.nifl.gov/nifl/facts/correctional.html#ed.

Rubin, R. J. and D. S. Suvak. 1995. *Libraries inside: A practical guide for prison librarians.* Jefferson, NC: McFarland and Company, Inc. (Reprinted from *Theoretical studies of the social organization of the prison*, pp. 5–19, by G. M. Sykes & S. L. Messinger, Eds., 1960, New York: Social Science Research Council.)

Rubin, R. J. and D. S. Suvak. 1995. *Libraries inside: A practical guide for prison librarians.* Jefferson, NC: McFarland and Company, Inc. (Reprinted from *The prison community*, by D. Clemmer, Ed., 1940, New York: Holt, Rinehart, and Winston.)

Rubin, R. J. and D. S. Suvak. 1995. *Libraries inside: A practical guide for prison librarians.* Jefferson, NC: McFarland and Company, Inc.

Snell, T. L. 1994. *Women in Prison.* Retrieved May 21, 2005 from http://www.ojp.usdoj.gov/bjs/pub/pdf/wopris.pdf.

Strom, K. J. 2000. *Profile of state prisoners under age 18, 1985–97* (February). Retrieved May 21, 2005 from http://www.ojp.usdoj .gov/bjs/.

Sullivan, L. 2000. The least of our brethren: Library service to prisoners. *American Libraries* 31(5). Retrieved January 3, 2005 from InfoTrac Web: General Reference Center Gold database.

Vogel, B. 1995. *Down for the count.* Lanham, MD: Scarecrow Press, Inc.

Wilder, S. 1996. The age demographics of academic librarians. *ARL: A bimonthly newsletter of research library issues and actions* 185 (April). Retrieved May 21, 2005 from http://www.arl.org/newsltr/185/agedemo.html.

4

Understanding the System

As much as any personal qualities, professional qualifications, or insight into the criminal mind, understanding how correctional facilities operate logistically and culturally and understanding the trends influencing library service to their occupants are key to working well behind their walls. And not all correctional facilities are created alike. Jails, prisons, community corrections, and juvenile detention centers differ as much from each other as public libraries do from academic libraries, corporate libraries, and school media centers. Certain features that impact the kinds of library services we can offer seem to be universal within similar types of facilities.

Different Types of Facilities and How They Operate

Jail

The last Bureau of Justice census of jails in 1999 found 3,365 jails in the U.S., with only forty-seven privately owned and operated and a scarce handful operated at the state or federal level (Stephan 2001). That means that the vast majority of jails operate at the municipal or county level, just like public libraries do! Fewer than 10 percent of American jails have average daily populations over 1,000 inmates, but these jails house almost half of the entire national inmate population. By contrast, the capacity of nearly half of all jails is fewer than fifty inmates. As a group, these small facilities house only about 5 percent of the entire national inmate population (Stephan 2001).

We don't bandy these statistics around for nothing. We want to show that the word "jail" is used quite accurately to describe everything from "super jails" housing thousands of inmates—more than some prisons—to mid-sized facilities in the suburbs, to Mayberry-style drunk tanks with one or two cells. Bigger, however, does not necessarily translate to better. Several years ago in San Francisco, we presented an ALA poster session on our innovative jail programming. We wish now we'd charged a nickel every time someone from the Department of Corrections said to us that day, "The state prisons here don't have anything like what you're offering at the county level." We've heard the same comments from many inmate patrons who have bounced around the state and federal prison systems and in and out of other jails for years.

> It's not what you've got. It's what you do with what you've got.

So what are the essential differences between jail and prison? Up until now, we have used both terms fairly interchangeably, as common parlance allows. The words "inmate" and "prisoner," also interchangeable in common parlance, reinforce this distinction. Occupants of jails are not technically "prisoners" since they have not necessarily been convicted (nor may ever be) and may bond out if they can afford to.

Jails are designed to be short-term holding places for inmates serving sentences typically shorter than a year and for inmates awaiting trial. Because jails are "take and release" facilities, the admission and population turnover rates are astronomically higher than in prison. Over 80 percent of new jail admissions will be released in less than five days.

In general, [annual] prison commitments . . . are about 50 percent of the average daily population (ADP). In rounded figures, the ADP of the nation's prisons in 1995 was about 1 million. Total admissions for that year were about 500,000. In contrast, the ADP of the nation's jail was about 500,000 in 1995, but the admissions to jail for that year were estimated to be between 10 million and 13 million. Stated another way, *it takes two years for the nation's prison population to turn over once, while the jail population turns over 20 to 25 times each [year]* (Schlanger 2003). (Emphasis ours.)

Additionally, jails often house convicted violent felons who have been transferred from state or federal prison back into the jail environment to await court hearings on other charges. Once they've been to prison, jail inmates tend to be more savvy about the system and the many ways to get around it. Classification of jail inmates isn't as discrete as classification in prison, so these inmates live right beside inmates who may never have served a day behind bars in their lives. This blend of convicts and "detainees" requires scrupulous scrutiny by the officers on watch. It is why one deputy told us once, "Jails are always maximum security. No one is allowed to walk around freely; no one has control over any doors." There's no such thing as a minimum-security jail, which differs greatly from the prison system with its many levels and layers of security.

Dozens of inmates and deputies have told us that jail time is much harder than prison time because of the level of security and the relative lack of diversions. We've been told that jail uniforms are less comfortable and more dehumanizing than prison uniforms. There is less privacy and greater crowding in jail than in prison. Jail routines are less regular than prison routines, resulting in lots of scrambling and juggling of people and schedules. Also, jail inmates are more likely than prisoners to be mentally ill, inexperienced with incarceration, drunk, high, or suicidal (Schlanger 2003). There's anecdotal evidence that jails are more dangerous than prisons, with one former prisoner saying, "I can only speak for myself as an ex-offender, jail was much more violent than prison, even though I was incarcerated in one of the toughest prisons in Georgia at that time" (Schlanger 2003).

Because they're operated by city and county governments, jails are situated within the communities whose taxes support them. Just like public libraries! Where jail librarians have an advantage over their public counterparts is in the captive nature of their audience!

The greatest influence upon library service in a jail is the short-term nature of the inmates' sentences and the high rate of turnover. Program series, such as a parenting class for women we tried several years ago, are very problematic due to the transient nature of inmate populations. Therefore, we concentrate on one-time-only programs. We may offer them more than once in the same cellblocks so different inmates may participate, but we don't do multipart programs any more. Also, our library does not offer interlibrary loan services to inmates for the simple reason that interlibrary loan is expensive, and many of our patrons will not be around long enough to receive items requested that way. Consequently, we do our best to purchase new titles for our own collection based on inmate requests. Collection development based on inmate input must take into consideration the relative obscurity of any particular inmate's request and the anticipated length of that inmate's stay in the facility. We have ordered some pretty weird stuff for inmates we figure will be around for awhile. By the same token, we order more popular mainstream titles for inmates whose length of stay is less certain; if they are not there when the book arrives, someone else will want it.

Prison

Undergirding most of the significant differences between jails and prisons is the fact that prisons are designed for people spending the better part of their lives there, while jails are way stations, either to freedom or incarceration elsewhere. Prisons are long-term holding facilities, although prisoners serving lifelong sentences are rare. Upwards of 95 percent of all prisoners will ultimately be released back into the community (Hughes and Wilson 2003). Although privately run prisons are becoming more common, the federal and state governments operate the vast majority of prisons. Therefore, the scope and perspective of prisons tends to be much broader than that of jails. One implication of this state and nationwide perspective is that where prisoners are sentenced—usually fairly close to home and family—often has nothing to do with where they will be sent to serve their sentences. Since state and federal taxes support state and national prison systems, people convicted of crimes in one corner of a state or one state in the union are often sent hundreds or thousands of miles away from home to serve out their sentences. The prison system lacks a community-level focus, and this creates devastating problems for prisoners, their families, and the communities they leave behind.

 The locations of prisons can affect the distribution of political cal power, the allocation of governmental resources, and the economies of the communities in which the new institutions are built and those from which the prisoners are drawn. Every dollar transferred to a 'prison community' is a dollar that is not given to the home community of a prisoner (*Prison Construction Boom* 2004).

On the other hand, because prisoner populations tend to be more stable than jail populations, and because any given prison building houses just one or two security classification levels of prisoners instead of the entire gamut of classification levels that jails do, prisons can offer different kinds of programs and services. For example, most prison libraries offer some form of interlibrary loan service. For some facilities, this can actually be more cost-effective than purchasing and storing an extensive on-site library. Prison libraries can also offer program series, such as multiweek classes on writing poetry, conducting legal research, and music appreciation. Because prisons tend to be larger than most jail libraries, they often have more floor space for their libraries, resulting in larger and more diverse collections. Perhaps most significantly, because prisons operate at discrete security levels, many low- and medium-security prisoners have access to materials such as videos, audiobooks, and vinyl records that jail inmates, at maximum security, are not allowed.

State prisons are also often associated with the state library or department of education. This can be an incredibly productive relationship in which both entities—the Department of Corrections and the Department of Education—are responsible for doing what each does best.

 "The heart of the Maryland prison system is the library."
– Motto of the Maryland Correctional Education Libraries

It can also be a drawback. In states hard suffering from economic decline and environmental disaster, like our home state of Colorado, prisons compete with other line items such as forestry, education, and health care. Prison budgets, unfortunately but perhaps not unexpectedly, are also often hard hit during such times.

There is a long tradition of libraries in prisons, to the point where the library has become an integral part of the institutional landscape. Historically, the provision of library services in prison has been taken for granted as much as the provision of GED classes, religious services, and dentistry. That is, until recently. Prison law libraries and recreational reading collections are being abbreviated or eliminated at an alarming rate all across the country. Three forces propel this trend. The first is simple economics. For example, Broward County, Florida, shut down all five county jail libraries in 2004 and replaced them with an online "service-on-demand" model, which is intended to save the county $150,000 (*Broward County Inmates* 2004). The state of Florida removed all typewriters, personal computers, and word processors from its prison libraries in 2001, saving $50,000 annually (*Typewriters Removed From Florida Prison System* 2001). Such scenarios are certainly not unique to Florida.

The second reason for the national shutdown trend is the 1996 landmark federal case *Casey v. Lewis*. It significantly limited the Supreme Court's 1977 decision in *Bounds v. Smith*, which held that correctional facilities of all types were duty bound to provide on-site law libraries adequately provisioned with legal research materials for inmate and prisoner use. With the *Casey* decision, correctional facilities still must provide either law libraries or legal assistance. However, the composition of an adequate collection or service is unclear and subject to broad interpretation. Inmates and prisoners may sue facilities for inadequate access, but only if they can prove they sustained actual harm due to insufficient legal resources (Wilhelmus 1999). If harm cannot be demonstrated, there is no recourse, even if the collections and services provided are obviously subpar. Many facilities have responded to this ruling by replacing prison law libraries with legal research services, as the state of Florida did. Inmates have sued over this change, fearing that the new model will slow down the legal research process (*Broward County Inmates* 2004).

The third reason prison libraries are closing is a shift in penal philosophy. In 1995, South Carolina's new governor shut down the state's lauded prison library system as part of a "get tough on criminals" campaign (Chepesiuk 1995). In an effort to curb "erroneous lawsuits" spurred by "somebody's personal set of issues," Iowa's Department of Corrections began phasing out state prison law libraries in 1999 (Rogers 1999). The *St. Petersburg Times* reported in 2001 that the Florida Department of Juvenile Justice prohibited juvenile offenders from having reading materials in their cells because "for the most part that privilege has been abused" (*Florida Inmates Sue* 2001). These scenarios and others point to the increasing appeal of the idea that libraries in prisons are a privilege, not a right.

Community Corrections

To our knowledge, partnerships between community corrections programs and public libraries haven't developed to the extent that jail and public library partnerships have. We think this is a service area full of possibility, however, so we include some basic information about community corrections to grease the wheels of your imagination.

Community corrections provides an alternative to incarceration. Its purpose is to reintegrate the offender into the community by allowing him to avoid incarceration while still under intensive supervision. Violent offenders are not usually eligible for community corrections, and often community corrections programs do not accept "repeat customers." Community corrections programs include halfway houses and work release.

In a work release situation, the offender spends nights and/or weekends in jail. The rest of the time, he or she is allowed to return to daily life if he or she has a job. Halfway houses, also termed "intensive supervision," are located in the community and provide a home and a home base for parolees and probationers. Most halfway houses have programs, like drug rehabilitation, that offenders are expected to complete as a condition of their release. Sometimes, people in work release and community corrections are monitored with ankle bracelets.

The most common library service available to work release inmates is whatever library service is provided to the correctional facility where they spend their nonworking hours. For halfway house residents, public library outreach departments sometimes provide deposit collections similar to those provided to nursing homes, donated collections similar to those provided to many county jails, or, in rare instances, bookmobile service. Depending on the nature of the halfway house, library-sponsored programs are possible. Our early childhood literacy coordinator regularly visits a halfway house for young moms convicted of drug-related offenses. Once a month, she conducts an infant lap-sit program that places a strong emphasis on parenting skills and demonstrates how to read to and interact with children.

We think community corrections programs also provide an obvious point at which corrections librarians and their public library counterparts can bridge the gap between inmates' incarceration and their lives outside. Many inmates have no idea how the information resources of a full-service public library can help them find jobs, places to live, financial assistance, and medical help. Cooperation between the librarians inmates get to know and trust on the inside and public librarians to whom they can be referred after release is largely uncharted territory and presents a great challenge and opportunity for us to help our patrons in new ways.

Juvenile Facilities

Jail and prison libraries are to juvenile detention center libraries what public libraries are to school media centers. The focus of the two latter is educational, nonlibrarians have a great deal of input into collection development, and the patrons are kids!

Probably the biggest difference between "juvie" and other correctional facilities is philosophical. Juvenile centers operate under the assumption that their detainees can be rehabilitated and returned to a normal functioning life. Influencing this belief is the idea that someone on the outside, be it parents, grandparents, teachers, or friends, might still care about juvenile offenders. Probably because they are still kids, these young inmates have not yet been written off by society, even if their crimes are heinous. Even the language in juvenile facilities reflects this philosophical difference. The residents are referred to as "wards," not "inmates." They have been "adjudicated," not "convicted."

The terminology implies both a responsibility for the child's well-being and a hope for rehabilitation.

Nine out of ten juveniles committed to adult facilities arrive without a high school diploma or GED. And adult facilities don't always offer the kind of educational support provided in a juvenile detention center. According to the Standards Commission of the Correctional Education Association (Corwin 2005), educational programs inside juvenile detention facilities must approximate those of the public schools. Unlike in jail or prison, inmates in juvenile facilities are required to attend classes, and the amount of time they spend in a classroom each day must meet the minimum requirements set by the state.

Because the primary goal of education programs in juvenile facilities is the achievement of the high school diploma, the programs are very similar to those of a typical high school, with classes in algebra, biology, English, art, physical education, and so on. Contrast this to most jails, which offer little more than GED classes, or most prisons, whose education programs may be more geared toward life enrichment than attainment of a diploma or degree.

Because of the emphasis on education that reflects the public school system, juvenile facility libraries should reflect school media centers in their mission and focus: curriculum support. And just as school boards govern what school media centers can have, the educational and social services departments in juvenile centers have a lot of say about what their libraries can offer young inmates. The collection must be strictly PG-rated; facility psychologists may be involved in determining if content meets this criterion. This may seem like an even greater measure of censorship than that found inside adult facilities. It's a fact, but not significantly more so than the censorship that goes on in school media centers. The overriding focus is educational, and the collection is selected accordingly.

Regulations and Standards

Correctional facilities of all kinds are governed by regulations and standards set by a variety of agencies. Standards speak not only to what goes on behind the wall, but to who is paying attention. And over time, they evolve to reflect the shifting political, philosophical, and moral landscape of the many decision makers who are watching. The American Correctional Association's (ACA) Commission on Accreditation for Corrections seats twenty-eight people from twelve different corrections associations, as well as health care, local government, and architecture associations, and the American Bar Association (ABA).

Some standards are mandatory for obvious reasons and focus on security and health. Others, like those concerning recreational programs for inmates, are optional. Administrative regulations (also called administrative rules, policies, directives, and rulings; director's rules; and commissioner's directives, among other things) are set by each state and govern procedural issues in prisons. Facilities seeking or reapplying for accreditation by the ACA are typically more motivated to meet the majority of national level standards set by that organization. The ACA employs a rigorous accreditation process for those facilities that elect to meet the standards; not all do.

There are different levels of standards that to a certain, but not exclusive, degree influence the level below them. The ACA sets national standards; state departments of corrections set their own policies and procedures based, in large part, on the ACA's standards. Individual facilities have their own policies and rules, usually detailed in inmate handbooks, that reflect state regulations and national standards to varying degrees.

The ACA, ABA, state departments of corrections, the Correctional Education Association, and the American Library Association all offer standards for correctional institutions that impact correctional libraries. A title search for "standards" in the ACA's online bookstore returns over two dozen manuals. Of particular note for correctional librarians are those titles that address inmate programs; often, this subheading includes library services. Among other titles setting standards for community corrections programs such as halfway houses and probation, ACA publishes the following:

- *Standards for Adult Correctional Institutions*
- *Standards for Juvenile Correctional Facilities*
- *Standards for Small Jail Facilities*
- *Performance-Based Standards for Adult Local Detention Facilities*

In addition to ACA's standards, states have their own regulations to govern activity at a more tactical level. State administrative regulations address much more than inmate-specific issues, often getting into the administration of facility staff, automation, public information and data reporting, and building management. Not all state departments of corrections' administrative regulations are created equal; some are far more detailed and comprehensive than others. Nor do administrative regulations necessarily carry the weight of law. Prisoners sometimes successfully sue states whose regulations exceed restrictions allowable by their own statutes or that violate federal or constitutional provisions for inmate rights.

Administrative regulations are readily available as .pdf files on most state government Web sites on their department of corrections pages. For a detailed example of an administrative regulations governing the provision of library services to state prisoners, we recommend you take a look at the State of Colorado's "Library Services" at www.doc.state.co.us/admin_reg/PDFs/0500_02.pdf.

The ABA's *Criminal Justice Standards* was described in 1968 by Chief Justice Warren Burger as "the single most comprehensive and probably the most monumental undertaking in the field of criminal justice ever attempted by the American legal profession in our national history" (*Criminal Justice Standards*, n.d.). Much of this mammoth work has no direct bearing on the work of correctional staff of any kind, but the section titled "Legal Status of Prisoners" does contain information relevant to corrections librarians. A short segment details acceptable access to legal materials, which can be provided by a prison law library. The remainder of the section addresses many issues of great concern for inmates and prisoners, issues like visitation, hygiene, medical treatment, and discipline. It behooves the librarian to be familiar with these issues, because you will get questions from inmates fighting for better living conditions, especially if you provide law library services. A thumbnail version of ABA's *Criminal Justice Standards* is available at www.abanet.org/crimjust/standards/home.html. It can also be purchased in print form.

Although the Correctional Education Association (CEA) has been accrediting correctional education programs since 1988, it's only been since 2004 that a discrete set of standards has existed for juvenile facilities (Corwin 2005). And while the American Correctional Association does have its own set of accreditation standards for education programs, it also accepts the audit findings of the CEA. Even if your facility is not ACA-accredited, you can still seek CEA accreditation. Information about how to do this is available at CEA's Web site, www.ceanational.org.

Finally, as we have already mentioned, the Association of Specialized and Cooperative Library Agencies (ASCLA) has three manuals of standards for libraries in correctional institutions. All are out of print, but are available at some public libraries and occasionally appear on Amazon.com and other online vendor sites.

Working with Other Staff

So far, we've talked as if the only people inside a correctional facility are officers, inmates, and librarians. Because correctional facilities are self-contained communities, there are many, many other departments, mostly staffed by civilians. So who are the people in your neighborhood? They are:

- nurses, doctors, and dentists
- teachers and tutors
- licensed clinical social workers, counselors, and psychiatrists
- chaplains and religious volunteers
- maintenance crews
- computer technicians
- finance staff, including those in charge of purchasing

A correctional facility's various departments, with their complex competing interests, are kind of like a big dysfunctional team, where everyone is basically there for the same reason—to take care of the prisoners—but few people really appreciate how all the players work together. In that sense, it's like any large organization. The nurses are there to make sure the inmates stay healthy, but underlying that is the desire to avoid lawsuits over "owies." The teachers would like to enrich the inmates' lives, but know that accreditation hinges in part on how many GEDs they pump out. The librarians are there to make sure basic American rights to access information are upheld, but realize that one of the things administration expects is to not get sued by inmates making ill use of legal resources. As with any organization, if the plumbing is out or the computers won't boot, maintenance and IT can make or break overall efficiency. And for anyone who has courted a recalcitrant accountant, staying in the good graces of the finance department also impacts the effectiveness of your operation.

What makes jail different from a large public library, for example, is the dramatic difference in status between the civilian and law enforcement staff. Although most of us pay due respect to our library branch managers and administrators, it is not the kind of deference civilians are expected to give the line staff inside a correctional environment. A closer analogy might be the deference afforded full professors in academic libraries. It requires perspective and not a little humility to accept your place as the lowly librarian in either of these scenarios. The payoff is how much you can accomplish when you learn how to cheerfully swing from the bottom rung.

Another difference is that all activities inside a jail or prison are rigorously scheduled. Certain activities overseen by officers, such as laundry exchange and mealtimes, take precedence over most other events. Different civilian departments have priority over others; if the dentist is in the building and half of your patrons have appointments, don't expect a busy day at the library. We have found that the education and chaplain's departments rank slightly higher than the library, necessary evils that are accommodated when all other activities have been scheduled.

If you take nothing else away from this book, do take note of this. The fundamental key to becoming an integral part of a correctional facility is to learn the facility's routine and keep yourself abreast of any changes. Be ready to change your own schedule at the drop of a hat. Don't get married to the idea that because prison is a structured place, nothing ever changes. Because of the precision with which activities need to be scheduled, a change in one department's routine can have a domino effect. If the chaplain wants to add a Mass to the weekly schedule and he wants it in the room shared by the library and the education department for literacy classes, you're probably in for some finagling. These moments, though exasperating, are wonderful opportunities for collaborating and building the relational bridges you need to function inside. They are also opportunities for refining your system-wide perspective.

Another piece of advice is that you pay attention to who has keys, both literally and metaphorically, and do everything within reason to stay on their good side. Crew leaders, maintenance workers, and IT staff juggling the demands of many different departments will usually respond according to the facility's pecking order: law enforcement first, then medical staff at close second, and then office and administrative staff, teachers, counselors, and librarians. But if you make good allies, you may be able to persuade a person with "keys" to prioritize you in a pinch or for good reason.

The shortest route to these alliances is flexibility, sensitivity to others' responsibilities, and willingness to accommodate. If others perceive you as easy to work with, they will go to greater lengths to accommodate you. Making these connections is as easy as stopping for a moment to say hello. Even if they question the necessity of the library in jail, your willingness to be flexible, to think outside the box, and to work toward win-win arrangements will inspire other staff to give the same consideration back to you. Take your staff on a tour of the facility. Encourage your staff to reach out to other departments. Don't wait for them to come to you.

"You had me at 'hello.'"

We remember when a new chaplain, within days of starting, stopped by the library to introduce himself and get an overview of who we were and what we do. We were absolutely stunned by his interest, because usually we are only a footnote in new staff orientation. Our appreciation of the chaplain's interest shows how civilian staff in jail respond to genuine interest by other civilians: very well indeed! We developed a very good relationship with the chaplain, which continues to this day. When he is unable to provide titles for his parishioners, he suggests titles to be added to our collection. If we notice a run on particular religious titles or subjects, we advise the chaplain of what might be an emerging religious focus that he needs to address. It's a win-win, and it began with "hello."

Ethics and Accountability

Ethics in correctional libraries is as complex a subject as it is in public libraries, but it is compounded by the fact that the codes of ethics governing librarians and law enforcement are dramatically (and necessarily) different. Librarianship is about service; we want to help our patrons, to offer them the keys to a wide world of information that can greatly enrich their lives. Law enforcement is about protection; they need to control inmates, and hold the keys to a facility to which judges—elected by the people—have sent offenders to punish them and protect others from further harm.

Many of the challenges that arise between correctional librarians and correctional officers have their root in fundamental opposing ethical values. Correctional librarians have many different ways of handling points of conflict, and there does not seem to be universal consensus about how to do it. Even among correctional librarians, there are questions about which of librarianship's ethical values to uphold and which to lay aside in the interest of safety. Even ASCLA's *Library Standards for Adult Correctional Institutions* (1992) points out in its statement of philosophy: "The librarian shall recognize that the library is a part of an agency with security priorities."

ASCLA (1992) also stipulates in its philosophy statement:

Services shall encompass the same variety of material, formats, and programs as available in the outside community and shall comply with the . . . Library Bill of Rights . . . Resolution on Prisoners' Right to Read . . . Policy on Confidentiality of Library Records . . . Freedom to Read Statement . . . [and] Freedom to View.

So perhaps a better way of approaching the ethics question is not to compare correctional libraries and law enforcement, but correctional libraries and public libraries. What ethical conundrums are common to both?

The most common ethical challenge in correctional libraries happens in the law library. The problem consists of knowing where to draw the line between providing legal information and providing legal interpretation or advice. Our experience has been that similar situations occur in the public libraries, especially when patrons are researching questions about health and taxes. The call librarians have to make about crossing the "advice line" is the same whether a public library patron is asking you, "Does this picture of melanoma look like my mole?" or a jail library patron is asking you, "Does *John Doe v. The City of Shangri-la* sound like my case?"

Another ethical question common to both public and correctional libraries is censorship. To those who frown upon jail librarians who refuse to order books containing martial arts demonstrations or pornography or vitriolic sentiments against certain ethnic groups or the government, we ask you to check with your local library and see how many copies of *Soldier of Fortune* and *Penthouse* they have available for checkout. Even if they carry those magazines, chances are about even that they store them behind the circ desk. The fact is, every library "censors" according to the accepted social norms of the communities in which they reside. Larger urban public libraries typically have the most diverse and encompassing collection profiles. They have to; they are serving many different communities. Small rural libraries, due to limited budgets and tight heterogeneous communities, make choices about their collections that are perhaps not as encompassing. Special libraries select and reject according to the subject specialty of the organizations they serve. Correctional libraries must build their collections with the physical safety of all stakeholders in mind.

Privacy and confidentiality issues have catapulted to center stage, thanks to the PATRIOT Act. At the risk of sounding cavalier about such an important issue, we'd like to suggest that privacy is a concept that evolves to meet certain ends; it is not, by itself, an intrinsic value. The idea of privacy has evolved from a concept of nonintrusion found in the Fourth Amendment, to noninterference as played out in cases like *Roe v. Wade,* to limiting access to information as in the 1974 Privacy Act (Moor 1997/2001). Even if privacy were an iron-clad, unchanging concept, there are other values that take precedence, such as the right to life and limb. "To be ethical, one must not inflict justified harm" (Moor 1999/2001). The corrections librarian is frequently confronted by a choice the public librarian must also make, but only in the face of a police investigation. Will withholding information about particular patrons' library usage lead to greater harm than the surrender of said information?

Here are the factors the public librarian must consider. As a tax-supported entity, are we first and foremost stewards of personal information, or can we assume that a criminal investigation is for the public good? As libraries, do we have a greater responsibility toward upholding Fourth Amendment rights, or, as government agencies, do we have a greater responsibility for public safety? And what do the prevailing opinions of the communities we serve say about our responsibilities? ALA and all of the state library associations are very clear about the answers to these questions. Our duty is to preserve privacy and confidentiality, even if it means in some cases to challenge a court order. Our primary responsibility is to the Fourth Amendment. And it doesn't matter what the community we serve believes. The reason for this is that ALA privacy and confidentiality policies, as well as the Fourth Amendment, are designed to protect the law-abiding majority.

Things can be different in jail, however. A corrections librarian must answer slightly different questions, and the answers are based on a different set of principles. Who is requesting patron information and why do they want it? Are there demonstrable security reasons for wanting the patron information? If not, what recourse do you have to challenge the request? You can go as far as demanding, and then challenging, a court order, just as the public libraries could. The decision to do so is where your own professional ethics will have to guide you. But unlike the real world, rules inside a correctional facility are most definitely not designed to protect a law-abiding majority. They are designed to control a criminal majority.

This raises perhaps the most important ethical question of all—access. To what extent do convicted criminals retain the freedom to read and the freedom to access information that the general public does? What does access even mean inside a jail or prison? We believe it consists of two things. First, access means the library is not a "perk" or part of a reward system for good behavior. Going to the library or having materials delivered by the librarian is as much a fundamental right as accessing religious services. Second, access includes what materials are accessible. This goes back to censorship. To have a truly accessible correctional library means that your patrons have access to a collection censored only by selection policies designed to protect physical safety.

Access also speaks to how much information inmates and prisoners can take back to their cells. Here, different but equally valid decisions can be made depending upon what the security concerns are and how much the deputies or guards want to keep track of. At our jail, no one may have more than five catalogued books in his cell at one time; other facilities might cap the limit at less than that or not impose a cap at all. At our jail, inmates are allowed to check out hardcover books; this is relatively rare since many correctional libraries only carry paperbacks.

One final ethical consideration concerns our stewardship of library materials. Most collections libraries are supported by inmate commissary funds. Inmates who appreciate the library often don't know how it is funded, but those who do express a great deal of pride and ownership. Because our constituents themselves are paying for the service, they are, in a very real sense, the inside equivalent of taxpayers. The difference between this arrangement and that of public libraries is that there is another, nonpaying group inside—the staff. Therefore, it is critical that we balance the need for good working relationships with those who accommodate the library's presence in the facility with the need to preserve our materials and services for those who are paying for them. Diplomacy, once again, rules in this situation.

Fine! Be That Way!

Making sure that materials purchased with inmate-generated funds actually go to the inmates is an ongoing challenge because we also consider other staff to be our patrons. And it's not always obvious to patrons, even in the public libraries, why some materials are available to them and others aren't.

We smacked (proverbially speaking) a deputy's hands once as he was absconding with a brand-new *Sports Illustrated* slated for distribution to the pods later that day.

He replied incredulously, "Are you telling me that I'm guarding you, but I can't take a magazine?" Ouch.

Sheila explained reasonably, "The commissary funds that pay for those subscriptions are inmate monies, and what those monies purchase should be reserved for inmate use." Not the response the deputy expected.

"Fine!" he said, obviously hurt. "I was going to give you a whole bunch of puzzles, but now I'll find someone else to give them to." Double ouch.

Sometimes sarcasm is your only defense.

"I'm sure," Sheila said solemnly, "that you will find another equally worthy organization that needs them just as much."

Ouch, ouch, ouch!

Perhaps the greatest ethical challenge for librarians behind bars takes place on a very personal level. Nonprisoners have a great deal of power over prisoners, and this goes for the civilian staff as well at the line staff. Jails and prisons aren't necessarily places where justice is rewarded. It is possible to cut a prisoner off from library service entirely for whatever cockamamie reason you want, and you very well might never be questioned about it. If the prisoner chooses not to file a lawsuit and the line staff are behind the decision, nothing more may ever be said about it. In other words, in jail and prison, librarians have opportunities every day to compromise with impunity every ethical tenet ALA holds dear.

There is no way for us to advise you about this. We want to assume that if you are reading this book and are interested in library service to inmates, you come to the table with the belief that they deserve fair and equitable access to library resources and as much privacy as the system will allow. Serving inmates you deeply dislike is no different from dealing with difficult patrons on the outside; the difference is that hardly anybody cares about how you treat inmates. If ethical corrections librarianship hinges upon anything, it is how you treat prisoners when no one is looking.

Challenges and How to Handle Them

In public library outreach, we provide services to people at the discretion of decision makers who will neither immediately nor directly benefit from those services. This does not mean that those decision-makers aren't stakeholders; they may, however, value the library for different reasons than you and your patrons do. In this section, we will look at common challenges and ways of communicating the library's value to these people.

We've talked a lot about challenges in terms of common difficulties or problems encountered regularly in jail, things like sexual harassment and intimidation. But there are also literal challenges inside a correctional facility. Especially if you're conscientiously trying to apply the public library model, there is a great likelihood that the library's presence in the facility and the materials it carries will be challenged by other, nonlibrary staff, especially the officers and often the administration. When the library's materials are challenged, it is a library issue and may be handled as challenges on the outside are. But if the library itself is challenged, a philosophical difference of opinion exists that will require a great deal of diplomacy to reconcile.

Challenges to Your Services

Let's be very clear on this point: A correctional library operates under the grace of facility administration that by and large is law enforcement in some manifestation or another. Even if the library is a co-endeavor, like ours is, with the public library placing staff trained to provide equitable access to services and materials, ultimately the facility gets to decide if the library stays or goes. Some access beats no access, and uncomfortable compromises may be expedient to preserve the correctional library's existence.

If you're very fortunate, the reason there is a library in your facility is precisely because the facility is run by administrators who understand its importance. This understanding will not be entirely altruistic. Libraries don't redeem souls, and no one knows that better than the people running a jail. But good libraries do help facilities get accredited; this is a bigger deal for some than for others. Hopefully, you will work for administrators who think correctional libraries are a big deal.

But, let's say you don't. Or you used to, but now there's a new administrator in charge of the library and he or she tows a hard line of retribution. Or let's say the county or state budget has been severely abbreviated due to economic downturn (you may have to use your imagination on this one). Or let's say there's been a recent increase in inmate violence and the officers, out of concern for civilian safety, are denying you access. In any of these scenarios, the library's existence could be in jeopardy. So what do you do?

Philosophical Challenges

This comes down to difference of opinion as to what people should and should not have access to while incarcerated, and which rights they should and should not be allowed to retain. Even law enforcement is divided on this question, and the country as a whole seems to swing over time from one extreme to the other. At the moment, most of us seem to be operating under a generally more punitive philosophy of corrections than that of just a few decades ago. Chances are, the pendulum will swing back, but if your library is on the chopping block, you can't wait around for national trends to support your efforts.

> *"Why do you work so hard for people who don't matter?"*
> A deputy once asked Sheila this question. He simply could not understand the long hours, the physical effort bookcart entailed, and the ever-increasing complexity of the library service offered to a population he obviously considered undeserving.

Sometimes, we do what we do because that's how we're made. So Sheila replied, "My self-esteem depends upon how much I get done each day."

But the deputy remained unconvinced.

"Do you have any idea what these people have done?" he demanded.

In all seriousness, Sheila responded, "If they've done what they've been accused of, then they are where they should be and we're all safer for it. But the reason I'm here is to make sure they get library books."

Another philosophical challenge came quite unexpectedly from the public library side when one high-ranking, albeit non-librarian, staff member approached us about the money we wanted to put toward life-enriching programs for inmates based on similar programs we were offering to the general public.

"Why in the world do you want to do programs for THOSE people?" she asked. I was the one who got nailed with that question, and my initial reaction was self-righteous indignation. But fortunately, Sheila has had many occasions to model more constructive responses than my first impulse, which was to wave my arms around madly and holler, "Kumbaya, people! Why can't we just all get along?" Taking Sheila's cue, then, I reiterated some basic values of the library profession, emphasizing equitable service to the underserved, while also acknowledging the commonness of the questioner's objection.

Acknowledging where the other person is coming from does not mean acquiescing. Merely listening respectfully to what a challenger has to say accomplishes two things. First, it creates an opportunity to educate others to our mission on the inside. And frequently, empathy diffuses tension and concern.

Fiscal Challenges

These kinds of challenges are not unlike those faced in the public libraries or in any special library in a business or hospital. When budgetary line items are on the chopping block, the question is one of value. So you must ask yourself: What is the added value of a library in a facility like this? We have already discussed at length all the reasons a corrections library is of value to its patrons, but they are not the ones looking to eliminate your service in this scenario. You must consider how the library benefits the facility, the other staff, and the taxpayers, and present those arguments clearly and respectfully.

"Is THIS where my raise went??"

ACDF's mobile reference unit is one of the most innovative ways in the country of providing inmates with legal research material, if we do say so ourselves. It took several years of pitching the idea to convince the facility's administrators that it would be well worth the financial investment. In a year when tax-supported agencies in our county were severely tightening their belts and evaluating which services might have to be eliminated, Arapahoe County Sheriff's Office (ACSO) spent over $30,000 on a wireless network with several site licenses to more than twenty WestLaw reference databases. The LAN was designed and intended for one user group only: the inmates.

The sheriff's office's investment, we are pleased to say, more than paid off. But it was a hard, bitter sell in the beginning. One deputy asked us, "Is this the reason we only got a 3 percent raise this year?" Another said, "Well, I guess I know now where MY raise went!"

These are hard questions to face, especially if the people asking them are good at their jobs and have earned your respect. The best thing to do is wait and see if their questions are purely rhetorical. Often, people just need to vent, which means all you need to do is listen. If the person asking really wants you to justify something, respond in terms of the value of the program or service to that person.

"You are not going to have to stand guard in the law library anymore," we told several deputies, "because we're bringing the law library to you now. Inmates aren't going to be moving back and forth all the time and if there's a problem, your backup is within earshot. We can accommodate more users this way, and that will minimize costly grievances against the facility about access."

Sometimes, there's nothing you can say. In those cases, you make sure you demonstrate how your program or service is beneficial. Actions can speak louder than words!

Challenges to Your Materials

Mutually Agreed Upon Selection Policy

In the previous section, we talked about how the ethics of censorship are similar between public and correctional libraries. There is a qualification, however. Even though most correctional libraries serve finite populations under 5,000 people, in a correctional library, like the large urban public library, people from many different communities and all walks of life comprise the library's service population. Consequently, if you really want to apply the public library model, keeping your collection development policies as open as possible are the only way to go. So we offer these guidelines.

- Write the first draft of your selection policy as broadly as you can; you will use this as a starting point should you have to negotiate for certain types of materials.
- Discuss your selection policy with the facility's administrator.
- Use common sense. No warden or lieutenant is going to let you carry books on locksmithing, and by including such topics under your selection policy, you will seriously undermine your credibility.
- Be prepared to defend your draft, and also be prepared to compromise.
- Keep your final draft handy so that when your materials are challenged, you will immediately be able to hand the challenger the policy that was blessed by the administrator.

Challenged Materials Process

The best defense is a good offense. But in the absence of a good offense, a good set of procedures works just as well. Most challenges will never turn into requests for reconsideration if you know how to neutralize the discussion simply by listening empathetically.

If the complainant insists that the material be removed from the library's collection, a set of written procedures is necessary to ensure proper treatment of the complainant's request. Again, behind bars very few people are watching to see if you're acting fairly, and sometimes it can be a challenge to do so even if you have the best of intentions. A reconsideration process helps guide your actions as well as protect your prerogative to select and keep appropriate materials for your patrons.

Most public libraries have a written reconsideration process, and you can certainly ask to see a copy of it. The process usually begins with a written request for reconsideration by filling out a form. Many examples of such forms can be found online. They typically consist of some or all of the following questions:

- What action do you want taken regarding this item?
- What do you find objectionable about the item?
- How would the action you are requesting improve the library's service to the community it serves? (Or, how would retaining this item hurt the community this library serves?)
- Have you read/viewed/listened to the entire material? If not, what parts have you read/viewed/listened to?
- Are you aware of the critical reviews and commentary regarding this material?
- What do you believe the purpose of this item is?
- Is there anything good about this material?

Once you have the form in hand, you should follow your library's procedures delineating the upward movement of the reconsideration discussion through the chain of command. Because the process could involve your facility's administrators, getting their input on and approval of proper procedure is important.

For everything you ever wanted to know about challenged materials and how to deal with specific situations, the ALA's Web page entitled "Dealing with Challenges to Books and Other Library Materials" simply cannot be beat: www.ala.org/ala/oif/challengesupport/dealing/Default1208.htm.

Conclusion

In the resolute pursuit of the public library model, it's sometimes easy to forget that a correctional library is an integral part of a unique organizational system whose purpose is very focused and straightforward. A juvenile prison librarian observed that both libraries and prisons are governed by "S" words, but they're not the same. In libraries, she told us, the guiding principle is Service. In prison, it's Security. If you can pay equal attention to both, you will probably achieve Success.

The fundamental keys to a correctional librarian's success are learning the correctional culture's peculiarities and routines, getting to know the people who walk its halls, and preparing yourself to respond creatively and respectfully to challenges to the library service and materials. The first two tasks require time and the latter requires practice. Prisons and jails are different from other organizations; give yourself the time and patience to learn to "do jail good," and success will follow.

References

Association of Specialized and Cooperative Library Agencies. 1992. *Library standards for adult correctional institutions*. Chicago: American Library Association.

Broward County inmates sue to prevent closing of jail law libraries. 2004. Retrieved December 23, 2004 from http://ala.org/ala/online.

Chepesiuk, R. 1995. S.C. scraps innovative prison library system. *American libraries* 26(6), 501–502.

Corwin, J. 2005. Juvenile correctional education standards approved. *Corrections today* 67(1). Retrieved May 23, 2005 from InfoTrac General Reference Center Gold database.

Criminal justice standards. N.d.. Retrieved December 3, 2005 from http://www.abanet.org/crimjust/standards/home.html.

Florida inmates sue over removal of typewriter. September 10, 2001. Retrieved December 23, 2005 from http://ala/org/ala/online.

Hughes, T. and D. J. Wilson. 2003. Re-entry trends in the United States: Inmates returning to the community after serving time in prison. Retrieved September 9, 2005 from http://www.ojp.usdoj.gov/bjs/reentry/reentry.htm.

Moor, J. H. 2001. Just consequentialism and computing. In R. A. Spinello and H. T. Tavani (Eds.), *Readings in cyberethics* (98–104). Sudbury, MA: Jones and Bartlett Publishers. (Reprinted from *Ethics and information technology* 1, 1999.)

———. 2001. Towards a theory of privacy in the information age. In R. A. Spinello and H. T. Tavani (Eds.), *Readings in cyberethics* (349–359). Sudbury, MA: Jones and Bartlett Publishers. (Reprinted from *Computers and society* 27(3), 1997.)

Prison construction boom reaches 3 in 10 counties. 2004. The Urban Institute (April 29). Retrieved February 20, 2005, from http://www.urban.org.

Rogers, M. 1999. Iowa prison law libraries on death row. *Library journal* 27(5).

Schlanger, M. 2003. *Differences between jails and prisons*. Paper presented at Prisons Seminar, Harvard Law School.

Stephan, J. J. 2001. *Census of jails, 1999*. Retrieved April 21, 2005 from http://www.ojp.usdoj.gov/bjs/pub/pdf/cj99.pdf.

Typewriters removed from Florida prison system. July 2, 2001. Retrieved December 23, 2005 from http://ala/org/ala/online.

Wilhelmus, D. W. 1999. Where have all the law libraries gone? *Corrections today* 61. Retrieved January 3, 2005 from InfoTrac Web database.

5

Facilities and Equipment

"People treat public places as they perceive them. To convey a positive effect on inmates and staff, the library should be maintained as an 'official' setting, much like a courthouse or other municipal building" (Vogel 1994).

As the low man on the totem pole, correctional librarians often find themselves housed in quarters resembling broom closets. Often, their offices and even the libraries themselves ARE converted broom closets. While those quarters are cozy, it's easier to cut a broom closet out of the budget than a proper library facility into which deliberate planning has been dedicated. If your operation is housed in digs completely inadequate to the service you know you should be providing, start lobbying for better arrangements.

Prisons, except maximum-security lockdown prisons, should have libraries that are accessible to the residents and are open evening and weekend hours to accommodate everyone. For lockdown facilities and jails, delivery services, such as bookcart, are adequate substitutions as long as you provide a browsing option. You can do this by regularly printing and distributing library catalogs that locked-down prisoners can consult in lieu of visiting the library and browsing the shelves. You may also take a well-loaded book truck into the living units for inmates to browse, though obviously this is a much-abbreviated browsing option.

The ASCLA's *Library Standards for Adult Correctional Institutions* (1992) gives generous guidelines for space planning. Keep in mind that for jails housing over 500 residents, ASCLA standards for prisons apply.

113

For smaller jails, refer to *Library Standards for Jails and Detention Facilities* (1981). Smaller prisons are treated in the ASCLA's 1992 publication. Timothy Brown's chapter in *Libraries Inside* (1995) summarizes the salient points of the ASCLA standards very nicely. To avoid reiterating these standards, we will take a look at how the standards might be applied with a particular eye to security issues and accessibility.

Physical Space

Seating

Square footage recommendations can be found in *Library Standards for Adult Correctional Institutions* and *Library Standards for Jails and Detention Facilities*. But what exactly does "twenty-five square feet per reader" look like in a correctional facility?

It's not a bad idea to start by considering how many patrons you'll allow in the library at one time. ASCLA recommends seating for approximately 10 percent of the general facility population since, obviously, not everyone is going to be using the library at the same time, even in small facilities. Keeping in mind that the fire inspector will have something to say on this topic, our opinion is that one person can keep track of about a dozen people at any given time. We'd say that for every inmate worker and paid staff member on the job at any given time, multiply their number by ten and you'll have a good, manageable number of patrons in your library. The longer you've been behind bars yourself, the better you'll get at detecting brewing problems, so manipulate the number according to your and your staff's experience and observational abilities. Obviously, these considerations are particularly applicable to larger prison and jail libraries.

"Twenty-five square feet per reader" does not necessarily mean "reading space." Your stacks will take up some of this space, computer work stations will take up some of it, and listening and viewing stations for music and movies will take up some of it. Stacks are a more efficient use of space; work and listening stations, because they have chairs and desks, take up more space.

If you want to approximate a public library as closely as possible, you want to create spots for people to linger comfortably. Soft chairs tend to take up more room than purely utilitarian ones. For your movie watchers and music appreciators who will spend most of their time in the library sitting down and plugged into headphones, comfortable seating is essential. It's a good idea to get upholstery that is waterproof or water-resistant and easily cleanable. Interestingly, some of the best ideas you might get for this kind of seating (barring the English floral patterns) can be found in assisted living residences. Your local bookmobile librarian would be happy to invite you on a ride-along!

Shelving

Security in your library begins with "visual control." When planning your library's layout, don't think vaulted university shelving; think elementary school. If you're going to have very tall shelving, keep it up against the walls so it doesn't impede your ability to see the entire room in one sweeping glance. Short stacks have the added bonus of being ADA compliant. Orient the stacks so that you can see between them from your office or circulation desk. Don't turn them into visual barriers; you don't want to create places where people can hunker down to swap contraband in comfort!

Literally, the nuts and bolts of shelving design poses a security risk, namely, the presence of nuts and bolts! But wooden shelving can be prohibitively expensive. One way around this for prisons with carpentry programs is to have the shop build your shelves to specification and cover the exposed bolts or nails with end panels. If you don't have this option, consider cantilever shelving. When planning the space in her juvenile facility library, Veronica Davis opted for cantilever shelving with colorful end panels as a safe alternative to industrial metal shelving (Davis 2000).

Your shelves should have load-bearing capabilities of 150 pounds per square foot. As with other aspects of space planning, don't forget ADA accessibility requirements. Keep your stacks at least thirty-six inches apart.

Lighting

We have found that the lighting in correctional facilities lives at two extremes of the visibility spectrum. Either the light is so poor that only a mole would be able to make out the sixteen-point font in a large-print book, or it's so fluorescently industrial it gives you a good idea of what reading on the surface of the sun would be like. As with all extremes, either can pose problems, particularly for those of us (and we suspect we are in the majority) whose vision isn't perfect to begin with.

In jail, not a week goes by that we don't meet an inmate who inconveniently enough got arrested without his glasses. (See amusing vignette in Chapter 6.) With the graying of our prisoner population in general, more people are entering jail and prison with older eyes that need optimum lighting. If you are serving your patrons in their living units, as we are, you and they will have to make do with whatever the lighting situation is in those areas. But if you have a library inmates can visit, strive for the optimum lighting recommended by the Illuminating Engineering Society in *Library Standards for Adult Correctional Institutions* (1992).

Do keep in mind that placement of light switches can be a security issue. Ideally, the switches for your entire library will all be located somewhere accessible only to staff. If they are not, and you do not have emergency auxiliary lighting, be sure to keep a flashlight and a radio with you at all times. You do not want to get caught in the dark with a room full of your patrons.

Staff Workspace

Any public librarian will tell you that if your patrons can see you, you're not really "off desk." But in jail and prison, you've got to maintain visual control at all times, even when you're not technically working the public service side. Because a lockable office door is a must, particularly in those facilities where the inmates visit the library, you want to be sure your office has plenty of windows so you see every corner of the library from your desk.

Securing your office doesn't end with a lock on the door. Every drawer and cabinet should have a lock, too. Building redundancy into your security procedures through more than one layer of locks will greatly reduce the chances that an inmate worker with ill intent will slip into your office and pilfer the scissors while you're not looking.

Staff workspace rarely meets all the optimum ergonomic requirements, and in libraries that too often get squashed into whatever empty room is left after all the other departments in the facility get their dibs, quarters can be cramped, windowless, and claustrophobic. Small comforts, like a little refrigerator and microwave (if administration will allow such things in your workspace), a snacks drawer, and colorful wall hangings go a long way to easing staff stress when they enter the office.

> *Home Sweet Home in the Big House*
> We've always decorated our library space with fun "library-ish" stuff, like READ posters from ALA and literacy posters featuring the words of our patrons' favorite authors, like Maya Angelou. We've also had bulletin boards displaying interesting news articles and the occasional prison-themed cartoon (usually supplied by a resident subscriber to the local paper).

But when we lost half our space and our patrons could no longer visit us, it was time for a decorating redux. The space remaining, though extremely small, was now all ours. We could decorate it for ourselves since it was no longer public space; it was our office!

Sheila got to work at once, making a brilliantly colored quilt to hang on one wall. Staff brought in houseplants and sometimes cut flowers. Erica contributed classy holiday decorations, like a talking resin skull at Halloween that spat out M&Ms. The library-ish décor that graced several walls in the old space now found a home at the end of one of our book stacks, the only one visible through our front door window to remind other facility staff and patrons walking by that the library is still in the building.

Making your work space as inviting as possible is particularly important in any far-from-ideal physical space. We remember from some years back our public interlibrary loan department. The office was in perhaps the worst location of any office in the entire library district. Behind a wall partition separating them from the main branch's reference department staff offices, three stalwart souls toiled in glorified closet space under glaring fluorescent fixtures, three rooms removed from the nearest natural light. One year, the supervisor bought a wall calendar featuring a photo of a different Tiffany window each month.

"The rest of the staff may be able to see the outdoors from their desks," she said cheerfully, "but my staff are the only ones with a Tiffany window!"

Computer Technology and Equipment

Basic—and Not-So-Basic—Equipment Requirements

Imagine yourself in an isolated rural public library. Imagine an enthusiastic clientele who bring to your desk all manner of requests, complex reference questions, the need for referrals to other libraries or nonlibrary agencies, interest in obscure authors and subjects, and the impatience typical of all library patrons ("NOW!"). Now imagine that your phone lines have been cut, a colony of prairie dogs just took over your satellite dish, the radio towers were recently uprooted by a visiting tornado—oh, and your copy machine is inexplicably hiding paper around rollers invisible to the naked eye. Welcome to a technology reality for many of us. Well, maybe except for the prairie dogs.

Perhaps this is not surprising since in jail and prison, we deal daily with decision makers who, while they often appreciate the need for libraries, have no real concept of what librarians *do*. Ask ten people at random on the street what librarians do for a living and nine of them will enviously reply, "They read all day." Ask the same people about the first word that springs to mind when you say the word "library," and nine and a half of them will say "Books." Responses like this lead us to believe that the general public still thinks of librarians as academic, introverted little troglodytes who rarely come up for air and avoid human contact at all costs. (Probably a result of early childhood traumatization at the hands of a librarian in whom "shushing" was an overdeveloped strength.) So, no wonder corrections administrators have a hard time understanding why we need phones and Internet access!

The soapbox speech on the shortcomings of the library profession's marketing of itself, sadly, will have to wait for another book. But as a consequence, we think popularly held misconceptions about libraries and librarians disserve corrections librarians more than they do librarians of other ilk. Again, this is a function of operating within a nonlibrary agency. You not only have to market your services to your patrons, you have to educate the decision makers who allocate your budget.

You cannot run a public library without a phone line to the outside world, especially in prison and jail. You cannot send your patrons blithely back to their dayrooms with a list of phone numbers and expect they'll be able to get all their questions answered over the phone. In many facilities, prisoners can only make collect calls. If someone has a question for the Social Security Administration, it's unlikely the SSA is going to accept that call. But you can call.

You need a phone for program planning as well. Presenters have to be able to get in touch with you. Your volunteers need access to you as well. If you work on any task forces or committees at a state or national level, meetings will be conducted via phone; you've got to be able to attend them in your own office, not be running around looking for someone else's empty space to do your daily work.

A computer with basic accoutrements (mouse and printer) is absolutely essential. Other equipment that a public library wouldn't think of going without can be shared between departments, so you may not need your own. These sorts of equipment include copy machines, fax machines, and paper shredders.

If your library carries media, you need to provide whatever it takes to play the various types you offer. This includes (for now) CD players,

VCRs, DVD players, audiocassette recorders, even special tape players designed to play cassettes for the blind. If your media collection is large, consider investing in CD/DVD and VHS cleaning kits, and perhaps even a videotape rewinder.

No matter what equipment you have, you need service agreements for all of it. Some facilities have a single department (usually in the finance office) to keep track of all maintenance and repair for all departments; in others, you might be in charge. Try to get direct access to the maintenance and repair plans yourself; response time will be faster if you're in charge of making a service call directly to the service company, rather than waiting for your another department to do it.

Build a replacement plan into your budget to ensure that you won't have to wait for hand-me-downs when your equipment wears out.

Computer Technology

For Staff

A prison librarian with well over a decade of experience recently told us, "Not a month goes by when the warden doesn't ask us, 'Now, exactly WHY do you need the Internet?'" Again, this reveals the generally held misconception that libraries are still hopelessly low-tech. But in a correctional facility, the Internet poses some very real security risks. Imagine an inmate sending threatening e-mails to her victim, or another trying to contact his ex-girlfriend when he has a no-contact order. Imagine an incarcerated sex offender in a chat room with children. Imagine offenders surfing through some of the Internet's most violent, salacious, and racist web sites.

By its nature, content on the Internet can't be selected by even the most vigilant and well-meaning librarian. Filters—regardless of whether you're "fur 'em or agin 'em"—are not foolproof. Determined patrons are not dumb. They will figure out how to get around them.

The key to getting and keeping Internet access for library staff is to address the security issues right off the bat. Keep the Internet computers in your locked office. Chain the keyboard, server, and monitor to the desk; a wireless mouse, though more expensive, can be stowed in a locked drawer when not in use. Keep computer screens out of patron view. Password protect access to Windows, as well as access to various applications. Resist suggestions to filter staff-only computers; librarians cannot do their jobs around filters.

In addition to any proprietary collection management software, like Innovative or Follett, which are essential, we recommend the entire Microsoft Office Suite.

For Patrons

Internet access aside, the sky's the limit in terms of what you can provide your patrons on a local area network (LAN). The Maryland prison libraries created a canned Internet training course on CD-ROM and offer classes to prisoners who have heard of the Internet but, having been incarcerated a couple of decades, have never seen it. Our jail library provides upwards of twenty WestLaw databases on a sixteen-laptop wireless LAN. These examples are all completely self-contained; no danger of anyone slipping into the World Wide Web to wreak havoc.

If you want to offer computer classes, an In Focus-type screen projector will make teaching much easier. If that's not an option but you have access to an overhead projector, you might try transferring screen shots to transparencies.

We conclude, however, with the technology that is most basic but that will best serve the most patrons the most easily. We're talking about a public access catalog on computers for patrons to use. The more patrons can do for themselves, the more positive their library experience will be. Even if they are computer-phobic, having computers available creates great customer service opportunities for the librarian willing to train patrons in their use. And as patrons self-serve, you have more time to do other things the patrons can't do (like supervise!).

Challenges and How to Surmount Them

If you want to bring computers into your library for patron use, you will have to convince your administration of the effectiveness of your security precautions. Questions your superiors will ask include:

- How will you keep track of peripherals, such as mice, floppy disks, and batteries?
- How will you keep the inmates from jimmying with your software?
- What will keep inmates from tapping into our administrative computer system?
- How will you monitor what they're working on?

The answer to the question about peripherals is inventory control. This is easily accomplished by requiring inmates to surrender their ID badges before signing on to a computer. When they are through, you can go over their computers to make sure everything is in its place. Some inventory items are easier spotted as missing than others, so you don't necessarily have to take badges if you know the groups you'll be working with are small enough for you to carefully observe. For example, our laptop batteries are enormous and leave a very obvious hole if they are removed. So we don't bother with badges for patrons who are just doing legal research. But we ask those who are using our computers to type legal briefs to exchange their badges for floppy disks so they can save their work and we can keep track of who has a small sharp metal object in their possession. As for mice, since we use laptops we don't bother with conventional mice. Finger mice take some getting used to for people accustomed to conventional mice, but those who have never used a mouse in their lives don't struggle any more with learning to use a finger mouse than they would to use a conventional one.

The answer to the second question is best answered by your IT people. Computers can be protected from hacking with passwords and security software—to a certain extent. These protections, combined with a guard card that will reset everything when the computer is turned off, are the best technical means by which to protect your computer settings. The exception is if someone figures out how to delete program files. Then you're looking at reloading your operating system, which is a hassle, but not the end of the world. Often, just good old-fashioned observation of what the inmates are doing can avert major technical headaches.

The third question might seem silly to those of you with a good understanding of administrative permissions. We can't claim to have such an understanding, and we work with plenty of officers who can't either. Again, here is where your IT people need to spell it out. This is a particularly important point to cover, since hackers will wreak absolute havoc on computer systems. If the hacker is an inmate who got to a facility computer without your knowledge and had enough unsupervised time to tap into the payroll system . . . well, you can imagine.

The last question begs the question of acceptable use, and can be answered by devising an acceptable use policy. Just as public libraries have acceptable use policies, you should write one with the help of your commanding officers if your patrons will have access to anything besides your catalog. In facilities (and this is close to almost all of them) that don't offer Internet access to prisoners, an acceptable use policy can be very short and sweet. In it, you'll want to specify:

- What kind of activity is permissible
- What kind of activity is not permissible
- Your right to monitor all activity and your right to terminate a computer session if you observe or even suspect unacceptable activity
- The consequences for unacceptable activity

You might even consider having new patrons sign an acceptable use agreement. But in the interest of minimizing paperwork, we recommend saving that action for patrons who have previously broken the rules but whose access privileges you want to preserve.

References

Association of Specialized and Cooperative Library Agencies. 1992. *Library standards for adult correctional institutions*. Chicago: American Library Association.

————. (1981) *Library standards for jails and detention facilities*. Chicago: American Library Association.

Brown, T. 1995. The facility and equipment. In R. J. Rubin and D. S. Suvak (Eds.), *Libraries inside: A practical guide for prison librarians* (156–176). Jefferson, NC: McFarland and Company.

Davis, V. A. 2000. Breaking out of the box: Reinventing a juvenile-center library. *American libraries* 31(10). Retrieved January 3, 2005 from InfoTrac Web: General Reference Center Gold database.

Vogel, B. 1994. Making prison libraries visible and accessible. *Corrections today* 56(1). Retrieved January 3, 2005 from InfoTrac Web: General Reference Center Gold.

Collection Development

If you are a librarian or correctional facility administrator, chances are you have had little, if any, exposure to some of the most popular materials in jail and prison libraries. Recreational reading collections differ from titles found on many white, middle-class public library shelves. Donald Goines and the many titles printed by Triple Crown Publications don't take up much space on the shelves of white suburbia's or rural America's public library shelves. Middle-class bias being what it is, you might be surprised to learn that inmates' reading tastes are incredibly broad, including everything from ethnic empowerment to love poetry, from freemasonry to colored-pencil drawing techniques, from parenting teenagers to residential floor plan design.

Well-stocked correctional libraries will boast legal research materials to rival any rural or suburban public library, and very good correctional libraries outdo a fair number of large urban libraries' legal collections. We have it on good authority from a local attorney that ACDF's law library is the envy of many small law firms. Unquestionably, the most comprehensive legal collection in all of Arapahoe Library District is provided to the inmates of the county jail.

Although collection development courses feature in all library science master's degree programs and there are principles that apply, a lot of collection development is an art form based upon a cognizance of what's hot in the publishing industry and popular culture, what's being taught in the education system, and what's happening to the people within the community the library serves. The most important thing to remember is that collection development is a process, not an event. It should be as regular a routine as checking books in and paying the bills.

This section is written with the seasoned public librarian and the novice or paraprofessional correctional librarian in mind. The former will benefit from knowing about authors and titles that mainstream publishing houses won't touch with ten-meter cattle prods and may also benefit from a review of the entire collection development process from beginning to end, since most public libraries have the luxury of delegating parts of the process to more than one person. The latter will benefit from knowing basic collection development principles and approaches.

The collection development process consists of six primary functions: community analysis or needs assessment; collection development policy; selection; acquisition; deselection (affectionately called weeding); and ongoing evaluation.

Community Needs Assessments

The world is full of truly superlative library collections, filled with nothing but the world's greatest literature and profoundest research, products of the loftiest of human mental machinations. But enough about the Library of Congress and the Bodleian. In the public library world, our commission is to provide collections that are as diverse as possible, catering not only to the higher mind but also to popular taste, entertainment, and recreation. Books that are not read are not worth the paper they're printed on. Because user needs and tastes differ from community to community, be it a community of scholars, school kids, business professionals, or prisoners, a book that is greatly valued in one library may be worthless in another. For that reason, we don't devote a lot of space to Susan Sontag, but Iceberg Slim has his very own shelf.

Our feeling is that unless you've got a professional consultant working with you, the simpler you keep the collection development, the better. Before doing anything, ask yourself a couple of questions:

- What is my goal in gathering this information?
- What do I intend to do with the information once I have it?
- Whom should I ask?
- How should I collect the information?

Patron Requests

There are lots of different ways to assess community information needs. The easiest way is to invite your patrons to request materials and provide input on an ongoing basis. Our own collection development process is strongly patron-driven. When we order a book, we have a real person in mind for it. We didn't always have such a user-centered approach, preferring the tried-and-true library school tactic of using book reviews and vendor lists. It took an eager paraprofessional staff member with no previous library experience whatsoever to turn us on to the effectiveness of actually listening and responding to expressed patron wants.

The advantage of this method is that it's a process-oriented model of user needs assessment. Ongoing input from your patrons will give you more information than the sort of snapshots surveys and interviews afford. Information needs and interests ebb and flow and, especially in jail, new people arrive every day so the population itself changes. The shortcoming of this method is that only your patrons have input; non-users don't have a proportionate voice. And to be really useful, user needs assessments must consider future users (presently nonusers) as well as current users.

Surveys

Another way of determining information needs is a survey. Surveying presents two primary temptations that will kill your ability to gather meaningful information. The first temptation is to ask every possible question you can think of that might have even the remotest relevance to your assessment. This approach will send your respondents running away as quickly as you yourself probably run away from the surveyors outside the grocery store who promise, "It'll only take five minutes." The second temptation is, in the attempt to keep it short and sweet, to ask this question: "What can the library do for you?" Absolutely dead-wrong question! How is Joe Public (or Joe Inmate) supposed to know what the library can do for him? He doesn't know any more about what the library does than we know about what he needs. Guaranteed, if you ask that question, you'll get a blank look followed by, "Uh, I guess the library can get me some books . . . if I ever decide I want to read anything." Your needs assessment is about *him*, not about the library. Better questions include the following:

- How do you like to spend your free (no pun intended) time?
- What kinds of TV shows and movies do you like to watch?
- What kinds of music do you like to listen to?
- In any given week, what three things are you most likely to buy from the commissary?
- What do you wish the commissary provided that isn't provided?
- How much formal education have you completed?
- What is your age/gender/race?

- Have you been sentenced? If yes, will you be serving your sentence at this facility and for how long? If no, please indicate your court date if one has been set. (This question is particular to jails.)
- Which clubs or groups do you belong to?
- If you have chosen to enroll in classes, what are they?
- Do you use the library? If not, why not?

These questions are good because they point to what the members of your community actually do with their time, what they're interested in, and what they're involved in. It also clues you in to population turnover rates, a particularly useful bit of information when considering how much individual patron input you want to include in collection development decisions.

The way questions are formatted and phrased is mission-critical to getting useful responses, and there are a couple of different ways to do it. Open-ended questions are good if your survey is very brief; ask your respondents to come up with too much original material and they'll abandon the exercise. For longer surveys, closed-ended questions answered with a simple "yes or no" or "agree or disagree" are better. If you want to get really scientific, you could even offer ranges of responses, ranking them from least to most importance, "strongly agree" to "strongly disagree," or numbering the strength of responses from 1 to 5, for example. Another option is multiple-choice responses. This is especially good for respondents, because it takes all the imagination and guesswork out of it ("What do they *really* want me to say here?"). The drawback is providing a broad enough selection of responses that you cover all your bases without swamping your respondents with choices that really have no bearing on what you intend or are able to provide. (For example, if you're querying interest in types of music, don't list "Norwegian Hunting Songs" if you don't plan to buy "Scandinavia's All-Time Greatest Hits" for your collection.)

Once you have a preliminary draft of your survey, we advise you to test-drive it on a sample of community members. The survey needs to be tested for the clarity of its wording, for the appropriateness of its length, and most importantly for how well it captures the information you need. You're looking for accuracy, but you're also looking for surprises; is the survey eliciting trustworthy responses that you didn't expect? If all of the responses merely parrot back what you already know, you need to go back to the drawing board and concoct deeper queries.

Along with working out the bugs, you need to decide how you're going to administer the survey. The easiest way is to just hand it to your patrons as they walk in the door. Again, however, this method fails to target nonusers. The importance of getting these people's input cannot be overstated. Satisfied customers are wonderful, but they won't challenge you to grow your service the way nonusers will. You might check with other service providers in the facility, like the teachers, to see if they will administer your survey to their classes. Another possibility might be to ask extroverted library users to administer the survey in their dayrooms. Inmates can be very charming and persuasive at getting others to do what they want!

Community Forums or Focus Groups

This assessment method lends itself more to prisons and longer-term juvenile facilities than to jails, where the population turns over so quickly, you literally might wind up with half the group members at the end of a two-hour meeting that you had at the beginning. In prisons, with their relatively stable populations, you can count on people being there throughout the process. Plan on a quick single-session meeting in jail and also keep in mind that housing restrictions being what they are, some of your best contributors might not be allowed in the same room together. Your focus group might need to be split up.

This approach benefits both the library and the participating group members in some significant ways. The library benefits by getting a lot of in-depth input that other methods fall short of providing. The participants get the satisfaction of contributing to a meaningful project, and their "ownership" of the process will almost certainly turn them into regular users, if they are not already. If they're already users, you might turn them into veritable evangelists for the library! This benefits everybody. One outcome might even be a safer library, since inmates who care deeply about the service will police themselves and other inmates to ensure it continues to be available.

Pulling together a focus group in jail and prison depends upon a combination of willing volunteers and careful screening. Advertise for volunteers; if the facility has an inmate newsletter, include a big advertisement. Posting flyers in dayrooms works too. You might also enlist officers, teachers, and the chaplain to talk up your project. In addition, you should consider personally inviting people to participate whom you know make extensive use of the library or a particular library service. Be sure you get a good cross-section of people, particularly if you're in an environment, like jail, that includes people of different races, sexes, ages, nationalities, security levels, and alleged (or convicted) offenses.

Before selecting your members from your volunteers and those you have invited to participate, you should get the approval of the officer in charge of the living units involved. You must be absolutely certain that the people you bring together have no housing restrictions that necessitate keeping them away from other inmates. If you are not holding the focus group meeting(s) in your library, also check with the programs department to be sure you have a room for the meeting when you expect to.

Interviews

Of all the needs assessment methods, this one is our favorite—and not just because we're both incorrigible extroverts with the gift of gab! When we have managed to carve out adequate time to listen to carefully selected interview subjects, we have learned amazing things about our jail community and our library service. Too often, we as information providers forget the perennial confusion of information users; we can't take for granted that any of them know what information they actually need, or that they even really understand their own questions. We can't assume that they are sufficiently trained to formulate research questions or to use the reference resources that might answer their questions. Interviews drive this point home in a way that is particularly applicable to your own library service.

When we conducted our last comprehensive needs assessment, we selected three inmates who were regular library users and who we also knew wouldn't be shy about voicing their opinions about all things good, bad, and ugly in the library. We decided to target just one of our services, the law library, because the circulation statistics for our bookcart service made us comfortable taking the success of that service for granted. Since we knew we'd be required to have a deputy present during the interviews, time was of the essence, so we kept the interview questions few and direct. The three questions we asked were:

- If you could create the perfect library for inmates, what would it be like?
- What is most difficult for you about using the law library computers?
- How could the library staff better serve the patrons here?

In devising interview questions, you should begin by questioning yourself. What exactly do you want to know? Our questions were carefully constructed to encourage different kinds of thought about very specific areas of concern. With the first question, our intent was to determine what kinds of services and materials the inmates really wanted by framing the question in a way that encouraged them to think beyond the limitations they perceived in the existing library service. The second question was posed to identify any interface and/or training issues to be kept in mind when implementing a computerized reference system. With the final question, we wanted to determine the perceived effectiveness and gaps in the library collection, services, and training.

Once you have your questions, you need to consider whom you will interview. The three participants in our interview were selected by us and the lieutenant in charge of library operations based on a number of factors. These included length of residence at ACDF (two had been housed at the facility for over four years), current awareness and patronage of a variety of existing library services, and availability to participate at the scheduled time. Each interview was conducted one-on-one by Erica. Two interviews were conducted with a deputy present; the third, with a low-security inmate, was conducted without a deputy. At this time, it is not felt that the presence of a deputy affected the inmates' participation. It may bear noting that the two interviews conducted with the deputy present each took less than twenty minutes apiece, while the third without a deputy present took almost an hour. We think this was attributable more to the personalities of the inmates involved than to any covert pressure by the deputy to expedite the interview. We mention it, however, as something worth paying attention to.

> *Ask and ye shall receive*
>
> Our interviewees delivered highly varied responses to our questions. Even though we asked the interviewees all the same questions, because we used the questions as jumping off points for considerable elaboration, the conversations went in their own unexpected directions. Some of the responses were universal. All three mentioned a need for better marketing of library materials and services and for training on using computers and understanding the Colorado legal system. One respondent pointed out that better training for inmate researchers would benefit the librarians since we would not constantly be running from patron to patron answering the same questions over and over! A couple of the respondents expressed frustration over the perceived lack of adequate site licensing for the law library databases, a problem we have since corrected.
>
> Many of our interviewees' ideas for better services are still on our back burner, awaiting the proper time to begin introducing them into a schedule already generously accommodated by the deputies. The respondents expressed a need for typing classes, writing classes, and English-language classes for native speakers wishing to improve their vocabulary. Again and again they pointed out the need for better training of both staff and inmates to improve their legal research skills and understand the legal system.

By far the most exhilarating responses were to the first question, "If you could create the perfect library for inmates, what would it be like?" Two of our participants had had ample opportunities to avail themselves of many other facilities' libraries, and all joking aside, they brought a perspective to the table that we could never have imagined. One of them envisioned a high-tech version of the traditional prison library, a computerized knowledge center "where you can visit, spend time, and study things of personal interest." Another stated baldly, "Very few people in jail have a high education. They need and look for all the guidance they can grasp." Definitely worthy goals for any of us in the library field, but particularly meaningful behind locked bars.

Collection Development Policy

Selection is one of the most fun parts of being a librarian, but before you give Ingram your credit card number, remember the goal: You must select materials that patrons want!

In Chapter 4, we talked about the importance of a collection development policy in confronting challenges to materials in your collection. But the primary purpose of such a policy is to guide your own purchasing decisions. Without a solid policy, regardless of your noblest intentions, the collection will inevitably start to resemble your vision of a perfect library . . . in your home. Collection development policies help us avoid bias in our collections. A correctional library's policy will also help us stick to the specified purpose of the collection by delineating the collection's scope. This contributes to better prioritization of purchasing decisions and lends credence to any defense we might have to give about prioritizing some materials over others.

Your policy should begin with a mission statement for the collection. What needs it is intended to meet? Is the collection supporting the education department's curricula, college courses, or vocational programs? Do facility administrators want benign diversions for inmates killing time before trial? Will the focus be on legal research resources? The decision about the goals of the library's collection should be shared by the librarian and the facility's administrators.

Once you have your goals in mind—and remember that everything about collection development is a process, so these goals will change over time—you can begin drawing up broad criteria for what your library will and will not purchase. These and other issues that should be addressed include (adapted from Colorado Association of Libraries Intellectual Freedom Committee 2004; Reese 1995):

- Community profile (based on data from your community needs assessments)
- Intellectual freedom statements, including the Library Bill of Rights, the Freedom to Read and Freedom to View statements, and the First Amendment
- Extent to which the library will provide interlibrary loan service
- Statement about who will have authority for selection decisions
- Titles and subjects that will be excluded due to facility security regulations governing inmate reading materials
- Different formats that will and will not be purchased, such as paperbacks, hardcover books, videotapes, compact discs, magazines, etc.
- Special needs formats, such as large print and foreign language materials
- Materials selected in support of other facility programs
- Guidelines about purchasing multiple copies of particular titles
- What materials, if any, will be provided for legal research
- How materials will be selected, i.e., from library vendor such as Ingram, other vendors such as Amazon.com and small press publishers, local bookstores
- Process for addressing suggestions for purchase by nonlibrary staff
- Process for handling donations
- Process for handling requests by nonlibrary staff to remove materials
- How often the policy will be reevaluated, and by whom
- Criteria by which materials will be mended, rebound, deselected, discarded, and replaced

Selection

How do you figure out what to buy, especially if you don't have the time or resources to conduct in-depth user needs studies? For good advice about where to look for book reviews, Evans and Saponaro's *Developing Library and Information Center Collections* (2005) can't be beat. However, many jail and prison libraries don't have much money to spend on *Library Journal* and *Publishers Weekly,* and the New York Times Bestsellers List doesn't always reflect the reading preferences of inmates. For these reasons, we strongly suggest you spend some time on Amazon.com. With scarcely any time to write purchase orders for books, let alone read book reviews, we have found Amazon.com to be an invaluable time-saver. The Listmania feature alone speeds up our selection immensely and we have stumbled on many popular little gems that were linked to the Web pages for books we already knew we wanted. Amazon also has corporate accounts for libraries to streamline the purchasing process.

Leisure Reading

Under the umbrella term "leisure reading," we include any books read in the pursuit of entertainment, life enrichment, or self-education. We believe the leisure reading collection is the very heart of correctional library service, particularly in prison systems that separate law library services from recreational library services, as in Colorado. Inmates desperately need psychological escape and emotional enrichment, needs found at all levels of incarceration. And no one is better equipped to provide constructive ways of doing that than a library!

In jail, as with any library, there are tried-and-true choices for a leisure reading collection. Fiction, as in public libraries, goes like wildfire. Certain authors, like Donald Goines, Stephen King, Harold Robbins, Louis L'Amour, Jackie Collins, and Sidney Sheldon are perennially popular. In women's facilities, mainstream romance novels are terrifically popular, but don't forget the burgeoning African American circle of contemporary romance authors like Eric Jerome Dickey and Sheneska Jackson. Genre fiction of all kinds, especially mysteries and science fiction, are popular with both sexes. Male inmates positively devour westerns.

Men tend to read for information over pleasure, so your nonfiction collection will be a particular hook for them. Subjects of universal appeal always circulate well, like religion (the broader your coverage, the better), poetry, and self-help. Histories and biographies are popular for both sexes as long as you select the right periods of history and the right biographical subjects. Your patrons will tell you who and what interests them. Your nonfiction collection can support self-education efforts to learn foreign languages, proper yoga and Pilates techniques, and managing personal finances. Women's facility libraries should stock many titles on pregnancy, childbirth, and menopause.

Children's books have their place even in adult correctional facilities, for people who prefer a fast, easy read and for those who struggle with reading adult-level books. Classics also have their place, since many inmates confess, "I want to read the books that that I never bothered to read in high school."

In Appendix A, we include lists of recommended leisure reading authors and subjects. These should not be substituted for a good hard look at your own clientele's preferences. Rather, they are meant to be a representative sample to get your own imagination flowing. If these work well in our jail, will they work in your facility? And what other kinds of materials will your patrons like?

Literacy

Many prisoners are functionally illiterate, so a solid literacy collection is something that will address universal user needs, regardless of what kind of facility you work in. If your facility has a literacy program led by the education department, you probably don't need to worry too much about stocking materials for teachers. But if you do happen to be in charge of literacy training, rest assured that bibliographic sources for teachers of literacy are abundant. The same cannot be said, however, of bibliographies on literacy materials for students. And having a good solid literacy collection for learners, both as a supplement to literacy classes and to support independent learners, is one of the hallmarks of a truly comprehensive correctional library collection.

In her article "Books That Speak to New Adult Readers" (1996), author Melissa Buckingham emphasizes two points in building literacy collections. First, a library's literacy materials must reflect the community it serves, which entails an understanding not only of community demographics but also of existing programs that serve the literacy needs of adults. She also points out that the best way for a person to achieve literacy is by reading extensively and recreationally, but that many literacy programs lack the funds to develop general collections outside their curricula. ALA's literacy brochure (2001) also emphasizes the need for collaboration between public libraries and existing literacy programs and advocacy groups. This is where the correctional library and the facility's education department can partner to greatest effect.

Selection guidelines can be adapted from the considerably dated but still relevant Literacy Volunteers of America's *Core Library for Literacy and Conversational English Programs* (1984) and from selection criteria established for the National Institute for Literacy's LINCS web sites (National Institute for Literacy 1999). Materials selected should meet most of the following criteria:

- Of interest to adults due to popularity of subject matter or life skills applicability
- Current and factual

- Well-written, contains appropriate vocabulary, and has a clear story line
- Depicts diverse cultural, ethnic, and social groups in positive ways
- Visually appealing and appropriately formatted
- Preferably nonworkbook formats
- Recommended by literacy experts or professional reviewers or is an award winner
- Supports existing curricula or independent learning

Reading teaches reading. For emerging and reluctant readers, careful selection of materials is particularly important. What you provide them can make or break their efforts to read better and more often. The biggest beef we have with publishers of literacy-specific recreational reading materials is that they look like literacy reading materials. The cover art is usually lousy and rarely sophisticated enough to even look like the book is meant for an adult audience. Pride can keep a struggling reader from picking one of these books up, for fear of the book being identified by others as a "dumb" book.

Your mission, therefore, is to identify mainstream authors and titles that emerging readers can check out and still save face. Poetry by writers like Maya Angelou, who present sophisticated (see: grown-up!) concepts in straightforward language, is good. Upper elementary- and young adult-level biographies are great, as are upper elementary- and young adult-level nonfiction titles. Don't forget about magazines and newspapers as literacy tools. Many of them are written at an upper elementary reading level, and their illustrations also help support the text.

If possible, don't classify or shelve literacy materials separately from the rest of the collection. Again, you must do whatever is necessary to maintain your patrons' dignity while still providing them with the materials they need. Make sure they know that you support their efforts as fully functioning adults. One strategy is to read several literacy titles yourself so you can say, "Hey, I read that one last week! You'll like it!"

A Brave Request

It can be very challenging to identify the emerging readers who need us most. It's embarrassing for adults to admit to a reading deficiency, especially if the adult in question is an otherwise macho guy and the person he needs to turn to for help is a woman.

One day, in a medium-security prison, an inmate cornered the librarian away from the rest of the patrons. As he leaned toward her face, she had a momentary feeling of panic. What's he doing? she wondered.

Very softly, the inmate said, "I don't want the other guys to hear this. I am forty-five years old and I don't know how to read."

The librarian's alarm turned to amazement and humility. "He trusted me enough to ask a woman for help," she said. She sat him down and asked him what he hoped to accomplish by learning to read.

"When I get out of here, I want to go to the grocery store and know what I'm putting in my basket," he replied.

So, for the next several months a brave and determined inmate sat with a savvy and sensitive librarian and a set of *Hooked on Phonics*. And he learned to read.

Legal Resources

The tools and techniques for locating publishers of legal resources are similar to those used for your leisure reading collection. Book reviews in *Library Journal* and *Publishers Weekly* will provide the most current information, an especially critical consideration when you're talking about the law. Contact your state law library, too. We have found the librarians at the State of Colorado's law library helpful and accommodating.

Keeping in mind that inmate patrons doing legal research are often at an educational disadvantage, thus making the complexities of the exercise even more daunting, we'd like to recommend a small core collection of materials more accessible to the nonprofessional than most law books. We cannot recommend highly enough the Nolo Press *Law for All* series for its readability and relevance. Nolo's commitment is to making the legal system as understandable and navigable as possible for the layman. In a correctional setting in particular, *The Criminal Law Handbook* and *Legal Research* should be part of your collection. If you provide law library services, you should read these yourself, too.

West Publishing's *Nutshell* series is written with law students in mind and is another good resource for self-practitioners. The books are highly focused on specific points of civil and criminal law so they are small and succinct and less daunting that many other law books.

West also publishes a wide variety of topics, including case law, statutes, digests, dictionaries, and encyclopedias. Many of their offerings are available on CD-ROM. West's target audience is the legal profession, so their publications are often very complex. But they are probably the most authoritative publisher of legal reference materials in this country.

At the very least, you need a West-published set of your own state statutes, as West heavily annotates these publications.

Two other books are essential core titles. A general dictionary is not adequate for supporting legal research, so you must provide one specific to the law. You'll need a law dictionary (preferably several), and *Black's Law Dictionary* is the one by which all others are measured. It will also be well worth your while to secure at least one copy of the out-of-print *Prisoners' Self-Help Litigation Manual*. This book is one-of-a-kind, geared directly to criminal offenders, particularly those already convicted. Although the indexing is extremely convoluted, no other single volume contains as much information with direct bearing on the lives of the incarcerated as this one. It's hard to find, and it's expensive. Get it anyway.

Although it does not necessarily constitute collection development, providing your patrons with research tools you yourself compile can be of great service in helping them navigate the complexities of legal research and can also cover your back in terms of the liabilities. The State of Florida provides clear stipulations on what unlicensed court staff may and may not do on behalf of *pro se* litigants in family court (Biro & Hill 2000). The list of rules applies so closely to what librarians may and may not do for their patrons, we include some of the most salient points here for your consideration.

As librarians, we may not:

- Give legal advice or advise a course of legal action
- Interpret legal terminology, statutes, case law, etc., or advise whether a particular definition is applicable to the litigant's case
- Record information on forms for a pro se litigant, with the exceptions provided by this rule
- Perform legal research on a litigant's behalf
- Encourage or discourage litigation, represent a litigant in court, or lead a litigant to believe that the librarian is representing him or her as a lawyer

But, as librarians, we can:

- Provide information about pro bono and low-cost legal services and lawyer referrals
- Provide definitions of legal terminology from authoritative sources, such as *Black's Law Dictionary*
- Provide approved forms and approved instructions on completing the forms
- Retrieve information requested by citation or subject
- Encourage *pro se* litigants to get professional legal help

With these rules in mind, let us suggest some subjects that lend themselves to handouts you can create:

- A glossary of commonly used legal terms, i.e. *habeas corpus, pro se*, and *mandamus*
- Citations of commonly referred-to statutes, such as penalties for felonies and misdemeanors
- Copies of commonly used legal forms, i.e. writs, motions, and transfers of power of attorney
- Instructions on using computer databases (if applicable)
- Contact information and addresses for judges, district attorneys and public defenders, the parole board, Health and Human Services, the ACLU, the Social Security Administration, etc.
- Lists of and contact information for prisoners' advocacy groups and pro bono and low-cost legal aid
- Annotated bibliographies of legal reference books you own or can get through interlibrary loan

Other Fancy Stuff

Magazines and Newspapers

In prison, newspapers pose an interesting collection development challenge not experienced in jail libraries. In jail, most of the offenders have enough connection to the county to have gotten arrested there! Inmates of jails are often incarcerated near home. But in prison, inmates come from far and wide; in the case of federal prisons, they very likely come from another state. So prison librarians have the challenge of figuring out where their service population comes from in order to purchase newspapers from "the state and regions most represented by the inmate population" (ASCLA 1992). Jail librarians, for the most part, can stick to purchasing the local papers.

Magazines often attract people who like to read but don't want to read books. They are a wonderful format for attracting reluctant readers as well as those nonfiction readers who want to stay current on subjects of interest in the outside world. You may evaluate the kinds of books that circulate well and select magazine titles accordingly or include magazines as part of your user needs survey. Don't forget foreign language magazines.

Because magazines are mostly pictures and are not bound to last anyway, inmates like to tear pictures out. This can inspire some resistance from officers trying to keep cells and day rooms uncluttered. Be prepared to defend the importance of magazines as part of what the library should be expected to provide.

Movies and Music

What most obviously distinguishes audiovisual materials from print materials is that their formats evolve more quickly and you have to plug them in. Collection development of movies and music depends upon reliable equipment that will play all of the formats you carry. Before you do anything, make sure you've got good equipment and a good service agreement (or money in the budget for replacement) if something breaks down.

Many correctional libraries do not purchase feature films on video, limiting themselves to educational films only. Before we get too bent about this, however, consider how many public libraries still do the same thing, preferring to emphasize the educational materials and leaving the entertainment to Blockbuster. Another advantage to educational films is that you won't have to worry about a questionable MPAA rating.

Another difference between movies and educational films is that feature films are rarely less than ninety minutes long. If inmates are only allowed access to the library for an hour per visit, it might be a disservice to them to offer movies they won't be able to finish in one sitting. Also consider how many viewing stations you have. Do you want two or three guys tying up your only viewing station for days on end to watch all nineteen hours of the extended edition of *Titanic*? You will need to work through these questions before you pursue approval to purchase feature films.

Audio recordings can be anything from books on tape to music CDs. If the inmates are not permitted to have compact disc or tape players in their cells, you will want to steer clear of any but the shortest books on tape. Be sure to query your population to find out what kind of music they like. A good question to ask is, "What are your favorite three albums of all time?"

Library Standards for Adult Correctional Institutions (ASCLA 1992) recommends a video collection of at least twenty titles and an audio collection of at least 100 titles. Because of the metal and plastic pieces comprising tapes, compact discs, and the equipment to play them on, librarians in jails and locked down, maximum security prisons might find it more difficult to convince administration that audiovisual materials should be included in the library's collection.

Foreign Language and Special Needs Collections

You're always going to have pockets of your service population who would be well-served by the library but might seem too small to justify investment in special materials. That's why, when you're considering any kind of special collections, you want to try for subject matter as broad as possible so even those who don't necessarily need special collections can use them, too.

The most obvious special collection is a non-English one. You should be able to get data on primary languages spoken by the inmates from the facility administration. If you simply cannot justify the expense of creating a foreign language collection of any kind (or if, in these times of increasing hostility toward the idea of libraries "wasting" money on foreign language resources, your administration will not allow you to do so), consider the interlibrary loan option. Even in jail, where we do not generally recommend using interlibrary loan services, making a policy-level decision to supplement your English (or in our case, English and Spanish) on-site collection with foreign language materials circulated by the public library will save shelf space and, hopefully, dollars.

Another special collection is large print materials. Determining need for these will be based on talking with and/or surveying residents. If you survey them, be sure the survey is in large type! Selections should be made with the entire facility in mind.

If you do not have enough foreign-language or large print readers to justify allocating adequate resources for them, consider ordering magazines for them.

Let There Be Light . . . And Pass the Large Print

Sometimes inmates are inconveniently arrested without their glasses. Fairly often, we are approached at bookcart by squinting patrons asking if we have any James Patterson or Louis L'Amour in large print.

"I don't need large print," one told us. "I'm only thirty-five. But I broke my glasses and the light in here is terrible."

Rising to the occasion, we supplied him with an array of best-selling large print titles for several weeks. Then one afternoon, we rolled into his dayroom to find him sporting a new pair of frames.

"I got my new glasses!" he announced happily as he handed the large print books back to us. "I don't need these big print books anymore."

"Hey, gimme those then!" another inmate hollered, peering through scrunched eyelids. "I got arrested without my contacts and the light in here is terrible!"

Curriculum Support

Juvenile facilities are required to provide educational programs reflecting the education provided in the local public schools, taught by certified teachers. In some facilities, those teachers are employees of the state department of education or the department of corrections. In others, they are employees of the local public school district. Either way, the local school's curriculum is the one used in the facility. Supporting the curriculum in your own facility begins with talking to the teachers in the facility, but you might also consider talking to the school media specialists in the public schools as well.

Many juvenile facility education departments have their own budgets and provide their own materials. The library's role is definitely one of support in those cases. Find out what the kids are studying and, at the very least, build a recreational reading collection to tempt them into pursuing topics of interest they're learning about in class.

In adult facilities, educational programs can be anything from basic GED prep to college courses for credit. Again, cooperation with the instructors will give you the information you need to build a relevant support collection for inmate students.

Forbidden Fruit

Selection is arguably just a politically correct term for censorship. All libraries make decisions about what they will and will not carry, and library school students spend countless classroom hours debating the difference between selection and censorship. We don't think there's any point in splitting hairs here, particularly since the security needs of the correctional environment sometimes overshadow the soundest library theory. So we'll just come right out and say it. Censorship is alive and well everywhere, but especially in jail.

Most verboten subject matter for a correctional library's collection is a no-brainer. Consider the following hypothetical list:

- Knot-making For Fun, Profit, Subduing Your Cellmate, and Sloughing Off Your Own Mortal Coil
- Houdini Factor: The Fine Art of Escape
- 1001 Pressure Points
- Martial Arts for Dummies
- The Complete Idiot's Guide to Locksmithing
- Pipe Bombs: They're Not Just for Terrorists Anymore
- The White Supremacist's Bathroom Reader

If you're unsure about a title or certain subject matter, just ask yourself this question: "Will the information contained herein result in an inmate getting loose or a deputy getting hurt?" If the answer is yes, buy something else. Safety has to be your first concern. Yes, the inmates have civil rights that we need to uphold, but human rights also matter. People can't be getting hurt because the library is providing how-to manuals.

The no-brainers are easy. But there are a lot of titles that fall into a muddy gray area. Just for the sake of the peace, you might avoid purchasing *The Very Best of Hustler, the Anniversary Edition.* But what about authors like Harold Robbins or books like *How to Draw Great-Looking Comic Book Women*? Is there that much difference between the visual content of *Playboy* and *Easy Rider* and the swimsuit edition of *Sports Illustrated*? You might shy away from *Turner Diaries,* but what about *From Niggas to Gods*?

This gray area is populated by authors and titles that affront mainstream cultural sensibilities. It is also the place where an overly rigid written policy can really tie your hands. If you make a blanket statement in your collections policy about not carrying any pornography or any politically or racially incendiary materials, you will definitely save yourself some headaches down the road. But we think that's the collection development equivalent of the old proverb, "To protect your feet, you can cover the world with leather. Or, you can wear shoes." We think a better tack to take is creating a policy statement that prohibits only the most explicit depictions and does not rule out the acquisition of controversial materials. You might make a statement to the effect of, "Material of a provocative nature will not be purchased if it advocates violence against women, other races, or the government. Material with illustrations depicting luridly provocative scenes will not be purchased." In this way, you can cover your bases while allowing yourself some negotiating room.

Banning Banned Books?

Several years ago, when we still had patrons coming into the library, Sheila decided to promote Banned Books Week. She managed to secure several feet of yellow police tape, which she lavishly draped over a bulletin board featuring Xeroxed covers of several offending titles. But then, a pang of uncertainty. We censor so much, she thought, are we being hypocritical by promoting books that have already generated controversy on the outside?

After careful analysis over iced tea, pitas, and hummus, we came to a couple of conclusions. The first was ethical. By banning banned books out of hand, we would not only be censoring them, we'd be *censuring* them. Considering that the subject matter of many of the books parallels our patrons' lives in so many ways, strong use of language and sexual proclivity especially, denying our patrons access to them just because somebody somewhere took umbrage to them just didn't seem right. The second reason was practical. Banned books, we reasoned, just by being banned could be one of the most effective hooks imaginable to get inmates to read.

In his book *Prison Ministry*, chaplain and former prisoner Lennie Spitale (2002) describes his predetainment attitude: "I took pride in being a misfit. I was an outlaw, and I had an outlaw's mentality. My perspective of life was viewed through a lens of rebellion ... I was restless, violent, and discontent. I *reveled* in being an outlaw." How like so many of our patrons, we thought. And if running contrary to white-bread values is a value unto itself among prisoners, what better way to turn them into readers than by offering them titles that have thoroughly offended mainstream cultural sensibilities!

Hardcover versus Paperback

A great many facilities forbid hardcover books for the simple reason that contraband can be easily concealed in the spines or dust jackets of hardcover books. We believe administration's concern about such activity can be allayed if you implement good circulation practices including careful inspection of incoming materials and good observation of patrons browsing books in the library. Limited materials budgets are also cited as a reason for not purchasing hardcovers, although we think that their durability justifies the additional purchase cost. Damage to hardcovers, when it does occur, is often more easily repaired than damage to paperbacks, particularly spinal damage.

An unequivocal benefit of hardcovers is that with a hardcover collection, you can get the very newest titles, hot off the New York Times Bestsellers List. Nothing will boost your circs like the newest James Patterson novel. The latest installments of spectacularly popular series, like *Harry Potter* and *Left Behind,* are anticipated as eagerly by people living behind bars as they are in the outside world. The ability to purchase hardcovers means you can respond to the reading needs of your patrons as quickly as the public libraries do.

Paperbacks aren't as durable, nor are they usually as current as hardcovers, but their relative cheapness packs a big punch. For the cost of a single hardcover, as many as half a dozen paperbacks can be purchased. And because they can't conceal as much contraband, they are a great format for deposit collections in the living units.

Deposit Collections

"Deposit collection" may be a public library outreach term without a direct corollary in jail and prison, but the basic concept is fairly common. In public libraries, deposit collections are often circulating materials, checked out to a facility (usually some kind of assisted living facility) for a finite span of time, and then regularly traded out for more materials. However, many public libraries' deposit collections consist of newly discarded materials that are no longer part of the circulating collection.

In our facility, "pod libraries" are essentially deposit collections consisting of paperbacks weeded out of our circulating collection and uncataloged donations. From time to time, we also purchase the most popular paperbacks, thirty copies of each title, so that each dayroom can have one copy. Sporadically, we send trusties into the pod libraries with a cart, shifting books between pods to keep the collections fresh.

The advantage of the pod libraries is that they provide an almost entirely cost-free way of doubling our collection. This is advantageous for a couple of reasons. First, we do not have the space in the library to store that many items, but the more stuff we have, the better we can serve our patrons' diverse reading interests. Also, for those patrons who read voraciously, the limit of three books per week from the bookcart is inadequate. The pod libraries provide a good supplement, since the deputies do not regulate quite as strictly how many pod books inmates can have. When patrons miss bookcart or if they are short-timing it, the pod libraries give them the option of selecting books to hold them over until the next week, or until their imminent release.

Acquisition

Purchasing

Shopping for books is one of the best parts of being a librarian, but you need to know where to start. If you're building a collection from the ground up and you're starting with a good budget, setting up an account with a reputable library vendor is a great idea because you'll be buying in volume, if only for that first purchase. Since we are part of a public library district, we began purchasing from a large vendor several years ago. But the large vendors suffer the same limitations of mainstream publishing houses.

> Because librarians tend to purchase whatever gets widely reviewed, their collections bulge with mainstream fare—works produced by the handful of giant conglomerates that own big publishing houses and, in fact, dominate global media (Dodge 2005).

Using a large vendor, such as Ingram, has its advantages, mainly the savings in volume discounts. But because of such vendors' mainstream bias, we have found it necessary to look elsewhere as well. Our patrons defy mainstream publishing's overwhelmingly white, middle-class target market and they don't always want popular mainstream titles. Consequently, our purchasing approach consists of placing several orders per year through a vendor, heavily supplemented with trips to our local bookstores.

You Reap What You Sow

Years ago, when Sheila worked at the jail library as a clerk, she spent months begging the library manager to let her go shopping at a local African American bookstore. The manager finally consented . . . and gave Sheila a whopping thirty dollars with which to purchase "a multicultural collection." Sheila decided to consider it seed money, a way of getting our collection started by allowing her to connect with the bookstore owner. She spent several hours in the Hue-Man bookstore in Denver, educating herself about what was available and grilling the owner about what was popular. Armed with this information, a new professional ally, and the fruits of her seed money (a Terry McMillan book and a collection of essays), she went back to the library prepared to push for more. Ultimately, the bookstore owner visited the jail and presented a number of book talks for the inmates. And those two little books eventually multiplied, growing into one of the best multicultural collections in the south metro Denver area.

Sniffing out small booksellers is as easy as opening the yellow pages. We look for bookstores in neighborhoods with populations our patrons represent. Be aware that these wonderful shops are often located in off-beat, even run-down parts of town; if you're nervous about venturing out alone, take a buddy along and make a day of it. Another great resource is neighborhood newspapers. Pay particular attention to the ads, since small stores often advertise there, bypassing the big city newspapers due to higher advertising costs.

It doesn't hurt to spend some time shopping online either. Amazon.com has impressive collections of African American, Asian American, Latino, and American Indian works, although they're deeply imbedded within the "Browse Subject" tree. You can find them by selecting "Literature and Fiction," then "World Literature," and finally "United States." You can also buy direct from the publishers, and the Internet is a great resource for finding them. A Google search for "African American Publishers" brings up several good places to browse for ideas and possible distributors. We suggest using Google to locate any out-of-mainstream publishers your patrons are interested in.

Booksellers' trade shows and the ALA's annual conference vendor exhibits feature many excellent independent and small press publishers. Even if you can't make these events, they often include lists of exhibitors on their Web sites, which will give you leads without your having to leave your desk.

One caveat we want to give you when you're building relationships with local bookstores and smaller publishing houses is not to get married to any particular retailer. Over time, certain ones may become less useful to you. Either your service population changes or their business model changes. Their publishing focus could evolve into something that doesn't serve your needs anymore. And remember that any smaller company is more susceptible to market fluctuations than larger companies are. A disproportionate number of these businesses go out of business, and there may not be a ready substitute. Our favorite African American bookstore went belly-up a few years ago, and we have yet to find another store that matches Hue-Man for selection and expertise.

> *Longarm and the Librarian*
>   Speaking of the sometimes vast differences in lifestyle and socioeconomic reality separating librarians from the nonincarcerated lives of inmates and the challenges to good collection development that separation creates, Sheila has often said, "Although we may not travel in the same circles, we all still have to go to the grocery store!" The fact is, our patrons would as likely as not never make use of a library on the outside. By going to grocery stores in neighborhoods representative of the communities our patrons come from, we get a first-hand look at what print materials are being marketed to them. The smaller the grocery store, the more targeted the print collection will be.

We've gotten all sorts of ideas about what to purchase, just by hanging out in the book and magazine aisle for awhile. Watch what people reach for, even if they don't buy it; that will tell you a lot about prevailing interests. By doing this, we figured out that even though Louis L'amour is still fairly hot, his contemporaries Matt Braun and Max Brand aren't. What guys were reaching for were western "romance" series such as *Longarm* (Tabor Evans), *Slocum* (Jake Logan), *The Trailsman* (Jon Sharpe), and *The Mountain Man* (William Johnstone). We purchased a few to try out. Suddenly, our western collection was the buzz of the building. The patrons positively swept them off the shelves! Now, we're not buying classic western authors as much, instead saving shelf space for these steamy little dime novels. We buy every new title as it hits the stands, and our patrons are thrilled.

Donations

Building your collection isn't entirely contingent upon your budget, since donations are relatively easy to come by. We indiscriminately accept private donations in all print formats—hardcovers, paperbacks, and magazines. We catalog any hardcovers worth keeping and send the rest to the public library for the annual book sale. We keep almost all paperbacks and put most of them in our uncataloged pod libraries. Magazines get thrown right into the dayrooms.

A few words of caution about donations, however. You should have a donation policy in place that states that the donations become the sole property and responsibility of the library as soon as they change hands and that what becomes of them will be entirely up to the librarian's discretion. This will help you avoid any outrage or insult if you pitch the twenty-five Reader's Digest Condensed Books that someone just cleaned out of their Aunt Mabel's attic. You also want to very carefully inspect all donations for contraband. We usually have inmate workers do this job for us. We also have our inmate workers remove any personal address labels from magazines and look for any pictures that might be problematic, especially in the sex offender dayrooms (e.g., pictures of children or scantily clad women).

You should have some sort of receipt you can offer a donor, for tax purposes. Because we are part of Arapahoe Library District, we use the library district's receipt. Your facility might have its own receipt that you can use, too.

Interlibrary Loan

Don't overlook the value of interlibrary loan as a way of filling in collection gaps and providing truly equitable access to your patrons. If you are part of a larger public library or prison library system, intralibrary loan is an economical alternative to trying to house everything your patrons could possibly need. If you're very lucky, you'll be able to access a statewide consortium, like the Prospector system in Colorado, which provides 95 percent of the scope of a true interlibrary loan system for a somewhat better price.

Interlibrary loan, especially when you're looking at going out of state, is pretty expensive pound for pound, particularly with rising postal costs. There's also the question of how accountable you can make your patrons. Despite ASCLA's recommendations that large jails follow the collection guidelines of prisons, we think true interlibrary loan is a risky prospect in jails. Once again, it's the movement of the population that complicates things. Reciprocal borrowing arrangements like interlibrary loan are built on relationships between libraries that can trust each other to properly steward other agencies' materials. If you can't reasonably ensure the safe return of another library's materials, you need to come up with other ways of giving your patrons what they need.

Cataloging and Classification

Librarians are famous for their ability to find things. This particular professional talent has more to do with how information is organized than by any miraculous scrounging abilities we might claim to have. When it comes to a well-arranged and well-maintained catalog of inventory, whether in print or electronic, librarians are experts at using the right phrases to turn up just about any information anyone might need. And then there's the Internet.

> I want to know what good is a web search engine that returns 324,909,188 'matches' to my keyword. That's like saying, "Good news, we've located the product you're looking for. It's on Earth."–Bruce Cameron

Don't get us wrong, Google is a great invention. But let's face it. The Internet is an immense and perpetually morphing blob of hopelessly disorganized and completely unregulated material, much of it more mental muck than actual information. Without standardized rules governing even the most rudimentary categorization of any of the nearly 137,000 new Web sites that appear every day, finding meaningful information is like looking for a virtual needle in a cyber-haystack.

Your physical library, even if it's small, can quickly become an unnavigable morass of clutter in which you won't be able to find anything when you or your patrons need it. The answer is good cataloging. Think of it as a roadmap between your patrons' information needs and just the right resources. A little conscientious effort applied to good cataloging will save you hours of frustration down the line.

We approach this next section with humility and caution. Neither of us went to library school with any intention, aspiration, or ambition to become catalogers, and we're proud to say that as classic overachievers striving for absolute ignorance of the exercise, we can't catalog worth a darn. Learning to become an expert cataloger requires sacrificing several graduate level credit hours to the arcana of Ranganathan and his estimable and inscrutable ilk. Go forth, little grasshopper, if you wish. Otherwise, here's our inexpert—but hopefully common-sense—take on cataloging.

Cataloging Nonfiction

Depending on the size and scope of your library, you might need greater or less complexity in your system. We admit a bias toward the Dewey Decimal system. It's familiar to many people, for one thing, even if they're unclear on the finer points. It's expandable according to clearly defined rules; but in a small collection, you might find that going out only one or two decimal places serves you just fine. Our nonfiction collection is about 3,000 volumes and we usually only go out two decimal places, though when our collection was twice that size, we sometimes went out four.

There are professional resources for catalogers, but even those of us who've passed through the library school hazing ritual known as Cataloging 501 rarely go into that kind of precision and detail. Instead, you can use a nifty little shortcut. When you get new books that you don't know how to classify, look them up on your local public library's online catalog. If they own the book, the call number is displayed right in the record. If it's not there, you can look the book up in a wider database, like WorldCat. Many public libraries offer free access to WorldCat for their patrons, but often, they won't let you access it remotely. Instead, you have to use the library computers on site. Of course, you can always call the librarian and ask him or her to look it up for you!

Where biographies are concerned, we apply the KISS method: Keep it simple, stupid! Biographies can be filed very simply by putting a "B" ahead of the name of the book's subject person. So a biography on Garth Brooks would have a spine label reading "B Brooks."

Classifying Fiction

Another advantage of the Dewey system is that it keeps nonfiction and fiction clearly separated, which we think is more intuitive for patrons. For collections of even many thousand fiction titles, alphabetization by the author's last name and then by title is the simplest way to organize. It's also easier on your inmate workers.

Genre fiction readers are well-served when you provide special sections of your shelves devoted entirely to mysteries, westerns, science fiction and fantasy, and romance. For larger collections, we recommend separating out horror, suspense, and Christian fiction, too. If you have a significantly-sized large print collection, it doesn't hurt to separate those titles. But we've found that marking our large print books with stickers to indicate what they are and interfiling them makes them readily available to all readers. Labeling genre and special-interest books is a great way to help your patrons find materials on their own. Affixing labels only takes a small investment of money and the time of an inmate worker or volunteer. Demco carries extensive lines of subject and genre labels.

Deselection

The year we lost half of our library's floor space to the expanding court services office, we culled our collection down to two-thirds its original size. It was a painful endeavor since we had long prided ourselves on the breadth of our materials and our consequent ability to meet our patrons' diverse interests. Most of our large print collection, a fair portion of our Spanish language collection, and an enormous chunk of legal reference materials went out the window. We figured our business was on its way out, too.

But at the end of the year, when we compared our circulation numbers to the year before, we were amazed to discover that our checkouts had actually *increased* by 8 percent, in spite of the fact that we'd slashed our holdings by 30 percent!

What this drove home was the most basic of collection management principles. A lean collection targeting the most expressed community interests will circulate much better than a fat collection choked with too much stuff that too few people actually want. The infamous eighty-twenty rule applies. That is, 20 percent of your collection will serve 80 percent of your users' needs, while the remaining 80 percent of your collection will serve the other 20 percent of users' needs. The problem is, without regular weeding, that ratio is easily compromised, with too few genuinely useful materials lost in a swamp of irrelevant junk.

We had to get rid of so much stuff in such a short time, it was easy to see immediate results. But the process didn't end when the new dividing wall cut our space in two. Keeping a library's collection healthy is like weeding a vegetable patch. Its success depends on regular and conscientious pruning. Turn your back for six months and titles that may once have flown off the shelves will have gone to seed, doing nothing but taking up valuable shelf space that could be devoted to something better. Even if you don't replace weeded titles, the remaining ones will be so much more visible to your patrons without the visual clutter of titles they have no interest in, books will begin flying off the shelves—even if they didn't before.

There are a number of criteria to look for when you're weeding your collection. Condition of the materials and popularity (usually inversely related) are the two most important. If you're discarding something in wretched shape that has circulated twenty times in the past year, consider replacing it. If you're discarding something in pristine condition that nobody has touched since the day you first shelved it, make a note to avoid purchasing similar items in the future.

Currency is important for certain nonfiction subject areas, particularly for medical topics. Nonfiction books are often revised and updated, so pay attention to what's being reprinted. Once you buy your reprints, get rid of the older editions. Dictionaries have a half-life of several years, but new words are always being added. Ready reference books like almanacs and even *The Guinness Book of World Records* should be kept current.

Also bear in mind that people do judge books by their covers. No one on earth is guiltier of this than teens, who are so very conscious of being "cool." If you're weeding a juvenile center's collection, be aware of the cover art. If it looks dated, get rid of it because the kids won't touch it.

Well-kept media can last a long time, but the rigors of public access do take their toll. If your facility allows compact discs and DVDs for inmate use, consider investing in a disc repair kit to extend the life of your materials. However, all it takes is one scratch to irretrievably compromise discs and LPs. Audiocassettes and VHS tapes can be more durable. Our rule of thumb in the public library is to discard most media materials after they've circulated 100 times.

We should warn you about the one cardinal rule governing any deselection process. With astonishing frequency, the moment you discard something that hasn't seen a day's action in three years, someone will request it. Don't let this extraordinary phenomenon rattle you. Far, far too many libraries are bursting at the seams with all kinds of useless stuff because the fear of getting rid of something that somebody somewhere might want someday has kept the librarians from actually discarding anything at all! Just accept the inevitability of this scenario and move forward. You can always order a replacement copy if you've really gotten rid of something mission critical. If you're in a prison, you also probably have the interlibrary loan option. In a real pinch, you can advise the patron on how he can purchase his own copy. Nobody ever died because a librarian threw a book away.

Shelve 'em, shelve 'em, shelve 'em (to the tune of *Rawhide*)

Shelve 'em, shelve 'em, shelve 'em, keep them book trucks movin'
Put those easy readers away!
No time to sit and visit, well, it's not much fun, is it?
Shelve that science fiction today.
Weed 'em, weed 'em, weed 'em, patrons do not read 'em
We don't think we need 'em, no way!
Put them on the sale cart, wait until it gets dark
Haul them out the back door—hooray! (Fetters n.d.)

Ongoing Evaluation

To close the circle of collection development, you should build ongoing evaluation into your process. You can certainly schedule regular audits of your collection, comparing your inventory to circulation statistics and conducting user satisfaction surveys. But you should keep an ever-critical eye on your collection in terms of the kinds of reference and readers advisory questions you get and are able to answer quickly and effectively, on the ratio of users to general population, and accessibility issues. Regularly review your acquisition policy to make sure it's still meeting the needs of your patrons.

Above all, listen to your patrons. To create a customer service environment that encourages input, you must not only invite input. You must be ready and able to act upon input quickly. The more responsive you are to your patrons, the more forthcoming they will be with their suggestions. And the more patron suggestions you use to build your collection, and all of your library's services, the more relevant it will be to your service population. Consequently, you will maximize the effectiveness of the library.

References

American Library Association. 2001. *21st Century Literacy @ Your Library.* Retrieved September 24, 2005 from http://www.ala.org/ourassociation/ governingdocs/keyactionareas/litaction/literacybrochure.htm.

Association of Specialized and Cooperative Library Agencies. 1992. *Library standards for adult correctional institutions.* Chicago: American Library Association.

Biro, N. and K. Hill. 2000. *Legal and ethical pro se issues.* Retrieved December 3, 2005 from http://www.ajs.org/prose/pro_legal_ethical.asp.

Buckingham, M. 1996. Books that speak to adult readers. *Library journal* 10(121), 73.

Dodge, C. 2005. Knowledge for sale: Are America's public libraries on the verge of losing their way? *Utne* (July/August), 73–77.

Evans, G. E. and M. Z. Saponaro. 2005. *Developing library and information center collections.* Englewood, CO: Libraries Unlimited.

Fetters, V. n.d. *Shelve 'em, shelve 'em, shelve 'em.* Unpublished.

Intellectual Freedom Committee. 2004. Elements of a materials selection policy. In *Intellectual freedom handbook.* Retrieved December 3, 2005 from http://cal-webs.org/ ifhandbook.html#elements.

Literacy Volunteers of America. 1984. *Core library for literacy and conversational English programs.* New York: Literacy Volunteers of America.

National Institute for Literacy. 1999. *LINCS selection criteria.* Retrieved September 24, 2005, from http://www.nifl.gov/lincs/selection_criteria_print.html.

Reese, D. 1995. Collection development. In R. J. Rubin and D. S. Suvak (Eds.), *Libraries inside: A practical guide for prison librarians* (156–176). Jefferson, NC: McFarland and Company.

Spitale, L. 2002. *Prison Ministry.* Nashville: Broadman and Holman Publishers.

7

Circulation and Cataloging

Circulation is one of those cornerstones to library service that no library school thinks of teaching. This is partly because circulation is based on policy, not theory, although certain ethical standards do apply. But we suspect circulation isn't mentioned in any library school because, as Anne of Green Gables would lament, it's not very romantic.

Some reference-only libraries don't have to worry about circulation, but they have problems of their own, like making sure the clientele keep their anti-microbial white gloves on while touching ancient manuscripts that are usually kept under lock and key. But in prison and jail, we are a) talking about the real world and b) definitely not in any danger of coming across anything antimicrobial (hepatitis notwithstanding).

Circulation policy and procedure is influenced by myriad factors and driven by different facility and patron needs. The following largely represents what we do in jail and what we've observed in prison libraries, and should not be taken as hard and fast gospel about what everyone should do. Over several years we have negotiated our way up to the level of circulation we are now able to achieve. We are also well funded and have the technology to support a large collection's circulation and maintenance.

Access

It's interesting to us how so much of what we do goes back to the concept of access. Perhaps it's the same in all libraries and it's just more obvious behind bars. But in applying the public library model in a correctional facility, at one time or another most of us face situations that call for an outreach approach. The most common situation in which this occurs is the delivery of library materials to inmate patrons. How do you get the books into their hands?

153

In minimum and medium security prisons, the answer is fairly simple. Prisoners have more discretionary movement in those facilities than they do in maximum security prisons and jails, which means in many cases you won't have to think about materials delivery at all. Your patrons will be able to come to you and browse your library shelves to their hearts' content, or until lockdown, whichever comes first. We have seen several libraries in the Colorado prison system and had we not had to pass through extensive security to get to them, we would have sworn we were standing inside small, well-maintained public libraries or school media centers. These libraries were positively teeming with patrons doing everything from studying to watching videos to reading the morning paper.

ASCLA maintains that for prison facilities housing more than 300 inmates, the collection should consist of at least 5,000 titles (Association of Specialized and Cooperative Library Agencies 1992). That doesn't sound like much, until you consider the alternative delivery method employed by maximum security prisons and many jails—delivery to the inmates' living quarters. Then you're talking about moving a lot of books!

Obviously, you won't wheel your entire collection down to the pods every time you deliver books. In many cases, you won't have the option of delivering a browsing collection of any size. Some facilities' library service consists of the librarian taking weekly requests for specific titles and delivering them door to door or via an officer. But others, like ours, are set up so that inmates may browse whatever can be crammed onto four book trucks. In a sense, it's like a bookmobile service where the browsing collection is driven right to patrons' front doors.

Circulation Policy

Along with your collection development policy, you'll need consensus from facility administration about your circulation policy. A circulation policy answers the following questions:

- Which materials do and do not check out (assuming you have a noncirculating reference collection or noncirculating materials like videos)?
- Who may check materials out and what is required to register as a patron?
- How many items may an individual have at one time?
- How long may materials be checked out?
- Are renewals allowed and if so, how many?
- What are the penalties for overdue, lost, and damaged items?

- For what reasons might checkout privileges be suspended and for how long?
- Are there any meaningful differences between facility-owned and interlibrary loan materials in terms of checkout times, limits, and penalties?

For the most part, administration is only going to care about the third question, which addresses the number of items an inmate may have in his or her possession at any given time. Deputies and officers have to pay attention to what's in prisoners' cells, and the less they have to keep track of, the easier their job is. A limit of two or three barcoded library books seems to be fairly standard, but don't let that keep you from negotiating for greater access. We broke through the two-book ceiling several years ago and have been checking out three items at a time ever since.

To maintain your trustworthiness, however, you have to stick by your own rules. Inmates exhibiting a pattern that indicates they are trying to get around circulation limits need to be confronted and, if necessary, cut off until missing materials are returned or lost or damaged items are paid for. In prison, with their predictable routines and long-term residents, you can be very strict about this, and we don't discourage you from doing so. But because inmates in jail live in an environment of upheaval and uncertainty unlike that of prison, we advise you go easy on those who have only one overdue or missing item on their records. When they get up to two missing items, your antennae should go up and you should issue a warning. If an inmate's record shows three missing items or more, you'd do well to cut him or her off until you get them back. The officers need to be able to trust your adherence to limits. Finding twenty books in one person's room and then discovering that ten of them are, in fact, checked out to him does a lot to undermine an officer's faith in the librarian.

> *"Help! Help! I'm being oppressed!"*
>
> A short-timer, Mr. L, was known for coercing other inmates in his dayroom to check things out for him since he felt the three-item limit on bookcart materials was unreasonably restrictive. We tried to counteract this, since we wanted everyone in his living unit to check out items *they* really wanted, rather than surrender the precious three books to which they were entitled. Some of the manipulation was a dead-giveaway, like when Spanish-only speakers checked out things like *The Rise and Fall of the Roman Empire* in English; we reckoned they were probably among those Mr. L was strong-arming.
>
> One day, after observing a lot of nudging and whispering by Mr. L at bookcart, one of our librarians decided it was time

respond. Later that day, she went to the deputy on duty in Mr. L's pod and said she strongly suspected Mr. L of hoarding library books, which really wasn't fair to the other inmates, now was it? The deputy promptly shook down Mr. L's room and found not three, not six, but twenty library books checked out just that afternoon! He just as promptly removed them, above Mr. L's lavish protestations.

The very next day, a written complaint awaited me.

"That librarian had no right to take away my books! She is oppressing my right to read!"

Now all librarians love it when people want to read lots and lots of books, and we have to admit, Mr. L's shenanigans were very good for our circulation statistics. But our circ rules exist for good and sensible reason, not the least of which is that we don't want to contribute to inmates being manipulated by other inmates. I wrote back, "The maximum number of bookcart books you may have at one time is three. However, we do invite you to peruse the pod library, since there is no limit—to our knowledge—to how many of those you may have. We appreciate your patronage." (Sheila)

Most correctional libraries we've seen don't charge overdue fines, but lost and damaged fees are another matter. In facilities where money is so tight that librarians repair and re-repair mass market paperbacks a dozen times before laying them to rest, accountability means replacement charges. The amazing thing is, though, and this plays out in public libraries all the time, when you finally convince the patron that he or she absolutely will not receive additional materials until the old ones are returned, nine times out of ten, the old ones magically reappear! It's one of the many small miracles of circulation policy.

Circulation Procedures

Routine circulation functions basically consist of three things: checking books out, checking them back in and putting them away, and registering patrons. All of these activities have their own natural flow that is unique to each library setting, so we won't go into great detail about them. But we will point out that all of these are typically paraprofessional tasks in public libraries, and student workers take care of them in many academic libraries. So circulation is a terrific place to plug in your more reliable trusties.

Checking Out

When checking out, the most important thing is to make sure the due date is very clearly marked. Make sure the deputies only need to glance at the date due slips to determine whether the books are overdue. A deputy who has to spend more than two seconds deciding whether an inmate has a book "legally" is going to err on the side of caution and take the book away. That's okay; you want the deputies or officers looking out for the library's stuff. But you always do yourself and your patrons a favor by making things easy on very busy officers.

We print small notes with the due date displayed in eighteen-point font. Nothing subtle about our slips, which is perfect. We tuck them into the pocket of each checked-out book, making sure to warn new patrons not to remove them or they'll lose the book during a shakedown or laundry exchange. This is a time-intensive way of indicating due dates, however, particularly if you check out between 200 and 400 books in less than two hours, like we do! Alternately, you might use the biggest date due stamp you can get your hands on. Just be sure, again with the officers in mind, to cross out all old dates to minimize confusion.

Checking In

What goes up usually comes down, and what goes out usually comes back. Sometimes, though, you get more back than you checked out! Books are great vehicles for moving contraband. Forget carving out the pages to make room for rock hammers. The spines and dust jacket flaps are primo places to hide notes, razor blades, and thin packages of tobacco. So are date due pockets. When checking for contraband, never—NEVER, NEVER, NEVER—sweep the pockets, spine, or flap with your finger! The worst we've ever encountered was a used Band-Aid, but in an environment rife with hepatitis, that constituted a major biohazard. If anything comes back even remotely damp, we advise you to get rid of it. Your health is more important than a discarded book.

Another thing you want to watch for are missing pages and missing parts of pages. This becomes a very big deal with books containing lots of illustrations. You can pretty well count on pictures being meticulously liberated from art books, drawing books, even some well-illustrated nature and history books. Unless your collection is very small and you are extraordinarily well-staffed, you won't have time to go through every single book. So you need to decide which books must stay intact. The criteria we use, and which we've seen applied in prison libraries, is to pay special attention to very expensive books and to very popular books. At one prison library, the librarian has certain books that she and she alone looks through when they are returned; they are costly investments in the collection, and she does not entrust her inmate workers to go over them with the kind of fine-tooth comb she desires.

Patron Registration

There's not much to registering patrons. The easiest way to do it, if you've got a computerized circulation system, is to use their inmate I.D.s as their library card number. Inmates are expected to have their I.D.s on their persons at all times, so you won't have to deal with forgotten library cards and the identification game as much as public libraries do. However, it can be more difficult to preserve patron privacy if you use inmate I.D.s; every officer and many nonlibrary staff members will know how to get an inmate's I.D. number. For that reason, we assign library card numbers different from our patrons' I.D. numbers. If you're in jail, you'll also need a system for keeping track of your patrons' movements, since most of them who stay for any length of time at all will be rehoused at least once.

Shelving Materials

We've already discussed cataloging and classification schemes. The whole reason for all of that is a circulation function: shelving! Accurate shelving is the key to patron access, since information might as well not even be there if patrons can't find it. But even with Library of Congress Classification and good old Dewey, you still need to decide how you're going to break up your collection into intuitive sections. It pays to consider what's most popular with your patrons and make that stuff especially easy to find. Your nonfiction can all stay together, but what about the biographies? Will you interfile them with the nonfiction or designate an entirely separate place? Fiction begs even more consideration. In jail and prison, with their largely male clientele, a separate section for westerns is almost a must. Even on our book trucks, with only fourteen shelves of books for patrons to choose from, we have one designated shelf for westerns. We also have a designated shelf for science fiction, and back in storage, science fiction/fantasy is far and away the largest segment of our genre fiction collection. Again, consider your patron base. If you're in a women's facility, westerns and sci-fi might be appropriately interfiled with general fiction, but the romances might need their own separate spot.

Preserving The Collection

By "preserving" we mean protecting, insofar as possible, the physical condition of the materials in your library. A library's collection is an investment made by the community for the greater good of all. But not everyone in the community understands or appreciates that, and that irritating phenomenon is as common in public libraries as it is behind bars. As stewards of materials that belong to our patrons, we have a responsibility for maintaining collections as close to par with public library collections as we possibly can. When weeding, the rule of thumb is this: if no self-respecting public library patron would touch a particularly mangled book, your patrons shouldn't have to either.

Preserving your collection consists of preventative measures and routine maintenance. We have found that inmate patrons are no harder on books than most public library patrons. Damage usually occurs as a result of poor binding and extended use. A correctional library's collection has to work harder than many public library collections; most of us don't have the budget to toss books because of a few torn pages or a slightly water-damaged cover. Whether or not you charge patrons for wear and tear damage is entirely up to you, but we advise against it.

Repairing books and magazines is as straightforward as cut and paste. We firmly believe the only trick to making the effort worth your while—and repairing books does eat up a considerable amount of time, even if your collection is small—is to invest in the proper supplies. A more expensive bottle of Norbond (a glue designed to dry flexible, not brittle, which makes it ideal for repairing broken spines) will ultimately save you money because you will not have to repair the same books over and over, as you would with an Elmer's-type adhesive. Real book tape, rather than packing tape, is more durable, it's stickier, and it also does not become brittle over time. Ninety-nine percent of your mending needs can be addressed with a bottle of Norbond, a couple of different sizes of generic book tape, and some plain Scotch-type tape for repairing torn pages, covers, and jackets.

If you have the money in your budget for some serious book bindery goodies, invest in some clear Mylar book jackets and some narrow strapping tape. Affixing book jackets over the paper dust jackets of your hardcover books will protect them from tearing and water damage. Mylar jackets are also easier to clean.

Those of you who have media collections will need to keep media repair materials on hand. These include disc repair kits, cleaning cloths, possibly even cleaning machines. If you're one of those who puts stock in the assertion that VHS rewinders extend the life of videocassettes, by all means invest in one.

Figuring an ounce of prevention is worth a pound of cure, take some basic preventative measures too. Keep in mind that some of your patrons have probably never used a library in their lives and have relatively little experience with books. Sometimes pages get dog-eared and spines split because patrons don't know how to treat books properly. (Frankly, some public library patrons could stand to take a refresher course themselves.) Make bookmarks readily available to your patrons and explain to new patrons how they are to be used. You can print them up yourself or purchase them. We like bookmarks because they not only protect our books, but they are something we can always provide our patrons even if we have to say no to other requests. They are also something inmates can send home to their kids; what a great way to carry the reading connection outside the facility walls!

If you're in a prison setting, you might have the opportunity to work a little library orientation into new inmates' general facility orientations. In small groups if you can, demonstrate the proper way to take care of books' spines and pages, explain the importance of using bookmarks, and spell out the consequences of deliberately or carelessly damaging a book.

Preserving the collection has to be a team effort. Inmates who make regular use of the library by and large learn to respect the value of well cared-for books and will do their part to keep them that way.

References

Association of Specialized and Cooperative Library Agencies. 1992. *Library standards for adult correctional institutions*. Chicago: American Library Association.

Staffing

In Chapter 2, we discussed the qualities that can influence whether a person will be successful as a corrections librarian. The people who possess most of these qualities are the people you want to attract when you're hiring. In many ways, the hiring process for corrections librarians is the same as for any librarian on the outside. A job description is written, the job is posted, candidates are interviewed, somebody gets selected, salary is negotiated, and the job is filled. But as with all things in corrections, there's more to it than that. Because corrections libraries fall under another agency's jurisdiction, county, state, and federal government may be involved in the hiring process. Sometimes there will be a question about which agency the new hire works for. For example, the state of Colorado prison system employs library staff who report to one of *three different agencies*: the state Department of Corrections, the state Department of Education, and the BOCES (Board of Cooperative Educational Service). In our county facility, the sheriff's office funds the library and staff salaries out of county tax dollars, but pays Arapahoe Library District to administrate the staff. Part of our library's offsite supervisor's salary comes from library district mill levy dollars, with a separate "compensation" fund paid by the sheriff's office. It can get a little confusing!

The Hiring Process

Any hiring process will consist of several steps, usually occurring in something akin to the following order: a staffing needs assessment, writing a job description, posting the opening and actively recruiting, the interview, and the reference check. In a corrections environment, there are two additional steps. The first, the "audition," is optional, but we cannot recommend it strongly enough. The second, the background check, is mandatory, and the facility itself will take care of it.

Staffing Needs Assessment

Before you do anything, you need to assess your current staffing situation and the evolving needs of the patrons you serve. It's important to give this ample thought. You might not need to advertise for the same skills you needed the last time you hired a particular position. You might also find that you need someone with entirely different skills. At times, we have needed to hire someone with at least a rudimentary grasp of the Spanish language; at other times, we're in greater need of someone who can tackle computer problems fearlessly. You should also consider the different talents of people with different educational backgrounds. If you have a larger staff and most of them have corrections backgrounds, you might want to emphasize a library or education background for your new hire. If you've got several staff with library backgrounds, a person with corrections or criminal justice experience can round your team out.

This is a time for reassessing the job duties and titles themselves too. Do you still need a library technician or has the job evolved to encompass supervisory responsibilities? Is your library looking at a remodel—or will its space be moved or downsized? Are you building a new library from scratch? Has the facility enlarged its offerings of programs and increased your materials budget to support it? Are people on your staff being laid off, leaving only one person in each library "branch"? In any of those cases, you might argue that you need an MLS librarian to manage the processes.

Part of the staffing needs assessment is to figure out what schedule the new hire will work. This is a great time to call your entire staff together to see if anyone is tired of working two nights a week, every Saturday, or wants to hand off a particular function or service. This is also the time to consider your vision for the library, whether that entails adding new services, and what that will do to the staff's overall workload, work flow, and the library's operating hours.

Phi Beta Con

We have one particularly challenging pod that we tend to foist on the newest staff member. The veteran staff joke that it's our "hazing ritual." The amazing thing is that the last time we assigned this pod to a new hire, she loved it! Now we have a very happy employee, some very well-served patrons, and a need for a new hazing ritual. Goldfish, anyone?

The Job Description

A job description is slightly different from a job posting in that it is a working document used by supervisors and employees, not a marketing tool used by human resources departments to attract new talent. Its content may differ somewhat from that of a job posting, and its format may vary a lot.

We like to write job descriptions like ambitious kids write letters to Santa. The job description is a wish list that not only specifies job duties and educational and experiential qualifications, but also the personal and professional qualities you want a new hire to bring to the job. Your staffing needs assessment and schedule will strongly influence what goes into the job description. In theory at least (which doesn't seem to hold during economic downturn), the better you write the job description, the closer your candidates will be to the ideal you're seeking.

A good job description won't be more than a couple of pages long. It's advisable to list job duties and responsibilities. You needn't list every possible microscopic task that might present itself, but you need to mention the mission critical tasks and those that will eat up most of the employee's time. You want to list the educational requirements for the job, preferred skills, qualifications, or previous work experience, and the position's title. Other components may include a statement of the position's role in the organization and the performance expectations of the person in this position. You might also include percentages to indicate how much time will be spent on certain tasks (or weigh their relative importance) and whether or not the tasks are considered essential or nonessential.

Once the job description is finished, you can transfer much of the information it contains into a sleeker, more focused job posting. Job postings should hit only the most salient points of the job description. Nonessential tasks unnecessarily take up space in job postings. Information not contained in the job description, but which should be part of a job posting, includes the name or position of the person to whom this employee will report, the work schedule, the address of the work location, the salary range, the application deadline, and instructions for how to apply.

Posting the Opening and Actively Recruiting

> The world is full of people walking around who have no idea they belong in jail. Yet.

Because correctional libraries attract librarians, paralegals, educators, and people with criminal justice backgrounds, you need to cast your net wide when you post a job opening. Chances are, the most effective ways of advertising public library jobs will not be as effective when advertising corrections library jobs. Certainly, the job lines maintained by state libraries and professional associations are good places to start. So is the local public library. But you also want to approach paralegal colleges and community colleges with pre-law courses. Colleges that offer degrees in education are another great recruiting ground. Post jobs in the local newspaper, or regional newspapers if a position is a professional one. Library listservs are good choices, too. Certainly the PrisonLib library listserv and the Association for Bookmobiles and Outreach Services' listserv would be appropriate places to post job openings. Some surprising candidates will come out of the woodwork when you post library jobs within the jail or prison facility itself.

If you are fortunate enough to have a library school in the general vicinity of your jail or prison library, make sure they know about any entry-level openings at your facility. Particularly for students with little or no library experience, working in a corrections library can provide invaluable experience in all aspects of library service, from collection management to customer service, from programming to hiring to interagency collaboration.

We have found that our best candidates come to us via word of mouth. But if that's the case, how do we find people to talk us up? It begins with us. Raising the outside world's awareness of jail libraries as something that even exists let alone great places to work, takes a lot of dogged salesmanship. Public tours of the facility are an effective way of getting your library on people's radar. Put your most avid jail library advocates in charge of leading them. Extend invitations to your counterparts in the public libraries (or school libraries if you're in a juvenile facility). Rarely does anyone turn us down because they are afraid or disinterested. Most of the time people say, "There's a library in the jail? That's something I've got to see!"

Another effective way of promoting the library is by offering library service to the facility staff. They have connections outside you don't even know about. If you can amaze and impress them with your materials, responsiveness, and customer service, they will remember. One of the all-time best employees we ever had came to us after her mother, who worked in the purchasing department and who appreciated all our hard work, told her, "You apply for that job. That library does good things and the gals who work there are great!"

Another Day in Paradise

The temptation on tours is to play up the luridly sensational-istic aspects of working in an institutional facility. The shake-downs, the take-downs, the lockdowns, the gruesome crimes, the lawsuits, and the heightened awareness of imminent threat all make for very exciting storytelling. But they can also scare the pants off people we are trying to win over! We've seen public library directors and board members nearly buckle at the knees when officers share graphic narratives about which gang member mauled which other gang member, who swallowed a Ziploc of several grams of pick-your-substance, and who did X number of former lovers in.

We recommend you collaborate with your law enforcement counterparts on facility tours, rather than turning tours over to them entirely or doing them all by yourself. You will be able to focus on the library's role in the facility, and the officers will be able to focus on corrections work and the facility itself. It's also a pleasant way for you to get to know the officers better and to gain more understanding of how the facility and all its various depart-ments operate.

Current facility volunteers are another wonderful source for new staff. A volunteer working out of the goodness of her heart can be your next great paid employee! Don't limit yourself to volunteers who already work in the library; let the other civilian departments know that you have a job opening, and ask them to mention it to their best volunteers. They might be hesitant to do so for fear of losing good help, so assure them that you will be more than happy to return the favor when they are hiring. Also make sure supervisors in the public library know about your job openings, and ask the same favor of them.

"Auditions" and Interviews

Once you've been deluged with applications and you've selected the ones that pique your interest, you could jump straight into the interview process, which in our situation is pretty well identical to that of our gov-erning public library. Applicants need to pass various diagnostic tests assessing their customer service skills, technology skills, emotional intel-ligence, and, at the supervisory level, management readiness. But before we put any of our jail library applicants through those particular paces, we insist on a preliminary acid test. We call it "the audition."

It's really not so much an audition as it is a glorified tour of the facility. We watch for two things when we do these tours: common sense and comfort level. We've already told the story about the candidate who showed up in the radically skimpy blouse. We've seen candidates obviously flirt with the inmates and deputies, volunteer personal information to or in front of inmates, and show up wearing outfits and makeup the women convicted of "working after hours" would be envious of. All of this points to either a fatal (to getting hired) lack of judgment or lack of understanding about the realities of the correctional environment. You can't teach someone common sense.

Plenty of candidates with loads of good judgment start out just fine . . . until entering the facility. As the minutes underground tick away, however, we've seen candidates lose color, visibly sweat, tense their fists, compulsively look over their shoulders, jump at the sound of a book slamming shut (let alone a dayroom door), stammer, and cringe within arm's reach of our patrons. The opposite end of the fear spectrum is still fear . . . masquerading as bravado. We've seen a lot of bluster that hides sheer terror.

We've also seen people's moods sink because of the lack of natural light, and we've seen people act positively claustrophobic in the small rooms with their low ceilings behind doors we can't control. There is a certain bit of the troglodyte in anyone who can work in a corrections environment and not go batty.

Thus the need for "the audition." We watch for all of the aforementioned things, and we also listen for genuine interest expressed during the course of conversation. Sometimes, we ask people to help a bit so we can see if they're comfortable taking initiative in uncertain situations. We try to show them both prongs of our library service, book cart and law library, so they will leave with a clear picture of the intensity and energy required. Then we ask them to ruminate for twenty-four hours. What seemed exciting and stimulating during the daylight hours can haunt people at night. We tell candidates if they are not sure they will feel okay in the environment, they won't enjoy the job. We don't have too many folks voluntarily drop out of the running after the audition, but there are enough we disqualify because of fear or lack of common sense that it's worth the staff time involved.

We advise you make the "audition" a part of every candidate's hiring process, even those with corrections experience. Different facilities have their own unique atmospheres and someone who feels perfectly comfortable in one facility might get the creeping heebies in another.

The Sweet Smell of Success

Environmental conditions in and surrounding a correctional facility have a lot to do with a person's comfort level working there. And sometimes comfort level has nothing to do with security. One of Colorado's minimum security prisons is located in a beautiful little valley of rolling hills, verdant flora, clear blue skies . . . and a dairy farm. The facility shares a parking lot with an enormous dairy, the existence of which can be detected from miles away if the wind is blowing in the right direction.

A corrections librarian with years of experience in all kinds of facilities almost walked away from a job offer at this prison. Forget the several hundred inmates walking around all the time; the aroma of several hundred cows doing what cows will do all the time nearly convinced her to refuse the job. Although she's glad she stayed, she still pinches her nose when she walks to her office.

Another librarian, however, working at the same facility considers her library one of the Colorado Department of Corrections' (DOC) best-kept secrets.

"If it weren't for that dairy," she says, "we'd have to beat back the crowds of people who'd want to work here!"

In Appendix C, we have included the interview questions Sheila has developed over the last several years. We'd like to make special note of the situational questions. They are designed to test how quickly someone can think on her feet—because every day in jail presents new situations you haven't dealt with before—and an applicant's confidence about making decisions without necessarily knowing the right course of action. We don't like to hear candidates respond to "What would you do if?" with "I can't really answer that because I don't know the policy." Sometimes you have to make a decision and hope for the best, and we need people who won't get too bent if they make the wrong decision and a deputy barks at them.

Because correctional libraries are often cooperative ventures between the library itself, the state library, the public library, a particular facility, the DOC, or the county sheriff's office, a panel of interviewers is desirable. Individual interviewers listen for different things. A law enforcement interviewer will pay particular attention to boundary issues, attention to detail, and respect for authority. A librarian interviewer will listen for library experience, common sense, and a real desire to do the job.

Because Sheila developed our interview questions with the help of our commanding lieutenant at the time, we do not always bring our current lieutenant in on the hiring process. Sometimes, it's just not feasible to coordinate our different schedules, especially if we're hiring an entry-level part-time position while he's occupied with higher priority things like ACA accreditation! Our library district, however, requires the position's supervisor and one other member of management to conduct interviews together. It's not always necessary for both interviewers to be intimately aware of all the subtleties of working in jail. In fact, we've found that experienced interviewers who are inexperienced in jail pick up on things—credibility, poise, articulacy—that we sometimes miss because we tend to focus on job experience and enthusiasm.

The Background Check

Some public libraries do background checks of new employees, especially those who work with children. We check outreach staff and volunteers who go into people's homes. Once you're hired to work in any correctional facility, there will be a background check. Don't worry if you have speeding tickets! That is not the kind of information that will keep you from working in a correctional environment. (Although it might be an issue if you want to be a bookmobile driver.)

Background checks can be basic or extremely comprehensive, depending on the position applied for, but what they basically boil down to is this: Does the applicant have a pattern of petty criminal behavior or a felony on his or her record? Depending on the position applied for, different histories might be tolerated. For example, author Lennie Spitale served three and a half years in a New Hampshire prison for armed robbery, after having served time in a Navy brig. He is now a full-time prison minister who has worked in nine different states.

Background checks don't take long to run. Once your candidates are cleared, you can decide whether to hire them.

Training and Motivation

Training New Staff

All right, we're going to assume you can get through the job offer and salary negotiation phase all by yourself, so we're going to skip right over into the subject of training. Obviously in any job the bulk of training happens in the first couple of months, when the learning curve is less a curve than it is a vertical line. Different correctional facilities deal with training in different ways, and the circumstances of each library, particularly in regard to how many paid staff it has, necessitate different approaches. That said, adult learning theory does apply. Most of us learn by doing. If you have an orientation manual, it should be a guide for the trainer now and a reference for the trainee later. You're not training if all you do is assign reading the manual as the day's homework.

We like to employ an informal "lead by example" strategy. New staff in particular find it extremely productive to work directly with the patrons from day one with an experienced staffer *shadowing them*. This way, new staff learn by doing but still have backup when they get stuck. And in the first several weeks, they get stuck often! We also serve the patrons better by making sure at least one person is on hand to help them out, even while we're breaking in a new employee.

Things that jail library staff should be trained on include:

- Reference interview skills
- Readers advisory skills
- Customer service, public library style
- How to deal with situations that test your boundaries
- The facility authority hierarchy and the most important features of the organizational culture
- General Web and Internet resources
- Proprietary or subscription-based software (at your facility and those you can access through the public library)
- How to assist legal research without giving legal advice
- Collection development, from acquisition to weeding
- Self-defense

Some facilities, like ours, are able to send new staff to "Librarian 101" classes in our governing public library. Some focus much more on safety and security issues and require new staff to attend "boot camp"-style training for several weeks before ever setting foot on the library floor. Another option we employ is using a required reading list; our Suggested Readings at the back of this book is a good place to start. The purpose of training new staff is not just about how to do the required daily tasks. You must also train public library values, heightened vigilance, and understanding the system.

Ongoing Professional Development

When there aren't enough hours in the day to get routine tasks done, continuing education is the last thing on your mind. But professional development is part of the public library model, from in-house classes to conference seminars all the way to the MLS itself. Ongoing education isn't just about you. It's an additional service you offer your patrons. The more you learn, the more you can pass on to them.

Continuing education begins with a commitment to lifelong learning. The easiest and cheapest way to develop yourself professionally is to read. Prison literature is a vast informational field that is ripe for picking, from memoirs and collections of prisoners' creative writing, to how-to manuals (like this one), to case law, to administrative regulations and statutory provisions for correctional library services, to Bureau of Justice and ACLU reports. Literature on correctional libraries is harder to find, but we have referenced a number of sources for you. Don't limit yourself to libraries behind bars. Get hold of your state library association's regular publications to see what's going on in the public and school libraries. *American Libraries* and *Library Journal* offer national perspective on issues impacting public and academic libraries. And frankly, don't limit yourself to libraries! Books written by and for prisoners' families, chaplains, social workers, teachers, volunteers, and even officers all contain information that can help you become a better corrections librarian.

Keep your eyes open for classes for staff offered in house, both at the facility and at the local library. We have attended classes at jail on everything from direct supervision of inmates to how to write a really effective incident report! The administrators might not think to invite you to classes geared toward law enforcement or other civilian staff, but ours have been most welcoming when we've asked to attend. If you work in the prison system, chances are you'll have ongoing training on subjects like "Effectively Using Pressure Points to Disarm an Inmate Patron Who Just Stuffed the Newest Harry Potter Book down the Front of His Pants." We've also attended library district classes on topics such as Internet reference, readers advisory, customer service, and dealing with difficult patrons. Your local bar association might offer classes for paralegals or law clerks that are open to anyone. Special interest law groups, like the American Association of Law Libraries, offer all kinds of topical classes.

Conferences are one of the very best ways to expand your knowledge and, not incidentally, your web of contacts. Prison and jail library work is quite isolated from the rest of the library community, from which much is to be learned. Even though your annual state library conference might not offer a single session on corrections libraries, there will be programs on collection development, curriculum support, engaging reluctant readers, literacy, ESL, collaborating with nonlibrary agencies, and grant writing, to name just a few general topics that can be applied in jail and prison. At the national level, in 2005 ALA offered a four-session track on library outreach, including a panel discussion featuring Maryland state prison library coordinator Glennor Shirley. In the same year, ACA's conference featured tracks on women working in corrections, developing cooperative relationships with noncorrections agencies, offender reentry into society, the challenges particular to jails, programs for adult and juvenile offenders, and, interestingly, a track on continuing education!

The important thing to keep in mind as you're striving to increase your expertise and experience is that compared to the grand total of professional development opportunities available to librarians, lawyers, and correctional facility staff, virtually none of it targets the job of correctional librarians. Rather than becoming frustrated, look at this as an opportunity to mine all kinds of sources for new ideas. After that, you just have to be willing and able to adapt other's good ideas to your environment.

Motivation

Jails and prisons generate more than their fair share of stress. Corrections librarians' low status, both within the facility and in the library community, contributes to this, as does the relatively low pay. Add to this the difficulty of moving "up the ladder," since professional positions are few, especially in jail, and you have a formula for staff discouragement and early burnout. The answer lies in motivating your employees.

Both of us employ several different techniques to motivate our team members, according to our own leadership styles and based not a little on what motivates us ourselves. The pillars of staff motivation are *recognition and reward*. Both must be specific and timely, and both are contingent upon observation. In our current situation with an offsite supervisor, frequent input from staff about the good things they have observed their coworkers doing often gives us more information than people are inclined to share about their own achievements.

There are lots of ways to recognize and reward employees and we think the best ways have nothing to do with money. Our library district has a staff kudos program that allows supervisors to reward staff with up to eight hours of administrative leave per employee (prorated for part-timers). We share everyone's stories of outstanding and personalized service during our staff meetings, to much praise and applause. We make sure to inform our superiors at the library and at the jail of the particularly good work individual team members are doing. We encourage our patrons to write letters of appreciation that we then pass along to our library director.

Fostering an atmosphere of *friendly competition* also works well to motivate our staff. We keep detailed circulation statistics every week and have, for years, striven for better and better ratios of inmate population versus patrons checking out. As our library has gotten better and better, the percentages keep rising. Each staff member sets a personal goal; in the very crowded pods, we always try for at least 80 percent of the inmates checking out at least one book per week. When the number is achieved, an e-mail goes out to everyone on the team. Hot diggity!

Mentoring and side-by-side training are the main methods for learning the job. Sometimes paraprofessional staff hesitate to coach others. When you *empower* your staff from the day they walk in the door to take initiative, learn as much as they can, ask questions, and share their own knowledge, they'll be less shy about offering each other advice. Empowering staff also gives them a sense of ownership over the library as a whole. When staff are invested in the library's success, the service will keep getting better and better.

Encouraging employees to coach each other is a great *team-building* exercise. Particularly in an environment that can be as oppressive as jail, you get by with a little help from your friends. A person who is not a good team player can wreak absolute havoc on the morale of your entire team, since the environment heightens sensitivity to differences in style, approach, and procedures. Staff have to be able to adjust the way they usually do things for the good of the entire team.

Another great team-building technique is regular staff meetings. Staff get acquainted by sitting together and paying attention to each other, which is hard to do when your job runs you off your feet eight hours at a stretch. Regular meetings provide staff with the opportunity to problem-solve, brainstorm, and catch up on what everyone is doing. To make meetings a little more palatable, no pun intended, encourage people to bring treats! If you employ a lot of part-timers, you may need to switch the meeting day each month so everybody gets to participate.

Leadership—or the lack thereof—can make or break the spirit of even the strongest teams. Knowing their leader's *vision* gives staff a sense of perspective and purpose. Whatever your vision, say it big! Goals have to be a little unrealistic; otherwise, they're not really goals, they're "to do" lists. Besides, what's unrealistic this year might be perfectly achievable next year. Be sure when articulating a vision that you state clear expectations of your staff.

Finally, we end with the tried and true, number-one best way to motivate staff: saying thank you. The work of a jail librarian, with all of its challenges, can be a thankless job. Thanking staff gives them a sense of their own value and the importance of their work.

Volunteers

Anyone who has worked in public library outreach can tell you that successful outreach services are built on the backs of volunteers. Armies of volunteers venture out of the library and into the community every day to deliver books and movies to housebound people, read stories to daycare children, and help with ESL and after-school programs.

Most correctional facilities have volunteers who do everything from teaching GED classes, to leading Alcoholics Anonymous meetings, to serving Communion. Library volunteers can be used for a variety of jobs, everything from shelving, to manning the circulation desk, to one-time special projects.

Recruiting volunteers to work in a correctional library can be tricky, because it doesn't seem to fit in with the dignified, behind-the-scenes, and predictable routine that attracts many volunteers to the public library. Still, it's worth jumping on the volunteer conscription bandwagon. If your local public library puts out a call for volunteers, ask them to include your need for volunteers in their advertising. Agencies such as Volunteers of America, which has chapters all over the country (VOA 2004), as well as correctional facilities themselves, also place volunteers.

Success with volunteers hinges upon their dependability, which can be a difficult thing to demand of people working for free out of the goodness of their hearts. The key is to tap into what matters most to them. Sit down with your volunteers and discuss their reasons and goals for wanting to work in jail or prison. That conversation should shed some light on their personalities and passions. Then you need to determine their particular skills set—and, more importantly, which skills they are willing to give away. A CPA might be perfectly willing to mend books on the weekends, but she's not going to balance your budget!

As with people interested in paid positions, potential volunteers need to spend some time touring your facility and talking with other staff. Volunteers go through a background check just as paid staff do. Once they are hired, some orientation will be required, but not to the degree you'll need to orient paid staff.

Sometimes, volunteers come in with huge hearts but no real idea of what they're getting into. The North Carolina Department of Correction has a good Web page for prospective volunteers that outlines different volunteer opportunities, ways volunteers can positively contribute to inmates' lives, and ways of effectively communicating with inmates (North Carolina DOC 1995–2005).

Inmate Workers ("Trusties")

In the public library world, the word "trustee" refers to someone on the library's governing board. In the correctional community, the homonym "trusty" refers to an inmate who works in and for the facility and who may have special privileges. We're not quite sure how that term came to be applied to inmate workers, and we have mixed feelings about using it. It implies someone who has been entrusted with something. And while we do rely on our trusties to help us provide the best customer service possible, we certainly don't trust them!

Beyond the invaluable help they provide, trusties can be ambassadors, bridging any gaps separating us, our patrons, and nonusers. Trusties can say things to us that the other inmates mention to them, but might hesitate to tell us. Trusties by their very presence also send the message to the entire population that the facility has a library and that the librarians are on site to provide good service.

Some correctional libraries are run by inmates who answer to a warden, sergeant, or other officer. Sometimes they report to the person in charge of the education department. And sometimes they report to the librarian in charge. Their duties can be as varied as the institutions in which they live and work. Some have acquisition and cataloging responsibilities. Some are trained to do legal research and in turn train other prisoners. Many do routine daily upkeep of the library, such as shelving, mending, and cleaning. Many also check materials in and out and, in a few cases, may even be called upon for network and equipment maintenance. Our recalcitrant copy machine limped along a lot longer than it would have if we hadn't been assigned an inmate worker who was a copier repairman on the outside!

Trusties come to work in the library in different ways, depending on the way each facility hires them. In some facilities, the librarian is in charge of the hiring process. Jobs are posted and inmates go through an application process that usually consists of an interview, certain diagnostic skill tests like typing and reading comprehension, and background checks (in the form of calling previous prison supervisors.) Sometimes, as in our jail, trusties are assigned by someone else, usually an officer in charge of inmate workers. For many reasons, the former method is preferable to the latter. We tend to get trusties who can't get clearance to work in the kitchens, usually because they have bad feet or hips or some communicable disease like hepatitis. Considerations such as good work ethic, ability to follow instructions, interest in and understanding of books, and customer service orientation don't really figure into our hiring process.

Hit the Road, Jack

One prison librarian told us about an avid library patron who applied for a library trusty job. Upon receiving his application, she called him to her office and told him she wasn't about to consider him because he cursed too much.

"Show me you can clean up your mouth and then I'll think about hiring you," she told him.

Not to be deterred, the inmate improved his language and when another job opened up several months later, he applied again. This time, he got as far as the background check. That's when the librarian called him into her office again.

"I talked with your kitchen supervisor," she said, "and he told me you got busted a couple of weeks ago for giving out extra pieces of pie. I'm not hiring you. If you're giving pie away, what's to keep me from thinking you won't give the library books away?"

Some months later, the inmate told the librarian that he was going to be released soon.

"Good," she said, "and I'd better not ever see you back here. If you come back, it means you didn't learn anything. If you come back, I'm automatically putting you on sixty days' suspension of library privileges."

Apparently that mess hall pie was really good, because a few months later, the guy came back to prison. The librarian ran into him in a hallway one morning and before she could open her mouth to speak, the inmate held up his hands and said, "I remember what you said when I left and I just want you to know that I won't be coming to the library for another couple of weeks."

"A couple of weeks?" the librarian said. "I told you I'd suspend your privileges for two months!"

"I remember, ma'am, and I've saved you the trouble. I've already been here six weeks and I suspended my own privileges!"

Needless to say, it's a crapshoot for us nearly every week. Since trusties are serving short-term misdemeanor sentences, some of them are literally here today, gone tomorrow. Training newcomers is an ongoing process that often has to be done with little warning or on the job. Having a checklist handy for last-minute training helps you remember the particularly salient aspects of the task at hand.

If trusties have been assigned to the library, chances are good they don't want to be there. Either they have no idea what a library is or have never had good experiences reading or have terrible memories of mean librarians who chased them out of the public library with brooms for talking too loudly. We have discovered that many of our trusties change their minds after only a few days of working with us. Part of what changes their opinion is the way we approach customer service. Libraries and librarians have evolved far beyond our "shushing" image, but a lot of people don't know that. Our trusties get to be part of a team that places excellent customer service above all other goals. They see the amazing response from our patrons and feel good to be part of something so meaningful.

We also work our readers advisory magic on them. Perhaps contrary to common supervisory approaches toward inmate workers, we try to actively engage ours in talking to us about their interests and books they have read in the past. Rarely do we encounter someone for whom we have absolutely nothing to recommend. Because our collection is built almost entirely on patron input, our trusties usually just need a little steering to find exactly what will interest them.

"Go toward the light!"

So many of our trusties have gone from unenthusiastic to positively evangelical about our library, we wish now that we'd exit interviewed every one of them. We have seen nonreaders suddenly jump on the reading bandwagon so they can start recommending books of their own to our patrons. Many others rediscover a love of reading that they lost after leaving school.

A few come to recognize the potential of books to transform lives. We will never forget one particularly colorful trusty who came to work every morning with a new poem about the library. Our personal favorite, which we heard him intone at bookcart once or twice, went something like this:

"Fee fie foe fum. If you stop reading, you'll stay dumb!"

Because trusties work alongside paid staff, they are the inmates you must watch most closely. Trusties have infinitely more opportunities for mischief than other inmates. And working side by side, you do get to know them better than your other patrons. It can be extremely tempting, therefore, to grant special privileges or even reward good work with favors. The results can be catastrophic. We advice you not to grant privileges to anyone, regardless of how deserving. Privileges are the province of the facility administrators and officers, not the librarians. And we cannot state strongly enough that you should never, ever reward the good work of trusties with favors. When asked, you may simply say, "Your hard work is excellent, but you know I cannot do that." You must also be extremely careful about what you say to and in front of inmate workers. Gossip spreads like wildfire in jail; don't say anything within earshot that you don't want to hear back six times in the next week.

Training trusties is a little different perhaps than training paid staff with library backgrounds, but it is remarkably similar to training paid staff with no library experience. They must be trained to respect the library's purpose and mission, coached on how to uphold it, and warned about compromising it through illicit behavior. They must be advised about privacy issues.

Obviously, they need to be trained on how to do their assigned tasks, and you should expect reasonably high-quality work from them, especially if you hired them yourself. Clearly state your expectations of them to diminish any misunderstanding about their role. Working in the library can be daunting for trusties, particularly if they did not choose the assignment. Assure them you want them to do a good job and that you'll welcome all of their questions about how to do it.

Exploiting Type A

Some trusties will quickly exhibit talents and skills that you can utilize beyond their normal duties. We had a trusty several years ago who was beyond obsessive-compulsive when it came to shelving. Our collection is small enough—and our staff have, by and large, been Type B enough—that we've always been fairly blasé about precise placement; as long as all the western authors beginning with "L" are in the same general vicinity, we don't get too bent. But this young trusty walked in one day and within a few hours declared the shelving situation a disgrace that he would personally see to remedying. Our collection didn't have a single volume out of place the entire time he worked for us. It hasn't looked as good since!

The Pursuit of Excellence

One prison librarian told us a story about an inmate worker she hired who barely knew how to type and had never used a computer. But he was chipper and had a sense of humor and, she discovered, was willing to learn. She worked with him for two and a half years, during which time he learned to type by writing memos. If he gave her a memo that wasn't up to snuff, she'd send it back for corrections as many times as it took to get it perfect. Ten years after his release, he called the librarian to tell her he'd landed a job with a real estate company that hired him because of his excellent office skills!

So how do you keep workers motivated who receive no or scarcely any pay, will never climb up the professional ladder (in your facility), cannot be provided with material incentives or privileges, and who may be working for you under protest? The response is the same as if you are supervising paid staff. You encourage the right actions and behaviors through positive reinforcement and say thank you as soon as you notice the good work they are doing.

Keep in mind that the average prisoner's self-esteem is zero or worse. When you praise their work, they feel better about themselves, their contribution to the library, and the library itself. The power of thanks cannot be overemphasized.

 [Your] words may carry more power than you realize...A word of acceptance and encouragement, of approval and pride, can go to the deepest places of a young man's or woman's heart and result in blessing and healing. They can bring hope, significance and a sense of identity. It means more than I think we will ever know this side of heaven. Just a simple, "I believe in you!" can change a person's life forever (Spitale 2002).

"Tap into people's dignity and they will do anything for you. Ignore it, and they won't lift a finger" (Thomas Friedan, quoted in Gilligan 2003).

Saying thank you costs us nothing and does nothing to imperil our own boundaries or safety. We have to watch trusties so closely to catch them if they do wrong, we should also be clueing in to what they do right. They, like paid staff, should be immediately recognized for their efforts and achievements. The rewards for paying that kind of attention more than compensates for taking the time to do so.

References

Gilligan, J. 2003. Shame, guilt, and violence. *Social research* (Winter). Retrieved May 14, 2004 from http://www.findarticles.com.

North Carolina Department of Correction. n.d. *Volunteers in prison.* Retrieved September 12, 2005 from http://www.doc.state.nc.us/DOP/Volunter.htm.

Spitale, L. 2002. *Prison ministry.* Nashville: Broadman and Holman Publishers.

Volunteers of America. 2004. *Finding a location near you.* Retrieved September 12, 2005 from http://volunteersofamerica.org/ext_locations.cfm.

Services and Programs

A lot of people, ourselves included, believe that the concept of libraries as information storehouses is obsolete. Sticking to the brick-and-mortar concept of libraries is a surefire recipe for the extinction of public libraries as we know them today. Rather, public libraries need to reenvision themselves as community meeting places, neutral sites for debate and for avocational learning opportunities, places that epitomize the concept of "people's university." This, we imagine, is the future of public libraries.

But aside from assuring the continuing existence of the public library entity, library programs provide an opportunity for building rapport between patrons and librarians, a necessary ingredient for sustaining the intercommunity dialog that keeps libraries relevant to the populations they serve. Programs are often special events, so they stimulate people to move outside their regular routines. Programs connect people with new ideas, to a larger world, in a high-impact way not necessarily achievable (or desirable) by people too busy to read a book or people who don't enjoy reading or people who can't read for whatever reason. Perhaps most importantly, programs catch nontraditional library users: nonreaders and the economically disadvantaged. For these reasons, programs allow libraries to meaningfully connect with all kinds of people in the community in new and creative ways.

Probably the biggest difference between public library and correctional library programs is the consciousness correctional library program planners have of the potential impact of programs on the participants' quality of life, both while incarcerated and afterwards. Writing about a series of Socratic philosophy classes he taught to inmates of a Texas state prison, Professor Lawrence T. Jablecki reports, "Most of my students 'see,' for the first time, the profound truth of Socrates' doctrine that the possession of knowledge and wisdom can lead to a radical and positive change in both thinking and behavior." This understanding was made possible in spite of the fact that most of Dr. Jablecki's inmate students come from intellectually and economically impoverished backgrounds that afford them few insights into noncriminal ways of living. "Humanities courses . . . are truly revelations, showing ways of living and thinking that they have not encountered before" (Jablecki 2000).

Of programs that diminish a released inmate's chances of recidivism and bolster their chances for better employment, Maryland's Correctional Education Libraries Coordinator, Glennor Shirley, states, "About 15,000 [Maryland] inmates go out every year. I prefer my tax dollars to go toward programs that will help the prisoner become a taxpayer later on" (*Connecting Inside* 2003). The Urban Institute, in a 2002 research report, cites preliminary evidence that prison programs, including educational and employment services to which libraries can contribute, can effectively reduce recidivism (Lawrence et al. 2002).

Logistical Considerations

In correctional libraries, there is often a resistance to the idea of offering the kinds of "life-enriching" programs that public libraries commonly offer. This resistance sometimes comes from facility staff and administration, but just as often (if not more so), it comes from potential program presenters themselves. By definition, our patrons are "bad guys." We have invited presenters to tell stories or lead workshops only to have them refuse, not because they didn't feel safe, but because they opposed on principle the idea of "rewarding" criminals.

Another difference correctional facilities sometimes face in providing programs is the number of logistical hoops to jump through to get approval. Even eager presenters can be put off by the level of security scrutiny they may have to undergo in order to even set foot in the building. Background checks are only the beginning. If a presenter comes in with a lot of props, there will be elaborate security checks and some of the props may be surrendered. It's hard to keep presenters excited about coming to the aid of prisoners if they're made to feel like criminals themselves!

If prisoners cannot visit the library itself, as is the case in our jail, but programs are still allowable, scheduling the common rooms can be a time-consuming negotiation process. The dividends programs pay in terms of morale and library usage more than compensate for the effort. Also, counselors or officers may need to give their approval for interested inmates to participate. This, too, might require some negotiation. The logistics involved with planning and presenting programs behind bars must be considered, along with your regular work load and energy level, in a way not necessarily considered by public librarians offering programs for their own patrons, so keep that in mind as you make your plans.

User Needs

By now, you've probably heard enough about user needs surveys. We agree that they are time-consuming and often tedious. We also acknowledge that a lot of public libraries seem to get along perfectly fine without ever systemizing their user needs survey process; many of them do little more than keep an eye on community happenings as reported in the local papers and an ear open for patron comments and come up with perfectly respectable programs for their communities. But we think really working at getting your patrons to identify what they want from the library is especially important in jail and prison. This is partly because, as we mentioned in Chapter 3, the shared demographics between most inmates and most librarians are rather limited. Many of us don't know who our patrons really are, and if we intend to serve them well, we need to put forth the effort to understand them and their needs. Another reason is perhaps even more important and may even be viewed as a value-added service of the correctional library. By surveying our patrons, by encouraging them to dialog with us about their library service, we acknowledge their humanity and respect their potential for contributing to something worthwhile. Many inmates have nothing to say about what books the library decides to buy because they are not interested in reading; many of them never read on the outside and have not yet discovered the joys of the printed word while incarcerated. But we're willing to bet that almost all of them have seen a movie or listened to a record at some point in their lives—and enjoyed the experience. We'd be willing to wager that they've petted a dog or seen a nature program about wild animals that interested them. Most of them will have doodled stick figures in math class. Many of them have children, spouses, partners, or parents they want to have better relationships with. Almost all of them have played board games, and many play *Wheel of Fortune* better than the contestants. These people, if given the opportunity, will have wonderful ideas for programs that may catch the imagination of even the most reluctant library nonusers!

So where do you go for ideas, and how do you enlist presenters? The weekend section of the local newspaper is a great place to start. Check out the listed events for the week for inspiration. Get on the mailing lists of local museums (even the smallest ones), zoos, community colleges and vocational schools, recreational centers, public libraries, and bookstores. Other nonprofit organizations, like churches, animal shelters, and schools, often do outreach of their own, and often for free. Potential presenters come from the ranks of librarians and other community members. Local business people hold potential, so you may consider attending chamber of commerce meetings to make connections. Don't forget to scout around inside your facility itself; facility staff and prisoners themselves have a lot to offer. One interesting program idea is to invite Toastmasters into your facility to teach residents and employees how to do good programs. Often, the biggest fear people have about presenting in jail is the fear of public speaking!

If you zero in on people who are already doing programs, you will eliminate one barrier right off the bat. When asking a presenter to consider coming to jail, be sure to emphasize how much more meaningful their expertise can be to prisoners and tell them about how appreciative inmate audiences usually are. If you have regular presenters who are willing to do a little evangelizing for you, ask them if you can refer potential presenters to them for personal testimonials about their experiences. The important thing is to keep the focus on the experience for both prisoner and presenter. Perhaps what makes programs particularly successful and rewarding behind bars are the human connections programs make possible.

The Cardinal Rules of Program Planning

We believe in six cardinal rules of doing programs in correctional facilities. Cardinal Rule #1: Get administration's approval first. Cardinal Rule #2: Keep everybody informed. Cardinal Rule #3: Never abandon your presenter. Cardinal Rule #4: Don't cancel regular library services to put on a program. Cardinal Rule #5: Consider the population movement in your facility. Cardinal Rule #6: Consider your staff turnover.

The importance of the first cardinal rule is amusingly elaborated upon in the sidebar. We should also mention that many facilities have "programs" departments to bring in visiting pastors, AA leaders, and tutors. Because of this, you need to make sure you're not reinventing someone else's wheel or overstepping into another department's territory. Consulting not only with your commanding officer but also with the head of the programs department allows you to avoid unnecessary duplication of effort. It also gives you an opportunity to dialog, particularly with the programs staff, about ways your two departments might support each other.

The second cardinal rule will encourage continued goodwill between you and the officers. If you have a program scheduled, particularly if it's being presented in the living units and not the library, get down there and talk to the officers who will be on duty that day. Tell them about the program. If they ask why you're doing it, tell them the expected outcomes or benefits in terms that will be meaningful to them. (For example, "We will be giving away as many paperbacks as these guys can carry back to their cells. That's a lot of quiet-time reading they'll be doing in the wee hours, instead of stuffing sheets down the toilets.") Ask them if they have any ideas about how to make the program run smoothly or any concerns about particular participants.

Keeping people informed doesn't end with the officers. You have to make sure the inmates know what's coming up or you won't have an audience! Particularly to patrons you know well, personal invitations are the best way to fill seats. Zero in on those pod fathers and mothers, the gatekeeper inmates who know a lot of people, exercise a lot of influence, and will be galvanized by your acknowledgement of those attributes to enlist participants on your behalf. Depending on the kind of program you're offering, other civilian staff could drum up interest. If it's a program on religion, the chaplain should be informed. If it's a program on diet or fitness, tell the nurses.

Goodwill goes a long way to keeping the doors open.

As for the third cardinal rule, we encourage you to go back in your mind to your first exciting hours on the job in your facility. (If you do not work in a correctional facility, please review Chapter 4: Understanding the System. You may also wish to rent *The Birdman of Alcatraz* to get a good grasp of the exhilarating atmosphere behind bars.) Now picture your presenter. Perhaps he is a college professor who has volunteered to teach a poetry class or an early childhood literacy specialist coming to coach inmates on the importance of encouraging their children to read. These people have no concept of the culture inside a correctional facility, and you must guide them. They also have no idea how subtly manipulative inmates can be, so you must chaperone them. You must also be the bridge between the earnest (and probably slightly nervous) presenter and the interested (but perhaps somewhat skeptical) audience.

Another aspect to taking care of your presenters is to prepare them in advance for the scrutiny they will undergo by the security staff. You need to reassure them that no one is implying that they're a criminal, but that for everyone inside to be treated fairly and to stay safe, everybody gets the red carpet treatment. So they might want to leave any suspicious-looking electronic devices like iPods and camera phones and any potentially incendiary print materials, like ALA's resolution against the PATRIOT Act, in their cars.

Your presenters, especially if they're planning on returning, will have a much easier time of it if you introduce them to other facility staff. Obviously, you will escort them in and out of the facility, but try to budget enough time to pause and introduce the presenter to some of the officers, key civilian staff, and your library staff. Presenters already feel like strangers in a strange land, so following a few simple social niceties will go a long way toward rehumanizing the environment and putting them at ease.

The fourth cardinal rule speaks to priorities. As much as we may believe in the power of programs, you are still the librarian and your role still has a lot to do with books. If you are a one-person operation, carving out the time to enlist, schedule, and chaperone outside presenters may be beyond the scope of what you can reasonably accomplish. Should you work longer hours to get programs to your patrons? That's entirely up to you, but remember, the burnout factor is powerful in jail and prison, and the best cure for that is to go home on time. Should you cancel regular services to accommodate a program schedule? We don't think so. Mainly, because there are ways of doing programs that don't require you to.

Mother, May I?

Don't do anything without running it past your commanding officer first! Sometimes, seemingly simple and straightforward programs can generate firestorms of controversy. For example, some years ago, following our fabulously successful book talks on "Macho Fiction," we decided to follow up with a series of book talks on Colorado mystery authors. The talk had been presented to much acclaim on the public library side, and we knew it would be a hit in jail.

So imagine our surprise when our cheerful recommendation to present this program was met with serious consternation on the part of the facility administrators.

"This isn't appropriate subject matter," one lieutenant said.

"What do you mean?" we asked, genuinely perplexed. "These are all local authors. We have a lot of them in our collection and have never had any complaints."

Turns out, the lieutenant took umbrage to the title of the book talk, "Rocky Mountain Murder." And upon reflection, we could kind of see his point. After all, in a Colorado county jail housing several hundred violent felons, there was perhaps enough "Rocky Mountain murder" talk going on already.

Seeing our gloomy dejection at the prospect of not doing our book talk, the lieutenant suggested a compromise. If we renamed the program, he said, we could go for it. We renamed it "Mystery Fiction by Colorado Authors," and it turned out to be one of the best attended series we've ever had!

The fifth cardinal rule addresses that pesky population overturn issue that most obviously differentiates jail from prison. In prison, where you can count on the stability of the population (in terms of their movement in and out of the facility—we reserve judgment on any other brand of stability), classes and seminars and projects that meet over a span of time are perfectly doable. Not so in jail. Some years ago, we decided to offer a three-week series on parenting for the women inmates. We started with twelve ladies, although in the ninety minutes we'd set aside for the program, two of the ladies were called out to meet with their lawyers. At the second session one week later, six of the original twelve attended, with the absent six either released, at the doctor, in other programs, or at court. By the third session, only three ladies remained. The experiment proved to us that one-shot programs lasting about an hour were the most appropriate format within the demands of the jail environment.

The sixth and last cardinal rule requires that you turn the spotlight on your staffing situation. Even if you're in a prison and you can count on all your program participants being in attendance for twenty years to life, if your staff turnover is high, complex or long-term programs will be harder to sustain.

Recreational Programs

Some programs have an obvious library angle, like literacy programs and reference services. But the really fun ones are the life-enriching recreational programs. These are the kinds of programs that might be offered by another department, so make sure before you get too involved in the planning process. They are also the kinds of programs that might be a little trickier to sell to a reluctant administration. Some arguments that have worked well for us are:

- This program has morale-building potential
- This program was successfully presented at (insert facility name here)

- This program will help the inmates stay connected to their families
- This program encourages constructive creativity/critical thinking
- This program builds life skills
- This program is free (administrators love this one)

Nancy Pitts' chapter on programs in *Libraries Inside* is a treasure trove of ideas and inspiration for anyone interested in prison programs, covering everything from writing and bibliotherapy, to athletics and crafts, to theater and pet therapy, to health fairs and horticulture. Kathleen de la Peña McCook's 2004 article in *Reference and User Services Quarterly* gives a good overview of the programs many public libraries offer to their county jails. To their good suggestions, we add the following:

Games

> Trivia contest
> Poetry slam
> Checkers championship
> Classic board games tournament

Books

> Discussion groups
> Movie tie-ins
> Dr. Seuss Read-A-Thon
> Summer reading programs
> Theme-driven book talks
> Read-to-your-children video- or audiotaping program
> Author talks
> Writing classes
> Writing clubs
> One Book, One Community
> Read alouds
> Readers' theater
> Comic books club

Not Requiring Much Staff Time

> Poetry and art publication
> Bookmark art contest

Daily or weekly crossword puzzle challenges
Daily or weekly word jumbles or word searches

Animals

Birds of prey
Reptiles
Insects
Visiting pets from animal shelters

Holidays

Martin Luther King's birthday
J.R.R. Tolkien's birthday
Four seasons
Hispanic history month
Black history month
"One world" multicultural programs in November and
December
Ghost stories
Day of the Dead
Banned Books Week

Crafts and Fine Arts

Storytellers
Music and art appreciation
Film festival
Miming class
Origami
Drawing

Lifestyles and Life Skills

How to write a business letter
Balancing a checkbook
Budgeting
Critical thinking
Parenting from a distance
Basic computer skills

Job seeking strategies
Interviewing skills
How to write a college admissions essay

Spirituality and Well-being

Meditation
Yoga
Journaling
Dream interpretation

Some of the most unlikely things become the most popular programs or program elements behind bars, so don't do anything to limit your thinking about the possibilities. There will be enough roadblocks with the logistics without you censoring your imagination!

A Cup of Sugar from My Dear Granny

Our favorite example of a surprisingly popular program is the storytelling part of our hugely successful "Begin With Books in Jail" program. Essentially, the program's focus is teaching inmates about the importance of getting their own children to read, but part of the program is a demonstration of a children's storytime. Close your eyes (after you read this) and envision thirty worldly, rough, and scraggly men in a room with a children's librarian and a grandmotherly volunteer. The volunteer, in a voice showing the wear of age, begins to read *The True Story of the Three Little Pigs*. Two things should give you pause as you consider this. First, these guys are being read a *children's book*. Second, it's a book that ends with an unfair criminal conviction. (If you've not read the book, the irony of that last statement will be lost on you.)

Amazingly and without fail, this story captivates our patrons by the third page. Men who've been in the system for years for strings of awful offenses sit absolutely enrapt. The obvious hook is the connection to their children. "My kid has got to read that book!" they exclaim. But we think something else is at work here, too. How many of them were read to as children? Those who were get to experience for five minutes the pleasure of having a trusted adult share quality time through the medium of a book. Those who weren't read to as children get to experience it for the first time and imagine the possibilities for their own kids.

Programs that Might Not "Go Over"

When considering the needs and interests of your audience, you must also keep the security priorities of the facility in mind. In order to minimize some of the guesswork, we have compiled a list of program concepts that might be better left on the other side of the wall.

- The Teddy Bears' Tattoo Party
- How to Stage an Escape with Things You Probably Have Around Your Cell
- I Do Not Want to Get Up Today: 101 Ways to Fake a Fever, the Flu, or a Grand Mal Seizure
- Murder Mystery Party: How to Host a Homicide
- "Find the Sally Port Key" Scavenger Hunt
- Urban Seuss Readers Theater Presents: Horton Hatches a Conspiracy Theory

Literacy Programs

Literacy programs are probably the easiest and most obvious program opportunities for correctional libraries. Because they provide opportunities for the librarian to collaborate with educators and outside agencies, you may not have to do anything more than get volunteers in and out of the facility and provide space for them to work.

Because many correctional facilities support literacy programming as an integral part of inmate continuing education, it often falls to the education department and not directly to the library to make it happen. If this is the case in your facility, the library will have more of a support role. Providing quiet reading spaces and materials for emerging readers to practice with, in addition to encouragement of their progress, are all nonprogram ways to support what the education department is already doing.

But there are programs you can provide above and beyond the classroom activities provided by many correctional education departments. In particular, correctional libraries can support *family literacy*. This can be as simple as helping inmates write letters to their children about their own reading experiences and the importance of reading. Or it can be as elaborate as the Maryland state prison system's family literacy events, where children of prisoners actually visit their incarcerated parents for a day of reading and literacy activities.

More and more jails and prisons offer reading outreach programs every year. Typically, volunteers with video recorders and/or tape recorders tape inmates reading books to their children. The videos and tapes are then sent to the children. At our facility, we offer this program twice yearly, at Christmas and at the beginning of the public library's summer reading program. Throughout the year, our early childhood literacy coordinator visits the inmates with a lively presentation on the impact of reading on the brain development of young children. In addition to emphasizing the need for children's literacy, she promotes adult recreational reading. "If your kids know you are reading," she says, "they will want to imitate what you're doing." It's especially meaningful when incarcerated parents have the opportunity to read the same books their children read, as a way of staying connected with their children's lives on the outside. This is also another way of helping emerging adult readers save face when they're reading children's books. "My kid is reading this in school and I want to know what she's up to" will shut up almost any bullying elitist.

Law Library

Reference Service

The ways in which the provisions of *Bounds v. Smith* manifest in correctional facilities are legion, which leads us to scratch our heads sometimes about why any facility would even bother. According to the ruling of this landmark case:

> The Supreme Court ruled that correctional facilities were duty-bound to provide offenders with on-site prison libraries that contain adequately stocked legal collections, although an alternative was allowed. Under the alternative, in lieu of providing the on-site law library, the prison would be required to make available to inmates trained individuals who knew legal research and writing procedures so that they might assist the indigent and the illiterate in drafting legal proceedings (Wilhelmus 1999).

The interpretations of "adequately stocked" and the "alternative" vary from the provision of a few copies of the state statutes to full-service law libraries run by legal paraprofessionals. Somewhere in between are law libraries operated by librarians, and even these run the gamut from poorly lit rooms with a few battered reference books and a place to sit and take notes, to state-of-the-art LANs and classrooms where detailed legal research courses are taught by experienced law librarians.

Legal research is one of those areas that strike terror into the hearts of many otherwise stalwart librarians. For one thing, legal research is hard! The law has its own vocabulary, and let's face it, lawyers and judges are the kings and queens of the interminable run-on, semicolon-dense sentence. (Those of us with an inclination toward paranoia sometimes swear that those paragraph-length sentences saturated with inscrutable legal terms are specifically designed to make nonlawyers admire the level of education required to practice law.) Legal research, like medical and tax research, also carries a certain measure of risk for the nonprofessional conducting it. Where do you draw the line between reference help and "the unauthorized practice of law"?

In jail and prison, helping inmates with their legal research also requires you to mine the details about some pretty lurid crimes. Can you do an in-depth reference interview with someone whose housing classification tells you he's been accused of sexual assault on a child? This kind of situation doesn't come up much, but can be extremely upsetting when you realize what a patron is telling you. Can you treat such a case with the professional detachment you'd bring to a reference question about high-altitude baking? In spite of the general tenor of humor we've presented thus far in this book, we are not being flip in this case. You must be able to discuss the details of violent crimes with your patrons as unflappably as you would discuss the details of a fourth-grader's homework assignment on penguins.

This sort of situation doesn't come up if your library service is strictly recreational in nature. Many jail and prison libraries do not expect their librarians to offer law library service; instead, they leave law library to legal professionals. In the state of Colorado's prisons, the librarians don't even have keys to the law libraries. The advantage of this to the facility is that they will never have to worry about "unauthorized practice of law" by nonprofessional library staff. The inmates benefit from professional legal help. And the librarians benefit from not having to deal with a particularly intimidating brand of reference service!

So we ask the obvious question: if you are not legally bound by *Bounds v. Smith* to even provide a law library, and you are not professionally bound to staff it with librarians even if your facility does provide one, why in the world would you want to? After all, it's difficult work and sometimes very dull, it carries a certain amount of legal risk because the line between reference and advice is sometimes unclear, and frankly, paralegals make more money to do it than we do. In response, we offer two arguments in favor of staffing law libraries with librarians. First, if you think legal research is difficult for you, put yourself in your patrons' shoes. They probably do not have your level of education, so the vocabulary you struggle with is absolute Greek to them. They are anxiously awaiting a decision about their lives—to convict or not convict—that they desperately want determined in their favor. They are part of a criminal justice system they profoundly distrust. They need training in how to think about their situations so they can think about how to frame their research questions, and they need coaching and encouragement to achieve both ends. Lawyers and paralegals aren't necessarily trained to conduct an effective reference interview or provide bibliographic instruction. Librarians are.

Secondly, and more simply, we believe that providing law library service to your inmate patrons fulfills a very basic function of librarians. We assist patrons with informed decision making. Inmates by their very nature have often lived lives marked by extravagantly poor decision making; once incarcerated, they often face the hardest set of decisions of their lives. How do I beat this charge? What will I do if I don't? How will I take care of my kids while I'm in here? Do I trust my public defender? If not, what should I do? While librarians cannot and should not answer any of these questions, we believe that we are duty-bound to provide our patrons with the research tools they need to answer the questions for themselves.

We don't need to make it harder than it is. Essentially, we just need reliable and current resources and the understanding of how to use them. This isn't fundamentally different from learning to use reference resources in the public library. You have to know the general content of the material and the audience to which it's addressed. You have to know how the indexing works. You should know how different resources supplement each other. And you must help the patron understand his or her own question. We often hear "I want to sue the sheriff's office!" Okay, we'll ask. Why? "Because I was the only tall guy in the lineup!" All right then. The first question, then, is what does a fair lineup consist of? What constitutes witness credibility? Answering legal questions is always, always process-oriented. This applies to both civil and criminal law.

Training for Legal Research

In prison, you can offer as many legal research classes as you can dream up. It's more difficult, as so many things are, in jail. Legal research is complex; a one-hour crash course could do more to confuse than clarify, but as we've said before, multi-part classes simply aren't feasible with a highly dynamic population. For a great model of how to teach prisoners to conduct their own legal research, we highly recommend you read William

Mongelli's article entitled "De-Mystifying Legal Research for Prisoners" (1994), keeping in mind that its design is prison-specific. For those of us in jail, Mongelli's article might seem to point out the hopelessness of even attempting to educate our patrons to research the law. But don't despair! You can help your patrons too. Some very succinct (no more than one page, and keep the text minimal) handouts about basic criminal or civil proceedings in your state, information sheets with commonly requested contact information (especially the names and courtroom numbers of judges), glossaries of commonly used legal terms, and quick how-tos on using the most helpful books or databases can be a reasonable substitute for classes.

None of this works without your own ability to guide your patrons through the process. And you must teach them well, because you can't do their research for them. That would cross the line into "unauthorized practice of law." If they need you to look something up for them, that's one thing. But the burden must be on them, and we must give them the tools—which include competencies—to fight their own cause.

Their training is built upon your own training, which as likely as not you will have to take the initiative to attain. Don't think you have to do this in a vacuum or that you even need to seek training geared toward librarians. Basic classes for paralegals and beginning law students are often open to anyone. Contact local bar associations for course offerings. Your local community college might offer introductory law courses. At the very least, you are looking for good legal research materials for the nonprofessional and teachable techniques for using those materials. Once you have your titles in hand, practice with them. All joking aside, we include in this section the ten most common legal reference questions of jail inmates; keep in mind that prisoners' questions can be different, because they have already been convicted. Also, some of the questions we hear most often pertain to civil matters, not criminal ones. Take your reference books and practice answering these most common questions, and you will have achieved 80 percent of "doing law library good."

Erica and Sheila's Top Ten List of Questions Asked by Jail Inmates

10. "What is the range of penalties for a conviction on my charge?" (Also phrased as "How long can they sentence me for?" and "How much time am I going to get?")

9. "How do I fire my lawyer?" (A corollary question is "How do I go *pro se*?")

8. "How to I transfer power of attorney/custody of my kids while I'm in here?"

7. "How do I get married/divorced while I'm in here?"

6. "How is good time credit/pre-sentence confinement credit applied?"

5. "How do I file a lawsuit against the facility?"

4. "I need information about the prison/community corrections program where I'm being sent."

3. "How do I challenge the credibility of a witness/material evidence against me?"

2. "How do I get a writ to another county?" (A corollary is "Why was my writ to this other county rejected?")

And the number one legal reference question asked by jail inmates:

1. "HOW DO I GET OUT OF HERE???"

The moment every reference librarian dreads most is hitting the wall with a patron's question, where you've exhausted every resource you can think of and still haven't come up with a satisfactory answer. As librarians providing legal reference help, that moment happens all the time. Give yourself a break and be gentle with your patrons, who are going to be very disappointed when you hit that wall. After all, the more success you have in helping them do their research, the more they are going to expect of you. That's okay! And it's also okay to know your limits. When you reach that point, remember your Customer Service 101 training: empathize with the patron's frustration and focus on what their legitimate options are. If you can't answer their question, can you refer them to another resource? Is there someone else in the facility who might be able to help? Do you know an inmate whose knowledge of the law you trust enough to pass stumpers along to? If these options don't work or aren't feasible, the final word on the matter is, "This question needs to be answered by a lawyer."

References

Connecting inside. 2003. *Library journal* 125(5). Retrieved January 3, 2005 from Infotrac Web General Reference Center Gold database.

de la Peña McCook, K. 2004. Public libraries and people in jail. *Reference and user services quarterly* 44(1), 26–30.

Jablecki, L. T. 2000. Prison inmates meet Socrates. *Humanist* 60(3). Retrieved May 9, 2005 from http://www.findarticles.com/p/articles/mi_m1374/is_3_60/ai_62111876#continue.

Lawrence, S., D. P. Mears, G. Dubin, and J. Travis. 2002. *The practice and promise of prison programming* (May). Urban Institute Justice Policy Center. Retrieved November 17, 2004 from http://www.urban.org.

Mongelli, W. D. 1994. De-mystifying legal research for prisoners. *Law library journal* 86(259), 277–298.

Pitts, N. 1995. Programs. In R. J. Rubin and D. S. Suvak (Eds.), *Libraries inside: A practical guide for prison librarians* (105–188). Jefferson, NC: McFarland and Company.

Wilhelmus, D. W. 1999. Where have all the law libraries gone? *Corrections Today* 6. Retrieved January 3, 2005 from InfoTrac Web database.

10

Budget

Budgeting and planning go hand in hand, and it's hard to say with which to begin. On one hand, beginning with your budget can provide a rational framework within which to make decisions about how your library will—or can—grow and change, especially if you have access to reliable financial projections several years out. But going about it in that way can also limit your thinking. Regardless of what your current budget is or where it comes from, regardless of economic recession and flat revenues, you owe it to your patrons to think beyond present circumstances. Think big, and the money will follow.

In this section, we will not go into lavish detail about how to create and manage a budget, because there are other books out there written by experts in such matters. What we will focus on here is how you should think about your budget in terms of what the budget is intended to accomplish, how you make a winning sales pitch to those who hold the purse strings, ways to deal with budget shortfalls, and where to go for more money.

Your Plan, Their Money

We believe your budget is part and parcel of your planning, not the other way around. Begin with a vision for your library. Then do your homework: What is the vision for the facility as a whole? What are the short- and long-term plans and goals of the sheriff or warden? Your task is to figure out how to marry their goals with your own. You also need to know what you might be up against. Is there a new sheriff whose election platform was his "tough on criminals" penal philosophy? Did administration just hire an adult education specialist to hugely expand the education program? Has the jail's budget been slated for demolition next year in order to put more deputies on patrol?

You also need a solid understanding of where exactly the money is coming from. This acknowledges the inevitable politics of money and is particularly important if your library is funded from multiple revenue streams, as ours is. For example, county taxes pay for our law library. So the people who are paying for it don't see an immediate return on their investment. The pot of gold is also parceled out to other county departments, many of which are more visible and valued by the general tax-paying public. Defending budget requests to augment our law library has to be treated as a political issue; we are stewards of tax dollars and must be able to, if not demonstrate real outcomes that benefit the public, at least compellingly demonstrate the ramifications of not receiving the funds we request.

But our recreational reading collection is paid for out of commissary funds. If the community purse is lined with dollars, the commissary purse is lined with potato chips. The amount of money generated by commissary (also called canteen) services to inmates is staggering. And that money is usually reinvested back into programs of immediate benefit to the paying customers. These include educational and chaplaincy services, as well as libraries. Asking for more money out of this coffer means competing with the people you work with every day. Talk about political! But here we're referring to office politics. Going back to the point we harped on in Part I about relationships being the cornerstone of successful correctional library service, you need to treat your colleagues' budget requests with respect while firmly asserting the importance of your own.

Presenting and Defending Your Budget

Stating Your Case

Don't get us wrong—it can be hard asking for money, especially when you're requesting changes or additions to your budget. We are reminded of a wonderful sound byte we heard at an ALA conference session on public library outreach: There's no such thing as a free lunch. But there ARE worthy investments!

You must present your budget proposal in terms that reflect the values and goals of the decision makers. And since we're talking about jail and prison, their values and goals might be very different from yours, at least on the surface. But there are corrections values and goals that you can support with your library materials and programs. Security needs can be met by keeping inmates constructively occupied through the provision of books and by offering enriching programs to improve morale. The provision of adequate library staff to meet inmates' research needs and support their educational goals might help the facility avoid lawsuits! Remember what is at stake for decision makers and tailor your arguments to those things.

Courting Strategic Allies

Working to expand your budget is an investment unto itself. Here, the quality of your relationships within the facility really can make or break your operation. We have a motto: Never get on the wrong side of the person who signs the checks. Your lieutenant may authorize the signing of the checks, but the folks in accounts receivable take care of the details. You need allies in that department. As with any relationship-building, emphasizing your own trustworthiness by being reliable, responsible, and honest works particularly well with the highly detail-oriented and deadline-conscious staff who pay the bills.

Even the best plan supported by a good budget requires follow-through to be successful. Make sure you follow all facility purchasing procedures to the letter. Prioritize money matters by sending invoices and packing slips back to the finance office at once so they can get the bills paid on time. (Accountants don't respond well to hate mail from vendors.) Keep your records accessible and in good order. Be responsive if anyone from the finance department asks you for information or paperwork.

Life is sure a lot easier when people like you.

Another way of building credibility is to approach your budget planning process with integrity. There are good arguments for and against padding your figures, but you'd better be prepared to use the money constructively if you get it. Unspent or misdirected funds send a loud and clear message, not only to the finance department but to your administrators, that you are not entirely serious about your own plans. Obviously, padding the numbers is culturally expected, if not entirely acceptable, in many organizations, perhaps especially in government ones. If yours is one of these, consider carefully if playing the numbers game will, in the long run, serve your patrons better than honesty.

What to Do When the Money Is Not Forthcoming

Let's face it. Money is a cyclical being. Even if you work in one of the handful of private correctional facilities, and inevitably if you work in a government facility, the economy will impact your inflows for good or ill. There will be years of feast and years of famine. Often, we create programs and services in fat years that come under fire in the lean years. What do you do when you're working with a flat or decreasing budget?

Before going on the offensive, you must pause and answer several questions. The more time you spend with these questions, the better prepared you will be to act. Consider the following:

- What are we doing well that we don't need to be doing at all?
- What can we outsource?
- Can we change the way we do things?
- What is being cut throughout the facility?
- What is being retained and why? (This will give you an idea about the priorities of administration, to which you can tailor your own arguments for funds.) What are we doing that could be funded by grants?
- Is staffing an issue? Can we make use of interns and volunteers?
- Whom can we collaborate with (either inside or outside) to save money?

Necessity being the mother of invention, we have found within our jail library and our public library counterpart that times of economic stress often result in some of our most creative problem solving. These times also reward collaboration.

There will be other times when the money you want is not forthcoming, even if your requisite services are well-funded. What do you do, for example, if your program's budget is spent by September, but you've just heard that Clive Barker will be in town for a series of Hellraiser programs in October? And he'd love to come visit you in jail . . . for a reasonable fee?

Grants

If you successfully win a grant, it will seem like a heaven-sent shower of free money . . . for about two days. Then reality kicks in: grants are hard work! The fact is, most grants, even teeny weeny ones, come from organizations that want to see demonstrated results. Before applying for a grant, be sure to read the fine print. What will be expected of you in terms of reporting? The expectations can be considerable, and meeting them can be time-consuming. If you know you don't have the time or staff resources to write four quarterly assessments, quantify your outcomes, and compile a final report, look for a grant with simpler reporting procedures.

Also consider what is and is not appropriately funded by grants. They should be projects or services that don't need to be sustained over time, such as special programs, the addition of nonserial collections, or new equipment. You're looking for one-shot or short-shot things. Using grant money to pay for regular library staff or your newspaper subscription is a risky business. What happens to those things when the grant money runs out? Too often there is no budget to sustain them, and they go out the proverbial window.

Not all grant requests are received the same. Foundations absolutely love funding anything that meets any of the following criteria (and the more criteria your project meets, the better your request will look):

- Innovative
- Humanistic (educational, life-enriching)
- Has quantifiable outcomes
- Not unique to your setting; in other words, can be replicated by others
- Showy (something to put a plaque on)

For more information about how to write grant proposals and to whom to write them, see the "Resources" section at the end of this chapter.

If you apply for grants to supplement your allocated budget, be sure the decision makers know about it. One of the wonderful things about writing grants is that sometimes the exercise pulls in money from the very administrators who told you there was no more money! When the decision makers know you are diligently seeking to make something happen (or effectively making happen) that they haven't funded themselves, they often get the message about how serious you are about making your library successful. Successful operations tend to become more successful because people are willing to invest in them further. Grant writing demonstrates a commitment that speaks well to decision makers, and those same folks just might surprise you down the line by finding money for you that didn't seem to be there before.

Resources

Gerding, S. and P. Mackeller. 2006. *Grants for libraries: A how-to-do-it manual.* New York: Neal-Schuman Publishers.

Hoffman, F. W. (editor). 1999. *Grantsmanship for small libraries and school library media centers.* Englewood, CO: Libraries Unlimited.

Reed, S. G., B. Nawalinski, and A. Peterson. 2004. *101+ great ideas for libraries and friends: Marketing, fundraising, friends development, and more.* New York: Neal-Schuman Publishers.

Taft Group for the American Library Association. 2005. *The big book of library grant money 2006: Profiles of private and corporate foundations and direct corporate givers receptive to library grant proposals.* Chicago: American Library Association.

11

Community Collaboration

Our concluding chapter could have just as easily gone into the first part of the book, since ultimately all collaboration is based upon human relationships. But since collaboration is the logistical cornerstone of library outreach—because whenever you're providing services on someone else's turf, you've got to build and sustain relationships unlike those required for traditional branch libraries to function—we place these thoughts here for you to take home.

Here we will tell you (at last) the story of how Arapahoe Library District and the Arapahoe County Sheriff's Office came to our rare partnership. We conclude with a list of organizations within which you can begin to build professional supporting relationships.

History of the Library/Corrections Partnership in Arapahoe County, Colorado

As with most public library outreach endeavors, the partnership between our library and our county jail began with an idea, a relationship, and an opportunity. In the mid-1980s, Arapahoe County's incarcerated population was increasing and the old county jail was bursting at the seams. The construction of a new jail facility was proposed and approved.

At that time, inmates all over Colorado were filing lawsuits to improve living conditions in the state's prisons and jails. Because the provisions of *Bounds v. Lewis* leave a lot of room for interpretation, a lot of facilities took a minimalist approach to providing inmates access to legal materials. The sheriff's office had been providing a few Colorado statues books and a *Black's Law Dictionary* that was only accessible through a blocked corridor. But in order to avoid costly litigation, our sheriff's office decided it was time to be more proactive. In 1984, despite the protests of a few deputies, the detentions captain at that time, Jeffrey Spoon, asked Arapahoe Library District for more materials.

Beginning in 1974, the Extension Services Department (now Outreach Services) of Arapahoe Library District had been maintaining a paperback deposit collection at the old jail facility in Littleton. When Spoon asked for more materials, hardcover books and the latest editions of popular magazines made their way into the jail for the first time as part of the library collection. But there still wasn't a proper site within the building for a library itself.

"We took donations and books discarded from the collection to the intake sally port door," recalls Brenda Carns, outreach manager at the time and now director of the Fort Collins Public Library in northern Colorado. "It was on the north side of the building, in total shade, and in the winter we sometimes stood in the cold, snow, and wind for fifteen minutes before anyone let us in."

This arrangement worked well enough at the time, but Spoon, looking forward to running a state-of-the-art new jail, decided they needed even more. He and Carns had a good working relationship, and he'd observed the positive impact that access to books had on the inmates. He also wanted to head off litigious inmates by providing them with good legal research resources.

"The library at that time was about fifteen by twenty feet and boxed off from the patrons by a caged window," says Carns. "The law library was adjacent to it, with the same setup. The only staff was one inmate trusty." Clearly, there was ample room for improvement.

Captain Spoon approached Carns one day and asked, "How would you like to have a REAL library?" He'd asked previous outreach supervisors before and had pretty well gotten the cold shoulder. But Carns recognized this as an altogether too-rare opportunity to really do some meaningful outreach.

"If you will pay for it," she told him, "we will do it."

Spoon, in a demonstration of political savvy and foresight for which we are eternally grateful, insisted that the library would need a good, solid contractual agreement with the sheriff's office if it was to sustain its funding. Carns did her homework by investigating Denver metropolitan area jails and other facilities across the country, and both she and the captain relied upon assistance from American Correctional Association and American Library Association publications to draw up the first contract. The language that opened that contract reflected the tone of the relationship between the two agencies.

"Whereas, it will be *necessary* for the County to provide a library and related library services to inmates . . ." was followed shortly by "Whereas the District is *able . . .*" The acknowledgement of responsibility of the sheriff's office and the expertise of the library district to provide good library service were established on the first page of the first contract and remain in force today.

While all this was going on, construction proceeded on the new detention facility. During the planning phase, an enormous storage area had been created. It was actually designed to be two rooms separated by a non-weight-bearing wall (a detail that becomes important later in the story). Captain Spoon, as, we suppose, only captains get to do, negotiated to have that storage space—a glorified closet—reassigned to the new library.

Carns went into high gear, hiring an MLS librarian with superlative collection development skills to build the Arapahoe County jail's first-ever selected-for collection. Castoffs and donations would no longer form the core of the library's collection. This would be a library built on the reading preferences of its users. Carns also applied for—and won—a grant to start up a good law library collection. The collection grew over a period of several months and was fully ready for patrons on opening day.

The library opened with the new facility in 1987. The first couple of years saw many community members touring the jail, and Carns recalls attorneys in private practice marveling at the quality of the law library collection. Success fuels (and often funds) further success, so over the next few years, and paralleling the continued growth of the inmate population, the little library's staff of one MLS and one part-time clerk grew to two full-time equivalent (FTE), then three, and finally to the four we have today. In 1996, funded by an Library Services and Technology Act (LSTA) grant, the law library went digital with the addition of six (eventually eight) networked computer stations featuring over seventy WestLaw databases in addition to the print collection so many attorneys had drooled over. In 1997, a new full-time on-site supervisor was hired: Sheila Clark, whose love of our particular library and of corrections librarianship as a profession had driven her to complete her master's degree in library science.

In 2001, while Sheila did a three-month internship at Arapahoe Library District's main branch, collection development was handed over (we thought temporarily) to one of our paraprofessional staff people. With no formal training in library science or collection development principles, she felt completely inadequate to the task and decided to take the path of least resistance. Every purchase made during those three months was specifically requested by at least one inmate. Our circulation statistics went through the roof. As degreed librarians who spent the first parts of our library careers as paraprofessionals, we feel justified in spotlighting this achievement as a testimony to the brains and creative problem solving of library paraprofessionals who are not overburdened by library science theory. We have used this technique, with a few exceptions, ever since. The ratio of our users to the entire facility population as a whole, broken down by living unit, ranges between 60 and 80 percent users to 40 to 20 percent nonusers. Granted, we have a captive audience, but the statistics are still impressive considering the population movements in jail.

In 2003, after years of hinting that this was about to happen, our captain informed us that the court services department was outgrowing its space and would need to dip into ours. The few months preceding this event saw the library staff in overdrive. We razed the recreational reading and print legal reference collections. Combined, the two collections had numbered over 13,000 volumes. In less than a year, those collections were pared down to 8,000 volumes. The legal reference LAN that had served thousands of patrons had to be completely dismantled. But again, opportunity was at hand.

Sheila, armed with an idea she'd been mulling over for some time, approached our lieutenant to wheel and deal. Our floor space was being overtaken; our law library service was facing serious compromise. That would never do! She proposed a mobile reference unit of laptops that we could roll into the living units, thereby preserving the law library service with the added benefit of eliminating the need for extra deputies to stand guard in the library itself while patrons were in the library. The lieutenant approved the project and in a year of flat revenues successfully secured the $32,000 required to make Sheila's vision come true.

The mobile reference unit debuted in 2003. Within the first year, we served twice as many patrons with the new service model as we'd ever been able to serve before. We also saw an 8 percent increase in circulation statistics from our recreational reading collection, a case study in the effectiveness of a well-weeded collection!

The nonweight-bearing wall that didn't get built in 1986 went up in December 2004, slicing our floor space in half. That same year saw radical changes on our public library side, as well, which seriously impacted the jail branch. An organizational restructure aimed at flattening the management hierarchy removed the on-site supervisor position from the library's management structure. For the first time in several years, the jail library would be overseen by an off-site supervisor. But it became obvious during the next few months that the restructure, which was improving operations on the public library side, was not working at the jail. Our Director of Libraries came up with a solution that surpassed anything we could have imagined ourselves, and we're jail librarians! He proposed that the jail library be removed from Arapahoe Library District's outreach department entirely. No longer would it be a functional unit of a department, but a fully independent library district branch with stature tantamount to that of any of our public branches.

We know of no other public library in the United States that has granted this kind of status to its jail library service.

Advocacy and Activism

Advocacy and activism are part of a continuum, although they influence each other to the point where they can start to look the same. Both of us love corrections librarianship so much, we often find ourselves promoting it without realizing it. We call this "unconscious advocacy," and everybody does it about something, be it greyhound rescue or organic gardening or skeet shooting. Because everybody does it, we're sometimes taken aback by the raised-eyebrow responses we get when we talk about jail, except that anything that can be taken as a boon to criminals can be a hot-button topic. (Which makes us want to talk about it even more, but we are obnoxious that way!)

The success story that is the Arapahoe County jail library was made possible by effective advocacy. As stated earlier in this book, you must advocate for your library both within and outside facility walls. The library's existence will be challenged by people whose personal philosophies of right and wrong, of crime and punishment, do not support the objectives of a public library for prisoners. A misunderstanding of the value of public libraries pervades correctional facilities, since a disproportionate percentage of nonusers, among staff and patrons alike, walk the halls.

To have a successful correctional facility library—and by successful, here we mean well-funded, continually evolving, and relevant to users— you must begin as an advocate for better services and better service provision. If you are operating your jail or prison library service as part of a public library, you will have to advocate on both the corrections and the public library sides. Both sides will ask the same question, and we offer some suggested responses for your consideration.

Corrections: Why do prisoners deserve any library services at all?

- Will help facility achieve/maintain accreditation
- Will help minimize the number of lawsuits brought against the facility
- Will support curriculum and classroom activities
- Will improve inmate morale
- Will also be available to facility staff

Public library: Why do prisoners deserve any library services at all?

- Supports the library profession's ethics of social responsibility and equitable access for all
- Helps prepare the 95 percent of prisoners who will eventually be released for life in the community
- Puts the public library "on the map" for the 95 percent of prisoners who will eventually be released, so they will know to turn to the public libraries for help once they are released

If advocacy happens on a daily basis as a regular part of the role of a corrections librarian, activism takes the message to the world. There are many activists working on behalf of prisoners; many of them are former prisoners themselves, while others are teachers and ministers. And let us not forget the contributions of the ACLU. Our own profession is fortunate to have a few strong voices, but it's high time more of us speak up. Remember, as librarians, it's not our job to save the world. It's our job to make sure every person in our information-driven society has access to the information he or she needs and that we keep the minds of our inmate patrons occupied as constructively as possible. An hour spent with the most blatantly pulp novel is still an hour better spent, we believe, than an hour watching "Survivor."

Public Relations

The second you take your message outside your facility, however, the Pandora principle comes into play. How much are you willing to share with the general public about what their tax dollars are providing to criminals? You have to be careful about what you share, and you have to be prepared for the questions.

Why are my tax dollars paying for perks for criminals? Why are you diverting money from cops' salaries to pay for reading programs for prisoners? Why are you providing prisoners with foreign-language materials, especially when so many foreign language-speaking prisoners are illegal aliens? Why in the world would you let an inmate charged with murder read Donald Goines books? Why are we paying for expensive librarians when other jails use inmates to staff the library for free? Why do the inmates have access to nicer computers than I can provide my kids with?

Before you panic, remember this: Public libraries and police departments get asked tough questions about allocation of tax money all the time. Sometimes, the questions will be obvious and clearly stated and you will be able to plan your response ahead of time. But some questions aren't really questions; they're verbal Molotov cocktails. "Why are you wasting money on the scum of the earth?" Such a question is posed for one reason only: to start an argument.

When facing any kind of question, but particularly a loaded one like this, we highly recommend the techniques of communication guru Arch Lustberg. If you can manage to attend one of his presentations, do so! If not, check out his Web site at www.lustberg.net. His advice, in a nutshell, is this: Figure out *in advance* what you can and cannot say about your organization, keep your responses focused on what your organization has accomplished, avoid getting defensive and thereby sucked into a debate, and above all, be pleasant as you're responding. The first two techniques establish your credibility and the latter two establish your likeability. And credibility and likeability will bolster your advocacy efforts.

Professional Organizations

Because working as a librarian in a correctional facility is such a multi-dimensional experience, you don't want to limit yourself to the professional resources of library organizations alone. But they are a good place to start. We realize that many if not most of you will be paying for any association memberships out of pocket, so this section highlights many free and inexpensive resources.

ALA and Company

The American Library Association's Web site at www.ala.org contains excellent resources on library ethics, intellectual freedom, and diversity. From ALA's Web site, you can access the Association of Specialized and Cooperative Library Agencies, ASCLA (www.ala.org.ala.ascla/ascla.htm.) From ASCLA's homepage, you can link to the Libraries Serving Special Populations Section (LSSPS), which addresses services to the traditionally underserved, including prisoners. This section includes the Library Services to Prisoners Forum, from which you can subscribe to the PRISON-L listserv. While relatively inactive most of the time, we believe this listserv has untapped potential as a support resource for corrections librarians and we strongly encourage you to contribute to it.

ALA's office of Literacy and Outreach Services (OLOS) at www.ala.org/ala/olos/literacyoutreach.htm is a treasure trove of information for any library involved in outreach. Under Director Satia Orange's stewardship, this Web site gets meatier every year with more and more information for jail and prison librarians appearing all the time. Of particular relevance are Glennor Shirley's invaluable articles on service to prisoners.

The Public Library Association (PLA) at www.pla.org does not address service to prisoners specifically (since that falls outside the scope of PLA's mission . . . for now), but you can find fact sheets and bibliographies as well as links back to ALA's Web site which should be of use to you.

State Library Associations

It's worth the effort to get to know your state library association. Spend some time on its Web site, paying particular attention to any sub-committees on outreach or interest groups on special libraries, or cooperative and contractual partnerships between libraries and nonlibrary entities. Watch for your state association's annual conference schedule and look it over carefully. As we've already mentioned, there's so little information out there specifically for people in the correctional library field, you need to use your imagination to apply lessons learned from other specialties or even other professions. We have taken classes at conferences on Internet search strategies, user needs assessments, giving presentations, bibliographic instruction in tribal libraries, how to form and sustain a writers group, and using anime to lure reluctant readers, and we have applied what we've learned to our jail library service.

Association of Bookmobiles and Outreach Services

One of the best national library associations out there has no affiliation whatsoever with the ALA. The Association of Bookmobiles and Outreach Services (ABOS) at http://abos.clarion.edu is a relatively new organization, only a couple of years old, and is run by members who, by and large, are still "working the floor" with patrons and have done so for years. The proximity of its members to the very patrons the association advocates for makes this small association a mighty one indeed. Combine that with the passion and energy unique to public library outreach staff and you have, hands down, the best library support system for outreach librarians in the country. And with a few members chiming in from the United Kingdom and New Zealand, ABOS can boast a truly international following.

The ABOS listserv is unquestionably the best thing going if you want to really learn how to do library outreach well. It costs $19 to get on the listserv and is worth every cent and then some. The listserv is a community of experts in the specialized field of library outreach, and although much of the conversation revolves around bookmobile and homebound services in the public library, since so many public libraries offer some kind of service to prisoners, questions about jail and prison libraries are always welcome. And, bookmobiles have a lot in common with jails. Their business depends upon parking on someone else's turf; often an inside administrator decides if they can park at all! Bookmobiles often serve economically disadvantaged and ethnically diverse patrons. And, like any special library in a business, hospital, or jail, bookmobiles are often considered bottom-rung budgetary line items that are easily slashed if money runs short. Bookmobile librarians spend a lot of time advocating for their patrons and their library service, just like we do.

The ABOS listserv members are articulate, knowledgeable, and invariably generous with their advice. If you have to break the pink piggy bank to scrape up the listserv subscription fee, do it. We promise you won't regret doing so.

ACLU

The ACLU obviously advocates for lots of people, but since prisoners' civil rights are under fire so frequently, the ACLU is a great resource for keeping up with legislation that may impact your provision of services, particularly as it relates to prisoner access to the courts. The ACLU operates the National Prison Project, which is the only national litigation program on behalf of prisoners in the United States. Visit their Web site and pay particular attention to the Web page about prisoner rights. ACLU advocates for civil liberties, which public libraries also strive to uphold. There is a lot of information here that will be useful to you.

American Correctional Association

The American Correctional Association may not at first glance seem to have much to offer the corrections librarian. But look again. If you want insight into the culture of correctional environments, the values, the issues, and the challenges corrections employees face all the time, this is your source. Of particular usefulness is the ACA publication *Corrections Today,* in which a few articles on prison librarianship have appeared in the last several years. Selected articles are posted on the association's Web site. The issues are thematic; as recently as October 2005, the magazine focused on the experience of women in the corrections profession, a topic many librarians behind bars can appreciate.

Conclusion

So, are you meant for corrections librarianship? We often wonder how the inmates wind up in jail; while writing this book, we began to wonder why staff wind up there. The answer may be a little more straightforward for law enforcement, for whom corrections work is part and parcel of "to serve and protect." More than one deputy has told us that corrections work is more interesting than working the streets; there's simply more to do in jail. It may also be fairly straightforward for social workers and chaplains, who see opportunities to know and understand scores of suffering souls every day, in a more direct and routine relationship than is possible for many on the outside. Teachers inside have the opportunity to dramatically change lives, by helping inmates get their GEDs or attain basic literacy or English-speaking skills.

But librarians? Why would any librarian in his or her right mind leave the tidy, relatively civilized world of school media, academic, public, or noninstitutional special libraries to spend their days behind bars, underground, surrounded by strange sounds and smells, dealing with people whose lives are unimaginable and crimes unthinkable? We're not teachers, we're not healers, we're not priests. We're not in there to save anybody. Why do we go there then? What is the draw? Why do so many of us stay for years? Why is it that many of us who leave never really get it out of our systems?

One of our former colleagues used to tell us that he could clearly see how his life could have led him to prison, had he made just a few different choices. "There but for the grace of God" is how his perspective might be described. And he was a great librarian because he served the way he would have wanted to be served—without nonsense but with a lot of humor.

My initial draw was the instant gratification of working with inmates. But I soon realized that working inside would test my assertiveness and character in a way the public library would not. And I wanted that testing, knowing that eventually I would find myself in public library management positions requiring the resolve and quick thinking I didn't possess before going to jail. With each challenge successfully met inside, I became a better librarian; more than that, I became a better person.

Sheila says that her blue-collar background predisposed her to working in jail. "They're my people," she often says. Her professional experiences and parenting life have also provided career direction. Years spent conducting research for the Department of Corrections, of working at a busy retail fabric store, and the challenges of raising a strong-willed child were the best possible training for a career on the inside.

Sometimes the motivation is purely pecuniary—a job presents itself, the dental benefits can't be beat, and the hours are preferable to those in the public library. The work is certainly preferable to most corrections positions. So the job is accepted without any particular vocational expectations; and many a true corrections librarian is thereby born.

What in your life has prepared you for a career in a corrections library? What events or experiences in your life would open the door, literally and metaphorically? We conclude this book with the following wish: that in time, the story about your journey to jail will fit into these paragraphs, and we'll know you as a member of this extraordinary cohort. We look forward to meeting you on the inside.

Glossary of Terms

ACA: American Correctional Association

ACDF: Arapahoe County Detention Facility, located in Arapahoe County, Colorado

ASCO: Arapahoe County Sheriff's Office, located in Arapahoe County, Colorado

Ad seg: Administrative segregation; housing arrangement wherein inmates or prisoners with codefendants or whose charges may put them in danger by other inmates are housed away from the general population.

Administrative Segregation: See "Ad-seg."

ALA: American Library Association

ALD: Arapahoe Library District, located in Arapahoe County, Colorado

ASCLA: Association of Specialized and Cooperative Library Agencies, a division of the American Library Association

CEA: Correctional Education Association

Cell block: Inmate or prisoner living unit, often comprised of more than one dayroom.

Community corrections: Alternative sentencing arrangement whereby convicted criminals are not housed in jail or prison, but reside in the community under surveillance.

Count: A routine procedure in which the officers going off-duty and the officers manning the next shift count all inmates in order to account for everyone.

Day hall: See "Dayroom."

Dayroom: A communal or semi-communal living area, often part of a larger cell block.

Deputy: A sworn officer, usually employed at the county level.

DOC: Department of Corrections

EDCU: At Arapahoe County Detention Facility, this stands for "Enhanced Disturbance Control Unit"; comprised of deputies specially trained to handle dangerous and volatile situations through interpersonal skills and, if necessary, use of force.

Guard: Common synonym for "deputy" and "officer," but generally considered derogatory.

Hole: See "Lockdown."

Inmate: A resident of a jail, usually prior to conviction. In common parlance, however, this term is synonymous with "prisoner" and in this book, we use the two terms interchangeably.

Jail: A county or municipal incarceration facility. Terms of stay are temporary as inmates await trial, adjudication, sentencing, release, or transfer to prison.

Kite: A form by which inmates and prisoners can communicate with facility staff.

Laundry exchange: Regular facility routine in which sheets and inmate uniforms are exchanged for clean ones.

Lockdown: In jail, either an in-house disciplinary procedure in which offenders are locked in their cells 23 hours a day or a security procedure in which all inmates are locked in their cells for counting, usually during deputy shift changes. in prison, It is often a condition of confinement as part of a criminal sentence, and can also be used as an in-house disciplinary procedure.

MPR: Multipurpose room; any community-type room that is used for a variety of purposes, e.g., programs, religious services, library book-cart services, classes.

Officer: Security personnel, often referred to by different terms, depending on the facility.

OLOS: Office of Literacy and Outreach Services, a department of the American Library Association

PLA: Public Library Association, a division of the American Library Association

Pod: See "Cell block."

Prison: A long-term incarceration facility for offenders who have been sentenced, usually administered at the state or federal level. Privately run prisons overseen by state governments or the Bureau of Prisons are becoming more common.

Prisoner: A resident of a prison, post-conviction. See "Inmate" for explanation of term usage in this book.

Shakedown: A procedure wherein inmate living units and/or cells are systematically searched, usually on suspicion of the presence of contraband.

Trusty: An inmate or prisoner who works within the facility or on the facility grounds. Common areas utilizing trusties are buildings and grounds, the kitchens, and the library.

Yard: Term used to describe an enclosed outdoor recreation area for inmates and prisoners; also used to describe the time inmates and prisoners spend in that area. ("Dayroom F *has yard* between noon and one o'clock.")

Appendix A

"Must-Have" Core Collection Suggestions

The closest corollary to a core collection list that we prefer to use is a list of popular authors and subjects whose popularity has either been long established, like Donald Goines and Stephen King, or whose popularity is emerging, like Teri Woods and Zane. Over the years, we have considered developing core lists but decided against creating anything too structured, since popular taste is a moving target. We serve this shifting bull's-eye by talking to our patrons all the time, actively soliciting their input into the collection development process. Their current requests have proved a more valued and efficient way of selecting materials than our stout devotion to a rigid list.

That said, the reading tastes of prisoners exhibit some remarkable consistency, whether they are incarcerated in a suburban jail or a rural supermax prison or an urban detention facility. Consequently, we can recommend authors, titles, and subjects that seem to withstand the tests of time and geography. If you find yourself building a collection from the ground up, begin slowly and thoughtfully. Buying books that never get read, especially when funds are limited, is a disservice to your patrons.

The differences in reading interests among women, men, and juveniles are slight and fairly predictable. Women have no problem openly reading romance novels, so the more of these you provide, the better. (Men do read them, but less often and rarely as overtly.) Women tend to read more for pleasure than men, who often read solely for information. Fiction collections for women should carry every conceivable genre, including action/adventure and science fiction. Remember to pay attention to multicultural authors since everybody likes to read about people like themselves. Women also tend to read more books about relationships and parenting, but you will need at least a representation of these topics for men, as well.

Some juveniles readily admit that they do not read very well, but teens embarrass easily and won't want other kids to know they are struggling. Your collection for them should include high-interest, low-reading level titles that don't *look* like high-interest, low-reading level titles. For teens, steer clear of titles that are too obviously geared toward literacy, relying instead on classics and adventure/sci-fi that appeal to all ages but are written for middle school or younger.

A core collection for legal resources is easier to build based upon that singular topic. The core collection would include:

- State statutes
- Federal statutes (which are easier to provide via CD-ROM due to the space required to store print versions)
- *101 Legal Forms for Personal Use*
- West Publishing's *Nutshell* series, especially titles on criminal and family law
- Nolo Press *Law for All* series, especially titles on criminal and family law
- *Black's Law Dictionary* and a general dictionary, like *Webster's*
- *Prisoner's Self-Help Litigation Manual* (out-of-print)

For recreational reading and nonlegal information, we have found the following consistently popular over the years. Any or all of these are appropriate for building your collection from the ground up.

Westerns: Tabor Evans, Louis L'Amour, Jake Logan, Donald Clayton Porter, Dana Fuller Ross, William Johnstone, Jon Sharpe

Science Fiction/Fantasy authors: Douglas Adams, Terry Brooks, Orson Scott Card, Arthur C. Clarke, David Eddings, Raymond Feist, Terry Goodkind, Robert Jordan, J. K. Rowling, R. A. Salvatore, Dan Simmons, J. R. R. Tolkien, Margaret Weis and Tracy Hickman, Tad Williams

Science Fiction/Fantasy series (multiple authors): Conan, Dragonlance, Forgotten Realms, Star Trek (especially the original series, *Next Generation,* and *Deep Space 9*), Star Wars

General Fiction: David Baldacci, Tom Clancy, Jackie Collins, Patricia Cornwell, Clive Cussler, W. E. B. Griffin, Janet Evanovich, John Grisham, Jerry Jenkins, Dennis Lahaye, Elmore Leonard, Robert Ludlum, Harold Robbins, John Sandford, Sidney Sheldon, Carl Weber

Horror and Suspense: V. C. Andrews, Clive Barker, Jeffrey Deaver, Thomas Harris, Stephen King, Dean Koontz, James Patterson, Robert McCammon, Anne Rice, R. L. Stine

Romance: Eric Jerome Dickey, Sheneska Jackson, E. Lynn Harris, Nora Roberts, Danielle Steel, Omar Tyree

Urban authors: Donald Goines, Iceberg Slim, Zane, Teri Woods

Urban publisher: Triple Crown

When considering your nonfiction collection, law-related or otherwise, it's important to remember that there's a greater imperative on currency with many nonfiction subjects (particularly computers and health) than others.

Nonfiction authors: Lee Ames, Jack Canfield, T. D. Jakes, Max Lucado, Joyce Meyers, Anne Rule, Ayanla Vanzant

Nonfiction subjects: computer hardware, computer software, computer certification study guides, astrology, meditation, anger management, philosophy, religion (especially Christianity, Islam, Kabbala, Paganism/Wicca, Buddhism, and Freemasonry), ready reference (almanacs, dictionaries, thesauri, encyclopedias, and rhyming dictionaries), world records, true crime, GED study guides, astronomy, animals of the world, automobiles and motorcycles, health (including fitness, diet, and illness-specific subjects like bipolar disorder, eating disorders, depression, and schizophrenia), pregnancy, parenting, business plans and entrepreneurship, personal finance, grant writing, drawing (how-to books and graphic-intensive titles, like *Spectrum*), board games and card games, music and music industry (especially hip hop and rap), poetry, history (military, Native American, and African American).

Appendix B

Job Descriptions

The following three descriptions are amalgams of job postings by Arapahoe Library District and the Colorado State prison libraries, specifically Fremont Correctional Facility Library in Cañon City, Colorado.

Generic Library Supervisor Position

Role: Oversees general library operations including provision of patron services, collection management, acquisitions, cataloging, budgeting, scheduling, supervision of library staff, and program planning.

Responsibilities:

- Hires, orients, trains, and evaluates both salaried library staff and inmate workers, annually appraises each employee's performance, follows proper procedures to correct staff performance issues, informs Human Resources when salaried staff performance warrants discipline or termination, and the officer in charge of inmate workers when inmate staff performance warrants discipline or termination.

- Acts as primary liaison between public library and correctional facility management by attending all facility supervisors meetings and keeping in regular contact with professional counterparts in the public libraries by attending supervisors meetings or participating on library task forces or committees or via active membership in the state library association.

- Coordinates daily operations by setting hours of operation, scheduling staff, tracking expenditures, ordering supplies and materials, compiling and reporting statistics, identifying and correcting operational or customer service problems, and setting policy and procedures in conjunction with supervising officer(s).

- Provides Internet and proprietary database reference service by researching patron requests for information on statutory and case law, general medical information, and other information as requested, providing directory assistance as allowed by facility

225

policies, locating and printing legal, tax, and Social Security forms, and keeping informed of new state and federal criminal legislation in order to provide the most current information to patrons.

- Plans informative and entertaining programs for patrons, such as book discussion groups and other literacy-based programs, by accessing resources in the collection and the community in order to promote use of library resources.

- Provides recreational reading material to all inmates, regardless of classification level, which includes verifying inmate locations and stocking book trucks for delivery to locked-down living units, ensuring accurate and timely reshelving of returned materials, selecting materials according to reader preferences, placing holds, procuring materials via interlibrary loan, maintaining collection through regular weeding and mending procedures, and checking books in and out.

- Facilitates inmate access to legal research materials by verifying inmate locations, checking law books in and out, regularly updating legal research databases, documenting inmate attendance, answering reference questions, instructing inmates on how to use computer software and printers, and collecting printing fees.

- Catalogs new materials by creating bibliographic records and processes new materials by printing and affixing labels according to the Dewey Decimal classification system.

- Weeds and discards items in collection by assessing the condition and suitability of items, and notifying the Collection Librarian of the discarded item in order to keep collection attractive, current, and useful.

Experience: Three years of supervisory experience with progressively greater responsibilities managing a library.

Education: Master of Library and Information Science preferred. Comparable combination of education and experience will be considered.

Interpersonal Skills: Significant levels of trustworthiness and diplomacy are essential, in addition to courtesy, tact, and strong customer service skills. Work involves extensive personal contact with others and can be of a personal or sensitive nature. Work involves motivating and influencing others. Fostering sound cooperative relationships with nonlibrary entities and personnel is necessary.

Other Skills:

- Initiative and self-motivation
- Creativity
- Emotional intelligence/good personal boundaries
- Commitment to the profession of librarianship
- Knowledge of public library reference service and/or law library reference service
- Skill in reference interviewing and readers advisory
- Knowledge of print and online reference resources
- Skill in collection management, including selection, acquisition, deselection, and evaluation
- Skill in using library cataloging and circulation systems
- Skill in customer relations, including dealing with difficult patrons and volatile situations
- Skill in computer and peripheral hardware troubleshooting
- Skill in Windows
- Skill in Microsoft Office Suite, especially Word and Outlook
- Skill in using the Internet
- Ability to operate common office equipment, including copiers, multi-line telephones, and fax machines
- Ability to lift at least fifty pounds and maneuver heavy book trucks between the library and the living units
- Ability to plan and implement age-appropriate programming
- Ability to work in a detention center environment
- Ability to scan books under laser wand
- Ability to sort books according to Dewey Decimal classification
- Bilingualism is a plus

Must be able to pass a criminal background check.

Generic Library Clerk/Library Assistant Position

Role: Provides readers advisory and reference services to the inmates and staff of This Facility.

Responsibilities:

- Provides recreational reading material to all inmates, regardless of classification level, which includes verifying inmate locations and stocking book trucks for delivery to locked-down living units, ensuring accurate and timely reshelving of returned materials, selecting materials according to reader preferences, placing holds, procuring materials via interlibrary loan, maintaining collection through regular weeding and mending procedures, and checking books in and out.

- Facilitates inmate access to legal research materials by verifying inmate locations, checking law books in and out, regularly updating legal research databases, documenting inmate attendance, answering reference questions, instructing inmates on how to use computer software and printers, and collecting printing fees.

- At the direction of the librarian in charge or library supervisor, catalogs new materials by creating bibliographic records, processes new materials by printing and affixing labels according to the Dewey Decimal classification system; weeds and discards items in collection by assessing the condition and suitability of items, and notifies the Collection Librarian of the discarded item in order to keep collection attractive, current, and useful.

- At the direction of the librarian in charge or library supervisor, assists with collection development by reporting patterns of inmate and staff requests for recreational materials and legal and nonlegal information.

- At the direction of the librarian in charge or library supervisor, assists with implementation of programs and enhanced usage of collection by creating and/or distributing marketing materials such as bibliographies, user's guides, and advertising for programs.

Experience: At least six months of related or similar experience.

Education: Equivalent to a college degree.

Interpersonal Skills: Significant levels of trustworthiness and diplomacy are essential, in addition to courtesy, tact, and strong customer service skills. Work involves extensive personal contact with others and can be of a personal or sensitive nature. Work involves motivating and influencing others. Fostering sound cooperative relationships with nonlibrary personnel is necessary.

Other Skills:
- Initiative and self-motivation
- Creativity

- Emotional intelligence/good personal boundaries
- Commitment to the profession of librarianship
- Knowledge of public library reference service and/or law library reference service
- Skill in reference interviewing and readers advisory
- Knowledge of print and online reference resources
- Skill in collection management, including selection, acquisition, deselection, and evaluation
- Skill in using library cataloging and circulation systems
- Skill in customer relations, including dealing with difficult patrons and volatile situations
- Skill in computer and peripheral hardware troubleshooting
- Skill in Windows
- Skill in Microsoft Office Suite, especially Word and Outlook
- Skill in using the Internet
- Ability to operate common office equipment including copiers, multi-line telephones, and fax machines
- Ability to lift at least fifty pounds and maneuver heavy book trucks between the library and the living units
- Ability to plan and implement age-appropriate programming
- Ability to work in a detention center environment
- Ability to scan books under laser wand
- Ability to sort books according to Dewey Decimal classification
- Bilingualism is a plus

Must be able to pass a criminal background check.

Generic Inmate Clerk Position

Role: Primarily responsible for routine clerical work in the library

Responsibilities:

- Checks materials in and out, shelves materials accurately and efficiently, collects required information from patrons who wish to register or update their library records.
- Handles library supplies and equipment correctly and appropriately, keeps work areas clean and clutter-free, files library paperwork

accurately, carefully and properly mends damaged items, performs routine "housekeeping" chores to keep the library neat and inviting.

- Becomes familiar with the library's layout and holdings in order to assist patrons in finding materials.
- Understands library policies and procedures and is able to enforce library rules in a courteous, consistent manner.

Experience: None required, although library, retail, or clerical experience is a plus.

Education: High school diploma or equivalent.

Residency Requirements: Must have at least one year left to serve at This Facility.

Interpersonal Skills: Significant levels of trustworthiness and diplomacy are essential, in addition to courtesy, tact, and strong customer service skills. Must be free of disciplinary reports for at least six months.

Other Skills:
- Punctuality
- Reliability
- Responsiveness to direction from paid library staff
- Ability to work well with library staff, inmate patrons, and non-library staff
- Excellent skills in alpha-numeric filing systems, keyboarding, and ten-key
- Good detail-orientation, attention to accuracy, and efficiency
- Neat personal appearance
- Good command of the English language; bilingualism is a plus

Appendix C

Sample Interview Questions

1. Why are you interested in this position?
2. Briefly describe any experience you have in the following areas:
   a. waiting on difficult patrons or customers
   b. suggesting books for people to read
   c. using or working at a library
   d. showing people how to use computers/troubleshooting computer problems
   e. using the Internet, MS Word, MS Office, Windows, circulation and cataloging software, and legal research sources (print and electronic)
   f. developing a library collection based on professional resources and patron requests
3. Are you able to:
   a. lift boxes of books or magazines using a dolly?
   b. push heavy carts full of books?
   c. work in a building with no windows?
   d. work in a building with strange sounds and odors?
   e. work behind doors with locking mechanisms over which you have no control?
   f. work under nearly constant visual surveillance?
4. A patron at book cart is being disrespectful to other patrons, e.g., making derogatory remarks, shoving. The deputy is preoccupied. What would you do?
5. A patron claims a book on his record is actually checked out by another person. What would you do?
6. How do you define outstanding and personalized service?
7. You have been standing at the pod door for more than ten minutes waiting to deliver books. What do you do?
8. Describe a difficult situation or conflict that you have experienced on the job and how you solved it.
9. How do you feel about providing library services to murderers, pedophiles, thieves, and rapists?

231

10. What is the purpose of a library in a detention facility?

11. A co-worker expresses being overwhelmed with the day's tasks. What would you do?

12. How do you handle and/or relieve stress?

13. Tell us how you would handle:
     a. being told about a problem with your job performance by your supervisor?
     b. being told the same thing by a co-worker?
     c. receiving a similar complaint from a patron?
     d. receiving a similar complaint from a deputy/officer?

14. What did you like best about your last job?

15. What did you like least about your last job?

16. How did you feel about your last supervisor?

17. What characteristics make a good supervisor? How do you like to be supervised?

18. If you find that you are finished with all of your assigned tasks, what do you do next?

19. How do you establish harmonious relationships with your co-workers?

20. Describe your computer skills.

21. A patron has asked a question for which you have been unable to find a satisfactory answer. What do you do?

22. If you could improve something about yourself, what would it be?

23. Leisure reading is important to our patrons. How do you keep current with the latest authors and titles? What resources would you use to help a patron find something good to read?

24. How did you come to work in a library, and why did you stay? (Or, why do you want to work in a library?)

Appendix D

Performance Measures

It's always important to keep in mind who's watching you and what they're grading you on. Often, these are not the things you *should* be graded on. There's no limit to what you can measure in a library: circulation statistics, facility use, program attendance, number of volumes added, deleted, modified, mended, dusted off, reshelved, or viewed askance. You need to decide what your goals are to determine what you need to measure.

The first question we pose is why should we measure anything anyway? The answer is easy in the public libraries. Because the state library makes us! No, seriously, measuring performance in a jail library is necessary for essentially the same reason public libraries measure: funds. You can't just know in your heart of hearts that you're good; you have to demonstrate continuous improvement so that when it comes time to ask for more money, staff, or space—or fight to the teeth to keep what you already have—you'll have a powerful tool at your disposal.

Before we get into what you should keep track of, however, we need to point out that pound for pound, library outreach is expensive. Those of you carting your materials around to your patrons' living units won't be able to run an operation as efficiently as those of you with libraries the patrons can visit themselves. The cost of circulation per item, per patron will be considerably higher if your patrons can't meet you 90 percent of the way. Consequently, statistics alone aren't enough to tell your story, and this of course applies to every correctional facility library. Statistics don't tell the stories of inmates who learn to read or learn to speak English or who stay in touch with their children through reading programs or who discover the joy of reading for the first time in their lives. Whether you love statistics (like Sheila) or hate them (like Erica), remember that they are only part of your library's measure of performance.

The statistics you collect will change based on the issues you're facing and the goals you wish to achieve. They are an important point of reference as you evaluate your services over time. If your circulation statistics begin to drop, what's going on to influence that? What has changed in the facility? Did you change something about the library that has impacted circulation?

233

You need to take a systematic approach when asking questions like this because your library is part of a larger organization—changes in one department are like pebbles thrown in a pond. The ripple effect can impact you when you least expect it.

So, without further ado, let's address performance measures specifically. Good things to keep track of include the following:

- Number of books circulated (be sure to specify time frames, which can range from hourly to yearly—decide what level of detail will be most meaningful)
- Ratio of users to general population
- Number of items in the collection versus number of duplicate copies
- Facility use (patron visits)
- Law library attendance
- Reference questions (if you run a law library, you may want to break these into categories: specifically legal reference questions and all others)
- Number of law library sessions
- Number of donated materials added to the collection
- Number of materials weeded from the collection
- Number of programs
- Number of program attendees
- Number of staff visits into the living areas to deliver materials
- Number of staff in library or in the living units during operating hours
- Volunteer hours
- Hours worked by inmate staff

Before you decide what to keep track of, you should ask yourself several questions. First, what matters to you? What information is going to mean something to you as a librarian? Second, who else needs or wants to know what's going on in the library? You're sure to have a facility administrator interested in the performance of the library; it's possible, especially if you're also affiliated with a public library, that the administrators there will also want to track performance. It's a good idea to check with those who might have a vested interest in the library to see what they really want to know. Third, at what level of detail should you keep track? Should you keep statistics for the entire facility or by pods or by living units? We think the size of your facility will help you answer that question. The larger it is, the more you might want to break down your performance measures.

The longer the library's hours of operation, the smaller the time incre-
ments for keeping track of reference questions or patron visits. If you
make deliveries to living units, you should follow the public library bookmobile model and keep track of activity per living unit. This will help you
identify use patterns and trends.

Suggested Readings

Correctional Libraries

Association of Specialized and Cooperative Library Agencies. 1992. *Library standards for adult correctional institutions.* Chicago: American Library Association.

———. 1981. *Library standards for jails and detention facilities.* Chicago: American Library Association.

Davis, V. A. 2000. Breaking out of the box: Reinventing a juvenile-center library. *American libraries* 31(10). Retrieved January 3, 2005 from InfoTrac Web: General Reference Center Gold database.

Rubin, R. J. and D. S. Suvak. 1995. *Libraries inside: A practical guide for prison librarians.* Jefferson, NC: McFarland and Company, Inc.

Sullivan, L. 2000. The least of our brethren: Library service to prisoners. *American libraries* 31(5). Retrieved January 3, 2005 from InfoTrac Web: General Reference Center Gold database.

Vogel, B. 1994. Making prison libraries visible and accessible. *Corrections today* 56(1). Retrieved January 3, 2005 from InfoTrac Web: General Reference Center Gold.

———. 1995. *Down for the count.* Lanham, MD: Scarecrow Press, Inc.

Correctional Library Programs and Services

Clark, S. and B. Patrick. 1999. Choose Freedom Read: Book talks behind bars. *American libraries* 30(7), 63–64. Retrieved December 3, 2005 from InfoTrac Web: General Reference Center Gold database.

Connecting inside. 2003. *Library Journal* 125(5). Retrieved January 3, 2005 from Infotrac Web General Reference Center Gold database.

de la Peña McCook, K. 2004. Public libraries and people in jail. *Reference and user services quarterly, 44*(1), 26–30.

Waites, M. 2004. Readers behind bars: Books can make a huge and positive difference to men and women in prison, as writer-in-residence [Editorial]. *The bookseller.* Retrieved January 3, 2005 from InfoTrac Web: General Reference Center Gold database.

Library Ethics and Principles

American Library Association. 1990. *Freedom to view statement.* Retrieved May 9, 2005 from http://www.ala.org/ala/oif/statementspols/ftvstatement/freedomviewstatement.htm.

————. 1994. *Freedom to read statement.* Retrieved December 15, 2004 from http://www.ala.org/ala/oif/statementspols/ftrstatement/freedom-readstatement.htm.

————. 1995. *Code of ethics of the American Library Association.* Retrieved December 15, 2005 from http://www.ala.org/ala/oif/statementspols/codeofethics/codeethics.htm.

————. 1999. *Libraries: An American value.* Retrieved February 7, 2005 from http://www.ala.org/ala/oif/statementspols/americanvalue/librariesamerican.htm.

————. 2004. *Core values task force II report.* Retrieved December 15, 2004 from http://www.ala.org/ala/oif/statementspols/corevaluesstatement/corevalues.htm.

————. 2005. *Dealing with challenges to books and other library materials.* Retrieved February 7, 2006 from http://www.ala.org/ala/oif/challengesupport/dealing/Default1208.htm

Library Operations and Staffing

Evans, G. E. and M. Z. Saponaro. 2005. *Developing library and information center collections.* 5th ed. Westport, CT: Libraries Unlimited.

Intellectual Freedom Committee. 2004. Elements of a materials selection policy. In *Intellectual freedom handbook.* Retrieved December 3, 2005 from http://cal-webs.org/ifhandbook.html#elements.

National Institute for Literacy. 1999. *LINCS selection criteria.* Retrieved September 24, 2005 from http://www.nifl.gov/lincs/selection_criteria_print.html.

North Carolina Department of Correction. N.d. *Volunteers in prison.* Retrieved September 12, 2005 from http://www.doc.state.nc.us/DOP/Volunter.htm.

Law Library Service

Bergman, P. and S. J. Berman-Barrett. 1997. *The criminal law handbook: Know your rights, survive the system.* Berkeley, CA: Nolo Press.

Elias, S. 2004. *Legal research: How to find and understand the law.* Berkeley, CA: Nolo Press.

Manville, D. E. 1986. *Prisoners' self-help litigation manual.* New York: Oceana Publications.

Mongelli, W. D. 1994. De-mystifying legal research for prisoners. *Law library journal* 86(259), 277–298.

Wilhelmus, D. W. 1999. Where have all the law libraries gone? *Corrections today* 6. Retrieved January 3, 2005 from InfoTrac Web database.

Prisoners and Prison Culture

Allen, B. and D. Bosta. 1981. *Games criminals play.* Sacramento: Rae John Publishers.

Chesney-Lind, M. and R. G. Sheldon. 1998. *Girls, delinquency, and juvenile justice.* Belmont, CA: Wadsworth Publishing Company.

Cooke, C. L. 2002. Understanding incarcerated populations. *AORN Journal* (March). Retrieved May 14, 2004 from http.//www.findarticles.com.

Facts about prisons and prisoners. October 2005. Retrieved December 3, 2005 from http://www.sentencingproject.org/pdfs/1035.pdf.

Foley, R. M. 2001. *Academic characteristics of incarcerated youth and correctional educational programs: A literature review.* Retrieved May 14, 2004 from http://www.findarticles.com.

Gainsborough, J. and M. Mauer. September 2000. Diminishing returns: Crime and incarceration in the 1990's. *The sentencing project.* Retrieved April 20, 2005 from http://www.sentencingproject.org/pdfs/9039.pdf.

Gilligan, J. 2003. Shame, guilt, and violence. *Social research* (Winter). Retrieved May 14, 2004 from http://www.findarticles.com.

Mallinger, S. 1991. Games inmates play. *Corrections today* 53(7), 188–192.

Memoirs and Personal Experiences

Jablecki, L. T. 2000. Prison inmates meet Socrates. *Humanist* 60(3). Retrieved May 9, 2005 from http://www.findarticles.com/p/articles/mi_m1374/is_3_60/ai_62111876#continue.

Leffers, M. J. 1990. Prison library—one day. *Special libraries* 81(3), 242–246.

Mantilla, K. 2001. Windows to freedom: Radical feminism at a jail library. *off our backs* 31(2). Retrieved January 3, 2005 from InfoTrac Web: General Reference Center Gold database.

Spitale, L. 2002. *Prison Ministry.* Nashville: Broadman and Holman Publishers.

Waites, M. 2004. Readers behind bars: Books can make a huge and positive difference to men and women in prison, as writer-in-residence [Editorial]. *The bookseller.* Retrieved January 3, 2005, from InfoTrac Web: General Reference Center Gold database.

Walker, J. 2004. *Dancing to the concertina's tune.* Boston: Northeastern University Press.

Personal Development and Personality

Autry, J. A. 1998. *Real power: Business lessons from the Tao Te Ching.* New York: Riverhead.

Covey, S. R. 1991. *Principle-centered leadership.* New York: Summit Books.

Goldberg, M. J. 1999. *The 9 ways of working: How to use the Enneagram to discover your natural strengths and work more effectively.* New York: Marlowe and Company.

Kroeger, O. 2002. *Type talk at work: how 16 personality types determine your success on the job.* New York: Dell.

Lerner, H. G. 1985. *Dance of anger.* New York: Harper & Row.

Loehr, J. E. and T. Schwartz. 2003. *The power of full engagement: Managing energy, not time, is the key to performance and personal renewal.* New York: Free Press.

Ruiz, D. M. 1997. *The four agreements.* San Rafael, CA: Amber-Allen Publishers.

Customer Service

Barlowe, J. and C. Moller. 1996. *A complaint is a gift: Using customer feedback as a strategic tool.* San Francisco: Berrett-Koehler Publishers.

Leland, K. and K. Bailey. 1999. *Customer service for dummies.* New York: Hungry Minds.

McNeil, B. and D. J. Johnson. 1996. *Patron behavior in libraries: A handbook of positive approaches to negative situations.* Chicago: American Library Association.

Rubin, R. J. 2000. *Defusing the angry patron: A how-to-do-it manual for librarians and paraprofessionals.* New York: Neal-Schuman Publishers.

Sarkodie-Mensah, K. 2002. *Helping the difficult library patron: New approaches to examining and resolving a long-standing and ongoing problem.* New York: Haworth Information Press.

Smith, K. 1993. *Serving the difficult customer: A how-to-do-it manual for library staff.* New York: Neal-Schuman Publishers.

Index

About the Authors

SHEILA CLARK holds a Master of Library Science from Emporia State University and a master's degree in political science from Southern Illinois University. She has been a librarian at the Arapahoe County Detention Facility in Englewood, Colorado, for more than ten years and has been the library supervisor since 1997. She spearheaded the nationally acclaimed *Begin With Books In Jail* and *Choose Freedom—READ!* programs. This is her first book.

Photo by Mitchell S. Wright

ERICA MacCREAIGH holds a Master of Library and Information Science from the University of Wisconsin and a B.A. in anthropology from the University of Colorado. She has more than fourteen years of public library experience in five different Arapahoe Library District branches, including the Arapahoe County Detention Facility library. She now supervises Arapahoe Library District's Outreach Services department. This is her first book.

Photo by Mitchell S. Wright